I0203291

THOMAS MARSHALL

DAILY MUSINGS FROM THE NEW TESTAMENT

DAILY DEVOTIONAL

DAILY DEVOTIONAL

Daily Musing From the New Testament

Thomas Marshall

Christian Publishing House

Cambridge, Ohio

Christian Publishing House

Professional Christian Publishing of the Good News

Daily Musings From the New Testament

Copyright © 2016 Christian Publishing House

Unless otherwise stated, Scripture quotations are from *The Holy Bible, American Standard Version (ASV)*, Public Domain, 1901 by Christian Publishing House, Professional Conservative Christian Publishing of the Good News!

DAILY DEVOTIONAL Daily Musing From the New Testament by Thomas Marshall

ISBN-13: **978-1-945757-33-4**

ISBN-10: **1-945757-33-7**

DAILY DEVOTIONALS

Table of Contents

Preface to Daily Musings

I have always believed that for one to acquire an understanding of the Bible, one must take the time to read the Bible. An old Preacher once said that he believed the Bible from Genesis 1:1 to Revelation 22:21 – and he believed the cover also where it said "Holy" Bible. Many of us might claim to believe all that the Bible says; yet, many have never taken the time to read this entire precious love letter from God. We enjoy the Gospels. We spend time in the book of Acts retracing the life of Paul. We seek to learn about the church in the Epistles. And who can resist looking into the future in Revelation. We need to daily spend time reading to strengthen our walk with the Lord.

Every part of the New Testament is important, and holds something that God wants us to know and understand about Him, man, creation, sin, salvation, and redemption. When we ignore sections of the New Testament, we are ignoring part of the sacred, holy words given by Almighty God. I have taught for years that God says what He means, and He means what He says. Moreover, the only way that we can hold this truth is by reading what He says – and then applying what He says to our lives.

D. L. Moody is quoted as saying, "This book will keep you from sin, or sin will keep you from this book." I have taught for years that there are two things that Believers should do every day – Read your Bible, and Pray. This is the way we keep in communication with the Father. He speaks to us in His written word, and we speak to Him in our prayers.

You hold in your hand a collection of daily ponderings based upon a passage in each of the 365 readings that will take you through the entire New Testament in One Year. Each of the consecutive daily readings starts with you reading the selected section of Scripture (example: January 1 you read Matthew 1), followed by a short devotional thought on a verse(s) from that day's reading. The day's musing will end with a short prayer starter from the devotional thought. In a footnote at the bottom of each page is a consecutive reading from the Old Testament should you choose to read the entire Bible in a year. Some use the New Testament reading and devotion in the morning and then close their day with the Old Testament reading.

Take a few moments every day to ponder the wonder of God's transcendent Word. Join me in musing over the truths that are contained in the marvelous Word of God.

1

JANUARY A Time for New Beginnings

January on our calendar marks the beginning of a new year. We look back in angst and longing for what has gone before us. We look forward in eager anticipation of what we can find.

We look backward, feel a mixture of happiness, and despair over the last year. We rejoice in the good things that have happened. We want to forget the hurts, tribulations, and troubles. We feel renewed over the things we did to advance the Kingdom, and regrets over the things that we did in sin.

This year, as we travel through the Old Testament, we need to look for the way that God has given us new opportunities daily (sometimes minute-by-minute) to be a part of His marvelous plan and majestic purpose for our lives.

Open your Bible, and spend time with God this month as you see the beginnings of everything, and ponder on how God makes each day a new beginning for you.

January 1

Daily Bible Reading: Matthew 1[1]

Verse of the Day: Matthew 1:23 – *"Behold, the virgin shall be with child, and shall bring forth a son, And they shall call his name Immanuel; which is, being interpreted, God with us."*

Immanuel. God with us. What a great and auspicious beginning for the New Year. To start this year with God in reading His Word – the reminder that God is with us in the person of Jesus Christ.

The prophet Isaiah predicted this in his writings. In the Old Testament, we find this in Isaiah 7:14. This is a Greek transliteration of the Hebrew word – עִמָּנוּאֵל – that is why Matthew gives the interpretation to his readers.

What a wonderful thought, God is with us, every day, in every place, and in the days to come. No matter what happens in this year, we can rest assured that God (Jesus) is with us every step of the way.

Prayer: Immanuel, I am so excited to take this journey with You through Your Word this year. Bless my reading and application. Amen.

January 2

Daily Bible Reading: Matthew 2[2]

Verse of the Day: Matthew 2:6 – *"And thou Bethlehem, land of Judah, Art in no wise least among the princes of Judah: For out of thee shall come forth a governor, Who shall be shepherd of my people Israel."*

Matthew 1 and 2 cover the birth of Jesus and the events that happen over the next couple of years. Of the four Gospel accounts (or as they can be understood as redemptive biographies), only Matthew and Luke cover the Virgin Birth of Jesus. This is such a vital part of understanding who Jesus is.

The Old Testament says to believe something only upon the word of 2 or 3 witnesses. We see this attested to by Matthew, Mark, and later by Paul in Galatians. The purpose of each writer of the Gospels also plays into this – Matthew pictures Jesus as a King, Mark as a servant, Luke as a man, and John as God. Matthew and Luke tell us important information for a King and a man.

---

[1] OT Reading – Genesis 1,2
[2] OT Reading – Genesis 3 – 5

Prayer: Jesus, as I look at your life, may it move me to follow and surrender wholly to You each day. I fully surrender all. Amen.

January 3

Daily Bible Reading: Matthew 3[3]

Verse of the Day: Matthew 3:16 – 17 – "*And Jesus when he was baptized, went up straightway from the water: and lo, the heavens were opened unto him, and he saw the Spirit of God descending as a dove, and coming upon him; and lo, a voice out of the heavens, saying, This is my beloved Son, in whom I am well pleased.*"

We find here the reference to all Persons of the Godhead. Jesus, the Son has submitted in voluntary humility to the Father, the Father has declared His endorsement and delight in His Son, and the Spirit desires to glorify Christ.

Today, as we go through our day, let us make it our desire and determination to give glory to Jesus in all that we think, say, and do. Let us seek to show those around us that we have been with God today, and He is pleased to work through us.

Prayer: Father, guard and guide my thoughts and mouth today. Allow me to show forth Jesus to any and all I can today. It is my heart's cry to follow Him. I thank You for Your direction in my life today. Amen.

January 4

Daily Bible Reading: Matthew 4[4]

Verse of the Day: Matthew 4:1 – "*Then was Jesus led up of the Spirit into the wilderness to be tempted of the devil.*"

Right after His submission to the Father in baptism, Jesus was faced with the temptations of Satan. Great spiritual victories are often followed by testing. The word used here *peirázō* in the Greek means 'to try or make proof of." It carries the negative context of "to entice, solicit or provoke to sin."

The Holy Spirit led Jesus into this temptation. Why? Many believe it was to show us that He was incapable of sin. Some believe it was to instruct us on how to defeat temptation in our lives. Jesus responded to each of the schemes of the tempter by quoting Scripture from Deuteronomy. We can have victory over the temptations in our lives

---

[3] OT Reading – Genesis 6 – 8
[4] OT Reading – Genesis 9 – 11

today by memorizing and applying God's Word when needed. Satan hates it when we stand upon the Word of God – so – make him mad and stand today.

Prayer: Jesus, guard my heart through Your Word today. Help me defeat Satan. Amen.

January 5

Daily Bible Reading: Matthew 5:1 – 26[5]

Verse of the Day: Matthew 5:1 – 3 – "*And seeing the multitudes, he went up into the mountain: and when he had sat down, his disciples came unto him: and he opened his mouth and taught them, saying, Blessed are the poor in spirit: for theirs is the kingdom of heaven.*"

Blessed – the word *makários* in the Greek means happy or fortunate. It is used about 50 times in the New Testament to describe the kind of happiness that comes from having God's favor.

In the Beatitudes, Jesus uses it nine times. I get the feeling that He is trying to teach us something. We can have true happiness by living in the favor of God, and He outlines different elements of life that will produce this.

Take some time today to review the Beatitudes (and the Sermon on the Mount) to re-discover how to have Divine Favor and inner happiness.

Prayer: Father, I desire to have this inner happiness that only comes from You. Amen.

January 6

Daily Bible Reading: Matthew 5:27 – 48[6]

Verse of the Day: Matthew 5:43 – "*Ye have heard that it was said, Thou shalt love thy neighbor, and hate thine enemy: but I say unto you, love your enemies, and pray for them that persecute you;*"

You have heard, but I say – a series of statements that Jesus gives in the Sermon on the Mount. The One who wrote the Scriptures now makes some serious points about them.

"You have heard" refers to the various teachings of the Rabbis rather than Moses. Jesus is questioning the scholars, not the Old Testament text. He is getting to the heart of the Scriptures – the spirit of the Laws, while

---

[5] OT Reading – Genesis 12 – 14
[6] OT Reading – Genesis 15 – 17

many previous Rabbis had worked on what they thought the letter of the Laws had taught.

The Law will help us to live right and provide and protect us, but, we find too quickly that we cannot live by it. We need Jesus to live it through us.

Prayer: Jesus, I submit my life to You. Control my life, live the perfect life through me, I can't do it. My life is in You. Amen.

January 7

Daily Bible Reading: Matthew 6[7]

Verse of the Day: Matthew 6:9 – *"After this manner therefore pray ye. Our Father who art in heaven, Hallowed be thy name."*

We refer to this as the Lord's Prayer. Technically this should be called the Model Prayer. It is the model Jesus gave His disciples on how to pray.

He builds it around 6 requests. The first three ask for the Kingdom of God to come (vv. 9,10) and the last three ask for God to meet our daily needs (vv.11 – 13).

The model starts with our acknowledgment of God as our Father, we must have a personal relationship with Him through Jesus Christ. Then, an imperative statement is used – "May Your Name be hallowed."

Begin in praise, bring your requests, and end in praise. What a great pattern for our time of prayer each day. Today, mark out time to do this pattern in your prayer.

Prayer: Glorious Father, I praise You that You do meet my needs each day. I praise Your Holy Name. I acknowledge Your greatness.

January 8

Daily Bible Reading: Matthew 7[8]

Verse of the Day: Matthew 7:7 – 8 – *"Ask, and it shall be given you; seek, and ye shall find; knock, and it shall be opened unto you: for every one that asketh receiveth; and he that seeketh findeth; and to him that knocketh it shall be opened."*

Ask, seek, knock. Receive, find, open. Sounds simple enough. If we ask, seek, knock, we receive, find, open.

---

[7] OT Reading – Genesis 18 – 19
[8] OT Reading – Genesis 20 – 22

As we muse over this section today, and as we ponder the depth of what Jesus is saying in our verses, I believe we can see that prayer is not complex, complicated, or beyond us. It is actually very simple. Prayer is simply talking to God as we would with others around us.

With a personal relationship with Him, we come as children to a Father with our requests. We come and seek His will for the desires of our heart, and then as a child trusts that their Dad can meet those needs, God will meet our needs.

Prayer: Father, as Your child I bring my needs to You today. I trust Your answer. Amen.

January 9

Daily Bible Reading: Matthew 8[9]

Verse of the Day: Matthew 8:1 – 2 – *"And when he was come down from the mountain, great multitudes followed him. And behold, there came to him a leper and worshipped him, saying, Lord, if thou wilt, thou canst make me clean."*

In chapters 8 – 10 we see the power of the King displayed in numerous miracles. We get a ringside seat to witness His miracles of healing, power over nature, and restoration of life.

As in His day, many focused only upon the miracle that was performed and miss the teaching that He gave with them. Because of His power over sickness, nature and death, He had the authority to forgive sin and restore a person to the right relationship with God the Father.

As you read these chapters, don't lose sight of the greater underlying miracle – the gift of eternal life.

Prayer: Jesus, I am so easily caught up in the glamour and wonder of the miracle to the loss of the greater miracle – I am God's child.

January 10

Daily Bible Reading: Matthew 9:1 - 17[10]

Verse of the Day: Matthew 9:9 – *"And as Jesus passed by from thence, he saw a man, called Matthew, sitting at the place of toll: and he saith unto him, Follow me. And he arose, and followed him."*

---

[9] OT Reading – Genesis 23 – 24
[10] OT Reading – Genesis 25 – 26

Jesus never begged His disciples to follow Him. He simply presented the offer – and they accepted. He offers us the same. Will we follow Him?

When He called them to follow Him, it was understood that they would leave everything behind. It was an all or nothing proposition. It is still the same today. Are you all in with Jesus? Or, do you pick and choose when you will follow? The problem is, it doesn't work that way. Follow or stay. Let Him change you or remain in your sin. You choose. Choose right.

Prayer: Jesus, today I choose You. I will surrender my thoughts, words, and life to You. Take it and change it for Your service and plans. I will seek to daily lay down my choices and pick up Your directions and Cross. I want to be all in. I want to see what You can do through me in this world. Use me. Amen.

January 11

Daily Bible Reading: Matthew 9:18 - 38[11]

Verse of the Day: Matthew 9:37 – "*Then saith he unto his disciples, The harvest indeed is plenteous, but the laborers are few.*"

Sad words. The question is whether that is still true today? Consider that for a moment. Pause and contemplate Jesus' statement.

OK. What did you decide? Is there still a harvest that needs to be reaped? With over 7 billion souls alive on earth, I would say that there definitely is. So, are there enough workers to bring in this harvest?

I believe that that is the sad part of this statement. Many could be reached for God, but there is not enough people seeking to reach them. I must stop and seriously look into my heart and life. Am I doing all that I can? Am I a serious and fruitful worker for my Lord?

Prayer: Father, today as I ponder this truth, I am ashamed to say that I am not doing all that I could to reach others with the Good News of the Gospel. I have discovered the hope for the world, and I shamefully hoard it up. May I reach out today and be Your worker.

---

[11] OT Reading – Genesis 27 – 28

January 12

Daily Bible Reading: Matthew 10:1 - 23[12]

Verse of the Day: Matthew 10:16 – "*Behold, I send you forth as sheep in the midst of wolves: be ye therefore wise as serpents, and harmless as doves.*"

Suspicion or discernment? There is a fine line between these two aspects in our lives. God expects us to be discerning, alert, and perceptive as we move through the world. He does not want us to be suspicious of everyone we come in contact with.

Suspicion can be defined as having or showing a cautious distrust of someone or something. Discernment can be defined as the ability to see and understand people, things, or situations clearly and intelligently.

We need to use discernment. We will face hatred and possibly violence from others, but we are to be pure and innocent in our interactions.

Prayer: God of all wisdom, grant me the ability to discern who, when and where I should be at all times in my walk with You. Give me a heart of love for others around me.

January 13

Daily Bible Reading: Matthew 10:24 - 42[13]

Verse of the Day: Matthew 10:39 – "*He that findeth his life shall lose it; and he that loseth his life for my sake shall find it.*"

In our passages today, Jesus was reminding His disciples that persecutions were coming – and we know that they did. He reminded them to fear God and not man, He challenged them to confess Him before men. In doing this, He said that division would come.

Today, we often think that plurality and unity at any cost is the right way. Jesus said that submitting to Him, standing on His truth, and speaking the truth in love is the only acceptable way. Sometimes this will cause division.

We need to learn to look at the eternal and not the immediate. Will temporal division provide eternal reward? Will temporal unity cause the loss of eternal rewards? We must choose the eternal over the temporal.

---

[12] OT Reading – Genesis 29 – 30
[13] OT Reading – Genesis 31 – 32

Prayer: Eternal God of Creation, I seek to submit, stand, and speak in the basis of Your love. Give me courage to follow through. Amen.

January 14

Daily Bible Reading: Matthew 11[14]

Verse of the Day: Matthew 11:28 – 30 – *"Come unto me, all ye that labor and are heavy laden, and I will give you rest. Take my yoke upon you, and learn of me; for I am meek and lowly in heart: and ye shall find rest unto your souls. For my yoke is easy, and my burden is light."*

Leadership often is associated with a tough, hard, bullish, rugged, demanding persona – Jesus is gentle. He is meek.

When we understand that meek is not weak, but strength under control, we can see that He is the kind of person we want to lead us. He is not legalistic in His demands. He invites us to "yoke" up with Him. Instead of increasing our stress and anxiety – He will make it lighter. He will walk, work, and weaken the things we are struggling with. Give them to God – and then let go. He's got it.

Prayer: Gentle and Meek Savior, I come today under a load of care and concern. I release them into Your hands, I take Your yoke, and I will walk and work with You as You weaken the load. I praise You – Amen.

January 15

Daily Bible Reading: Matthew 12:1 – 21[15]

Verse of the Day: Matthew 12:8 – *"For the Son of man is lord of the sabbath."*

In today's readings (vv. 18 – 21) Matthew quotes Isaiah 42:1 – 4. Jesus had just had some run-ins with the Pharisees – first in a field over the disciples plucking grain and eating it on the Sabbath, then in the Synagogue over His healing a man with a shriveled hand on the Sabbath.

The Pharisees and Sadducees had developed an intricate system of what was considered work and what was allowed on the Sabbath day. This placed a great burden upon the average Israelite of that day. Jesus here is teaching that He is the Lord of the Sabbath. He is the One who created the Sabbath – and it was created for people's good.

---

[14] OT Reading – Genesis 33 – 35
[15] OT Reading – Genesis 36 – 37

When we place rules and regulations, when we put manmade laws, when we refuse to help and minister to others, we are not following the lead of our Lord. Be an imitator of Christ today.

Prayer: Jesus, I seek to imitate You in all.

January 16

Daily Bible Reading: Matthew 12:22 – 50[16]

Verse of the Day: Matthew 12:31 – 32 – *"Therefore I say unto you, Every sin and blasphemy shall be forgiven unto men; but the blasphemy against the Spirit shall not be forgiven. And whosoever shall speak a word against the Son of man, it shall be forgiven him; but whosoever shall speak against the Holy Spirit, it shall not be forgiven him, neither in this world, nor in that which is to come."*

The unpardonable sin. Some worry over if they had committed it.

Jesus teaches that the stubborn refusal to heed the Holy Spirit's convicting urgings and accept the forgiveness that Jesus offers is the unpardonable sin. In other words, if one dies without accepting the free gift that Christ offers through the Holy Spirit, there is no second chance.

While you are alive (and if you are reading this, you are), do not delay. Receive the free gift of Salvation today. You may not have another chance.

Prayer: Jesus, I accept Your gift now. Amen.

January 17

Daily Bible Reading: Matthew 13:1 – 32[17]

Verse of the Day: Matthew 13:3 – *"And he spake to them many things in parables, saying, Behold, the sower went forth to sow;"*

I love to study Jesus and His methodologies of teaching. He is THE Master Teacher. He knew exactly how to communicate. We live in a word that communicates by digital format in many instances. Still there are many times that we communicate in a face-to-face interaction.

Jesus might give us the following advice in our communications – make it clear. Make it simple. Emphasize the essentials. Minimize the non-essentials. Don't communicate to try to impress others. Be content to leave some things unsaid.

---

[16] OT Reading – Genesis 38 – 40
[17] OT Reading – Genesis 41

How does my communications stand up to this review? How does yours? Consider this, Jesus' teachings and words still are communicating to millions, shouldn't we learn from this.

Prayer: I come to You, the Word to learn from You how to communicate the message to others around me. Amen.

January 18

Daily Bible Reading: Matthew 13:33 – 58[18]

Verse of the Day: Matthew 13:57 – 58 – "*And they were offended in him. But Jesus said unto them, A prophet is not without honor, save in his own country, and in his own house. And he did not many mighty works there because of their unbelief.*"

This is the second time that Jesus has gone into His hometown. Because of their familiarity with Him they refused to recognize Who He really is. They may have admitted that He was a Rabbi, but knowing His lack of training may have rejected Him as one. They definitely rejected Him as God.

And, in turn they took offense that He would present Himself in this way. Their unbelief blinded their eyes to who He is. Many take offense at Him today, and their eyes are blinded to who He is. They reject the One who could be their answer and hope.

Prayer: Father, open my eyes to see all that Jesus is. He is God, the very God who can offer the solution to every issue. The One who can direct and guide my life. I want to see Jesus. Amen.

January 19

Daily Bible Reading: Matthew 14:1 – 21[19]

Verse of the Day: Matthew 14:20 – "*And they all ate, and were filled: and they took up that which remained over of the broken pieces, twelve baskets full.*"

In this particular miracle, we can lose sight of an important concept given here. What is that you say? It is the fact that Jesus is enough!

We find the disciples and Jesus teaching 5,000 men plus women and children (some say this may have been as many as 20,000 people). When

---

[18] OT Reading – Genesis 42 – 43
[19] OT Reading – Genesis 44 – 45

it comes time to eat, where would they ever find supplies enough to feed this crowd? Jesus knew – the need could and would be filled by Him.

Notice, he provided food for all these people, they ate until they were full, and there was still a large supply left over. Jesus is enough. Got it? JESUS IS ENOUGH.

Prayer: Jesus, there are times when I am not sure that You can fill the needs that I have. My lack of faith is the reason that I often worry and lack to see You provide what I need. I need to trust You more. Amen.

January 20

Daily Bible Reading: Matthew 14:22 – 36[20]

Verse of the Day: Matthew 14:27 – "*But straightway Jesus spake unto them, saying Be of good cheer; it is I; be not afraid.*"

It was a dark and stormy night.

How many books have I read that start this way. Yet, as you read today's passages, your mind will see the picture of a small fishing boat on the sea of Galilee engulfed by a vicious storm. Seasoned fishermen are frightened for their lives. Yet, they are exactly where Jesus told them to be.

But, what I have learned from this passage is that when I am in the midst of a "vicious storm" in my life if I will stop and look and listen I will find Jesus coming to me through the winds, rain, and storm. He will always show up right on time in just the right way. If you are facing a storm today, stop, look, and listen. He is there.

Prayer: Great Encourager, Jesus, I am looking for you in the midst of the storm. You promise to be there. You bring cheer and courage when most needed. Come, Lord Jesus.

January 21

Daily Bible Reading: Matthew 15:1 – 20[21]

Verse of the Day: Matthew 15:18 – "*But the things which proceed out of the mouth come forth out of the heart; and they defile the man.*"

A children's song goes like this:

---

[20] OT Reading – Genesis 46 – 48
[21] OT Reading – Genesis 49 – 50

"O be careful little mouth what you say, O be careful little mouth what you say. There's a Father up above, And He's looking down in love. So, be careful little mouth what you say."

Jesus warns us that the words that we speak come from the depths of our heart. If our heart is clean – we will speak words of praise. If our hearts are defiled – our words will display this.

We need to see that the root issue is not our talk, but the depth and depravity of our hearts. Only One is capable of cleansing a heart. Only One is able to make what is defiled presentable again. Jesus. Come to Him today and ask Him to clean Your heart and full being.

Prayer: Jesus, clean me. Take the dirt and evil from within me and clean it into what will praise and honor You. May others see You through me and the words that I speak today. I trust You as able to do this. Amen.

January 22

Daily Bible Reading: Matthew 15:21 – 39[22]

Verse of the Day: Matthew 15:28 – *"Then Jesus answered and said unto her, O woman, great is thy faith: be it done unto thee even as thou wilt. And her daughter was healed from that hour."*

Jesus continues to heal multitudes of people in our passages today. Of all the ones that could have been discussed, Matthew tells of a Gentile (non-Jewish) woman from Canaan and her daughter. After some back and forth discussion with Jesus, He heals her daughter.

Some think Jesus cruel for not just healing the girl, but rather debated with the mother. But, understand that the miracles that Jesus performed where also teaching moments. He sought to show that this Gentile woman had great faith in who He was. He was pointing to the fact that all of us need to have faith. Our salvation is based upon Grace that comes through Faith. How great is your faith today?

Prayer: Jesus, I come to You in faith today. Help the areas of unbelief that struggle in my being. Allow me to only believe. Each day I seek to trust You fully. Grant my request. Amen.

---

[22] OT Reading – Exodus 1 – 3

January 23

Daily Bible Reading: Matthew 16[23]

Verse of the Day: Matthew 16:18 – *"And I also say unto thee, that thou art Peter, and upon this rock I will build my church; and the gates of Hades shall not prevail against it."*

In Aramaic (the language Jesus spoke) the words for Peter and rock are same. We lose the wordplay in English. The Greek word for Peter is *Pétros* (a pebble), and the word for rock is *pétra* (a cliff or boulder). Some misinterpret this verse to mean that Jesus was going to build His church upon Peter, but the wordplay shows that He will build His church upon Peter's proclamation – "Thou art the Christ, the Son of the living God." (Matthew 16:16)

The people of God will be joined in Christ's Church because they believe and accept that Jesus is God. The Church is not man's design or making – it is the divine structure that Jesus Himself has established for His followers.

Prayer: Jesus, help me to see the truth of the importance of Your Church. This assembly that You created is based upon the pétra that Peter displayed that evening with Jesus. May I be a pétros of this great design. Amen.

January 24

Daily Bible Reading: Matthew 17[24]

Verse of the Day: Matthew 17:3 – *"And behold, there appeared unto them Moses and Elijah talking with him."*

The Mount of Transfiguration account. Jesus takes His inner circle of disciples up on a high mountain. While they are there, Jesus "peels back" his humanity, and they get a glimpse of His majesty and glory. What an awesome privilege that must have been.

While He was transfigured into His Glory before them, Moses and Elijah appear on the scene and talk with Him. These two are representatives of the Law (Moses) and the Prophets (Elijah).

Jesus instructs them to remain silent about what they had witnessed until after the Son of Man had risen from the dead (Matthew 17:9).

---

[23] OT Reading – Exodus 4 – 6
[24] OT Reading – Exodus 7 – 8

The disciples missed the reference to His rising from the dead. The Law and Prophets looked forward to the Messiah, we look back to the Messiah.

Prayer: Jesus, grant us the vision of Your Glory. May we have eyes to see You. Amen.

January 25

Daily Bible Reading: Matthew 18:1 – 20[25]

Verse of the Day: Matthew 18:1 – *"In that hour came the disciples unto Jesus, saying, Who then is greatest in the kingdom of heaven?"*

Greatness. We live in a world that seeks greatness. We are challenged and coerced to seek that mysterious, elusive entity called greatness. Exactly what is greatness? You will find that different cultures define it differently. Even in our country, we have varying degrees of what people call greatness.

Jesus, in this passage defines it in Matthew 18:4. Purity, innocence, humility, and trust like a child. When a father holds out his arms and says "Jump!" A child trusts and does just that.

Are we willing to surrender to Jesus and become like a little child? If not, we will never know or achieve the true measure of greatness in the kingdom of God.

Today, when the Father says "Jump!' Do it!

Prayer: Heavenly Father, I seek today to be Your child, to live like Your child, to talk like Your child, to trust like Your child. I surrender my will to Yours, and seek to obey. Amen.

January 26

Daily Bible Reading: Matthew 18:21 – 35[26]

Verse of the Day: Matthew 18:35 – *"So shall also my heavenly Father do unto you, if ye forgive not every one his brother from your hearts."*

Have you ever really stopped to think about how much God has forgiven you? I don't mean a surface check, but a deep down, gut level realization of what God has done in forgiving you?

---

[25] OT Reading – Exodus 9 – 10
[26] OT Reading – Exodus 11 – 12

His forgiveness cost Jesus His life. He died for us physically and spiritually to restore us to the Father. In celebration of the magnitude of what God has done, we should be the first to forgive others. Forgive and forget an action that a spouse, friend, or neighbor has done against you. In comparison, what they have done in minuscule to what God has forgiven us.

Today, if you harbor ill feelings or refusal to forgive someone, compare with God's forgiveness – and let it go. Forgive and forget.

Prayer: Jesus, thank You for taking my sin and my shame. Thank You for making me right with the Father. Help me to forgive others.

January 27

Daily Bible Reading: Matthew 19:1 – 15[27]

Verse of the Day: Matthew 19:5 – 6 – *"and said, For this cause shall a man leave his father and mother, and shall cleave to his wife; and the two shall become one flesh? So that they are no more two, but one flesh. What therefore God hath joined together, let not man put asunder."*

Jesus is questioned on the importance of marriage by a group of Pharisees. They are seeking to entrap Him and create division among His followers. Jesus, as was His custom responded with a quotation from the book of Genesis (2:24).

Whenever we are confronted with challenges of what we should do or believe, let us always return to the source – the Bible. Whatever God desires for our best can be found in His Word. That is why it is important for us to read and heed this precious book.

How much time are you spending acquiring the truth and wisdom available to you from God?

Prayer: Father, open my eyes and mind.

January 28

Daily Bible Reading: Matthew 19:16 – 30[28]

Verse of the Day: Matthew 19:25 – 26 – *"And when the disciples heard it, they were astonished exceedingly, saying, Who then can be saved? And Jesus looking upon them said to them, With men this is impossible; but with God all things are possible."*

---

[27] OT Reading – Exodus 13 – 15
[28] OT Reading – Exodus 16 – 18

In this last part of chapter 19, we read the story of the rich, young ruler. The disciples were shocked by Jesus' response to this man. Many today would have gone out of their way to accommodate him. Jesus told it straight and to the point.

One thing that I have always noticed in this passage is the question here and the answer of Jesus. Who can be saved? When we look at people around us, do we try to decide who can and who won't be saved? Jesus reminds us that salvation is entirely in the hands of God. Man can't save himself, and others can't make the choice. God is author of salvation, the provider of salvation, and the keeper of the saved.

Prayer: Father, I thank You that salvation is all from You and that I can rest in that assurance for all eternity. Amen.

January 29

Daily Bible Reading: Matthew 20:1 – 16 [29]

Verse of the Day: Matthew 20:16 – *"So the last shall be first, and the first last."*

In our reading today we hear Jesus tell a parable about the Kingdom of Heaven. He often uses parables to take the visible world to teach about the invisible.

In this parable, the worker's with the contract (the first one's selected) are the nation of Israel. They have the covenants and promises. The latter workers are those whom God has brought in – namely the Gentiles.

Jesus wants us to see that all who believe and obey God will receive the same rewards and promises. The Church did not replace Israel, and the Church will not receive anything that Israel will not receive in the coming Kingdom Age.

Spend some time today meditating upon the glorious and marvelous riches that are promised to those who are God's children.

Prayer: Gracious King, as Your child I come today in grateful adoration for the promises that You have made for all who believe. Amen.

---

[29] OT Reading – Exodus 19 – 21

January 30

Daily Bible Reading: Matthew 20:17 – 34 [30]

Verse of the Day: Matthew 20:18 – 19 – *"Behold, we go up to Jerusalem; and the Son of man shall be delivered unto the chief priests and scribes; and they shall condemn him to death, and shall deliver him unto the Gentiles to mock, and to scourge, and to crucify: and the third day he shall be raised up."*

Today, Jesus tells His disciples for the third time (16:21; 17:9. 22, 23) about His anticipated arrest and death. This is the first time that He reveals to them the method by which He would die – crucifixion.

They should not have been taken by surprise at His death, burial, and resurrection. He spelt it out plainly. Yet, they are as human as we are. God in His Word has told us of His power and might, yet we are so surprised when He answers our prayers. Before we are too hard on the disciples, consider this – we have the rest of the story and still are taken by surprise at His promises.

Prayer: Jesus, I am sorry that I so often pray and then are surprised that You answer. I need to have my faith strengthened to believe You.

January 31

Daily Bible Reading: Matthew 21:1 – 22 [31]

Verse of the Day: Matthew 21:6 – *"And the disciples went, and did even as Jesus appointed them,"*

In this account by Matthew of what we term the Triumphal Entry of Jesus, we find this simple statement. They went and did as he appointed them. Simple. Concise. To the point.

As I have pondered on this statement, I asked myself – could this be said of me? As I walk through life today, do I do as He has appointed me to do? Am I one that could be labeled faithful and true?

Today, pause and ask yourself that same question. What would you answer honestly?

As I mused over this, I realized that, no, I do not do this all the time. I fail often. However, I am reminded that I have a God who forgives and restores.

---

[30] OT Reading – Exodus 22 – 24
[31] OT Reading – Exodus 25 – 26

Prayer: *Forgiving and gracious Father, today I ask You to forgive and restore me. May I seek You each and every day to do as You have appointed me to do. May I be a pleasant follower of You in all areas. Amen.*

FEBRUARY Love Letters From God

February – considered by many to be the month of love. We celebrate St. Valentine's Day in the middle of the month. The Bible is God's Love Letter to His children. It is His way of connecting us to Him, to understand His plan, His purpose, His heart, His Love, His acceptance, His way of restoring us to a fullness of His love.

All through the New Testament God is showing His great love for His created beings – and especially to those who are His. The Gospels are sometimes called Redemptive Biographies, because they are biographical accounts of Jesus' life – but more than that, they are the account of the provision of Redemption provided by God.

As we read the passages this month, pause and consider how that they can show God's love by provision and protection in our lives. Spend some time thanking God that He does care so much that He provided the way to be reconciled with Him.

Now, let us begin this month of love receiving His love and giving our love to Him.

February 1

Daily Bible Reading: Matthew 21:23 – 46 [32]

Verse of the Day: Matthew 21:45 – *"And when the chief priests and the Pharisees heard his parables, they perceived that he spake of them."*

Parables. Jesus often used these heavenly stories to explain earthly concepts. The Old Testament is written to those who thought in stories. Jesus at this point is still in the Old Testament economy of God. Thus, He uses stories – but not only stories, stories that are like wrapped gifts. The package needs to be peeled off to reach the wonder of the gift inside.

These stories reach different people in different ways, and effect each differently. The parable of the soils can reach 4 different types of people. The Prodigal Son reaches the father, the prodigal, and the jealous older brother differently.

Prayer: Father, as I ponder and study the stories (parables) that Your Son shares in the Gospels give me wisdom to understand. And, once I understand, give me strength to apply what You are teaching me in the correct way. My I have true ears to hear His Words. Amen.

February 2

Daily Bible Reading: Matthew 22:1 – 22 [33]

Verse of the Day: Matthew 22:14 – *"For many are called, but few chosen."*

In this parable of the Wedding Banquet, Jesus makes this statement at the end. He has just spoken of one who was bound "hand and foot, and cast him out into the outer darkness" (22:13).

The Greek word, κλητοι, means invited. It is not used in the same sense as Paul uses it (Romans 8:28 – 29). Jesus is specifically speaking of Israel at this point, and He is saying that all of Israel has been invited into the Kingdom, but only a few will believe and follow Him. Thus, God will not bring them into the banquet of the Kingdom.

In a way we can understand this of all people also. God has made His invitation open to anyone (John 3:16), but only a few will believe and receive this gift (Matthew 7:13 – 14).

---

[32] OT Reading – Exodus 27 – 28
[33] OT Reading – Exodus 29 – 30

Have you believed and received? Today will be a great day to settle it.

Prayer: Jesus, I bring my heart to You to cleanse and claim as Your own. Amen.

February 3

Daily Bible Reading: Matthew 22:23 – 46 [34]

Verse of the Day: Matthew 22:23 – *"On that day there came to him Sadducees, they that say that there is no resurrection: and they asked him,"*

I remember in one of my Seminary classes the instructor said, "The Sadducees were exactly that, they were sad you see." He went on to explain that they based their beliefs solely on the Pentateuch (the first five books of Moses) and rejected all other writings. They thus did not believe in angels, demons, the resurrection or an afterlife. Thus, they were sad you see for a lack of a promise for the future. They basically saw any reward and success to be in the here-and-now only. Thus they lived an opulent lifestyle and found the teachings of Jesus a major threat.

When we muse over this religious thought pattern today, do we harbor it? Do we act as if we believe that today is all there is? Do we forget the promise of Eternal Life and the Kingdom?

Prayer: Eternal King, help me to focus on You and Your future rewards. Amen.

February 4

Daily Bible Reading: Matthew 23:1 – 22 [35]

Verse of the Day: Matthew 23:13 – *"But woe unto you, scribes and Pharisees, hypocrites! because ye shut the kingdom of heaven against men: for ye enter not in yourselves, neither suffer ye them that are entering in to enter."*

We often look with disdain at those who are very evident in their sinful lifestyle. But Jesus used His harshest and longest sermons, not for struggling sinners, prosperous people, or discouraged disciples – He spoke the strongest against the glory-hogs, legalists and religious hypocrites.

When we struggle, God knows our hearts. When we are discouraged, God knows our inner being. God comes to give rest and encouragement

---

[34] OT Reading – Exodus 31 – 33
[35] OT Reading – Exodus 34 – 36

to those who truly seek Him, no matter where they are in life. But, to those who wear a mask and pretend to be perfect and above others – He sends strong words of condemnation.

Prayer, Father of Grace and Mercy, I come as a humble sinner before You today. Seek out the sin in me, cleanse it, remove it, take control over that area of my life. Amen.

February 5

Daily Bible Reading: Matthew 23:23 – 39 [36]

Verse of the Day: Matthew 23:37 – " *O Jerusalem, Jerusalem, that killeth the prophets, and stoneth them that are sent unto her! how often would I have gathered thy children together, even as a hen gathereth her chickens under her wings, and ye would not!"*

The Greek word, ορνις, translated "hen," simply means "bird." It is the base of our word for the study of birds – ornithology.

The Old Testament has many references to God's care for His people in the same way that a mother bird cares for her chicks. (Deut. 32:10 – 12; Psalm 36:7; 61:4; 91:4; Isaiah 31:5; and Malachi 4:2). The passages bring to mind how birds shelter their young under their wings and compare this to God's protection. Jesus here says He wants to give people this same kind of protection and love, yet they so frequently reject what He offers.

Prayer: God of protection and love, I come today asking You to cover me with Your wings of shelter in this time. May I gain the assurance of Your protection and shelter in the midst of the storms in my life. Amen.

February 6

Daily Bible Reading: Matthew 24:1 – 22 [37]

Verse of the Day: Matthew 24:3 – *"And as he sat on the mount of Olives, the disciples came unto him privately, saying, Tell us, when shall these things be? and what shall be the sign of thy coming, and of the end of the world?"*

Chapters 24 and 25 in Matthew is the End Times course that Jesus taught His disciples. They ask Him these questions, and in response He shares an insight into the chronology of eschatology (end times).

---

[36] OT Reading – Exodus 37 – 38
[37] OT Reading – Exodus 39 – 40

Three indicators of time are given in Matthew 24:6 – 14. Read and consider these. In Matthew 24:6 – "the end is not yet." The second is in Matthew 24:8 – "But all these things are the beginning of travail." And the third is in Matthew 24:14 – "and then shall the end come."

Consider these as you muse over what Jesus is saying in this important passage.

Prayer: Father, open my eyes to see the truth in Your Word. May I understand the lessons that You proclaim. May the reminder that Jesus is coming back challenge me today.

February 7

Daily Bible Reading: Matthew 24:23 – 51 [38]

Verse of the Day: Matthew 24:36 – "*But of that day and hour knoweth no one, not even the angels of heaven, neither the Son, but the Father only.*"

Jesus again restates this in Acts 1:7 – "And he said unto them, It is not for you to know times or seasons, which the Father hath set within His own authority." Some manuscripts do not include the phrase, "neither the Son."

When He was here upon the Earth, Jesus voluntarily restricted His use of some of His Divine attributes (John 17:4, 5; Philippians 2:5 – 8). In this way He became hungry, thirsty and tired. Luke speaks of Him growing in knowledge and wisdom (Luke 2:52).

It appears that Jesus surrendered His use of omniscience in this matter. He is stressing that the date is not important – our being ready for His return should be at all times.

Prayer: Heavenly Father, may I spend each day as if Your Son could come back at any moment. In fact, the truth is that He could. May I live expectantly and ready to greet Him.

February 8

Daily Bible Reading: Matthew 25:1 – 30 [39]

Verse of the Day: Matthew 25:1 – "*Then shall the kingdom of heaven be likened unto ten virgins, who took their lamps, and went forth to meet the bridegroom.*"

---

[38] OT Reading – Leviticus 1 – 3
[39] OT Reading – Leviticus 4 – 6

In this chapter we find the parable of the Ten Virgins. Jesus uses the phrase "the kingdom of heaven" here (βασιλεια των ουρανων). The Jews in reverence to God avoided saying the name of God, so this is a Jewish way of saying the "kingdom of God." Matthew uses this phrase about 33 times and it is found basically in his writing alone.

This points out to us that the kingdom of God is not a political entity, it is a heavenly, spiritual one. Contrary to what they were looking for, Jesus did not come as a political deliverer, but a spiritual deliverer. We often make this same mistake today. He did not come to change governments – He came to change men's hearts, and this in turn will change the world.

Prayer: Jesus, help me to seek You to change my heart. May I seek to walk in Your truth. Amen.

February 9

Daily Bible Reading: Matthew 25:31 – 46 [40]

Verse of the Day: Matthew 25:40 – "*And the King shall answer and say unto them, Verily I say unto you, Inasmuch as ye did it unto one of these my brethren, even these least, ye did it unto me.*"

Probably a well known verse, our passage today contains the Lord challenging us to reach out to those who truly have needs, no matter what they are. We are called to provide help to the people we are aware of that need it.

In this verse, He uses the Greek word, ελαχιστων, which can be translated as smallest in importance; in authority; in the estimation of men; or in rank and excellence. We can find it easy to help those who can reciprocate while ignoring those who are most in true needs.

Jesus states that when we do it to those who are most needy, we are doing it as if it were Him receiving the help. Today, consider someone around you that needs a helping hand.

Prayer: Jesus, give me Your eyes to see the needs of friends, co-workers, and strangers that You bring into my sphere. Amen.

---

[40] OT Reading – Leviticus 7 – 9

February 10

Daily Bible Reading: Matthew 26:1 – 19 [41]

Verse of the Day: Matthew 26:14 – 15 – *"Then one of the twelve, who was called Judas Iscariot, went unto the chief priests, and said, What are ye willing to give me, and I will deliver him unto you? And they weighed unto him thirty pieces of silver."*

How could one who was close to Jesus, who apparently was considered by the Disciples to be a person of integrity (he was allowed to be the treasurer), and was considered one of His specially selected followers (a Disciple) so callously seek to betray Jesus into the hands of His enemies?

Maybe, a better question we should be asking ourselves today is – how could I, one of His followers and family so easily betray and disobey Him? Before we cast the first stone at Judas, we need to examine our lives.

Judas betrayed Him and so did Simon Peter. And, when we are honest in our personal scrutiny, we are guilty also.

Prayer: Father, examine me, expose how I so easily disobey and betray my Savior. Amen.

February 11

Daily Bible Reading: Matthew 26:20 – 54 [42]

Verse of the Day: Matthew 26:36 – *"Then cometh Jesus with them unto a place called Gethsemane, and saith unto his disciples, Sit ye here, while I go yonder and pray."*

This is the account of Jesus' final night, the night of betrayal and trials. Jesus, being fully aware of what was about to take place goes to the Garden of Gethsemane (Greek word for "Oil Press"). Sin and death began in a garden, and now the Victor over sin and death battles in a garden. In this place where olives were crushed into oil, the One anointed with oil would be crushed under the burden of our sin.

The first people (Adam and Eve) betrayed God the Father by disobedience and brought sin and death into this world. Now, God the Son would be faced with a betrayer, and He will steadfastly obey the Father and destroy sin and death.

---

[41] OT Reading – Leviticus 10 – 12
[42] OT Reading – Leviticus 13

Prayer: Jesus, I bow humbly before You today. Because of Your obedience I am redeemed. Because of Your obedience I am forgiven. Because of Your obedience I have a future with You and Your Father. Amen.

February 12

Daily Bible Reading: Matthew 26:55 – 74 [43]

Verse of the Day: Matthew 26:69 – 70 – *"Now Peter was sitting without in the court: and a maid came unto him, saying, Thou also wast with Jesus the Galilaean. But he denied before them all, saying, I know not what thou sayest."*

Hours earlier Peter had declared that he would "die with thee, yet will I not deny thee." (Matthew 26:35). Now, faced by a young female slave (Greek παιδισκη), Peter begins to deny that he knew Jesus. In our reading today, we see him increasingly vehemently denying any knowledge or relationship with Jesus.

We need to stop here and consider our own lives. Day-to-day do we act, speak, and live like we know and obey Jesus? Or, in our own ways do we deny any relationship with Him? If someone asked those you come in contact with about your relationship – what would they say?

Prayer: Holy Spirit, come into my life and give me the confidence and boldness to constantly acclaim Jesus. May I humbly be seen as a true follower of the King. Amen.

February 13

Daily Bible Reading: Matthew 27:1 – 31 [44]

Verse of the Day: Matthew 27:27 – *"Then the soldiers of the governor took Jesus into the Praetorium, and gathered unto him the whole band."*

The Praetorium was the palace in which the governor or procurator of a province resided, to which use the Romans were accustomed to appropriate the palaces already existing, and formerly dwelt in by kings or princes. At Jerusalem it was a magnificent palace which Herod the Great had built for himself, and which the Roman procurators seemed to have occupied whenever they came from Caesarea to Jerusalem to transact public business.

---

[43] OT Reading – Leviticus 14
[44] OT Reading – Leviticus 15 - 17

A magnificent palace that became a scene of brutal treatment of the King of the Universe. The soldiers mocked and abused Him there. The creature desecrated the Creator. And yet, this was all in the plan and purpose of God. Our forgiveness and restoration will come from this treatment. We may not always be able to understand God's method, but let us trust Him to provide for us.

Prayer: Father, thank You for Your plans.

February 14

Daily Bible Reading: Matthew 27:32 – 66 [45]

Verse of the Day: Matthew 27:55 – *"And many women were there beholding from afar, who had followed Jesus from Galilee, ministering unto him: among whom was Mary Magdalene, and Mary the mother of James and Joses, and the mother of the sons of Zebedee."*

Today is Valentines Day. A day that we celebrate love. It almost can seem like this is a strange section of Matthew to read today. Yet, when we stop and ponder the importance of what is taking place in this passage, we realize that this is the fulfillment of what we consider in John 3:16.

What is taking place on the hill called Calvary is the visual portrayal of the grand and endless love of God. "For God so loved the world that He gave His Son." There really is no greater image for understanding the grandeur of love – God's love for us.

Prayer: Heavenly Father, as we ponder the fullness of Your love, it is not displayed in any other place as grand as in the Cross on Calvary. May I pause today in the thoughts and celebrations of love to remember this truth.

February 15

Daily Bible Reading: Matthew 28:1 – 20 [46]

Verse of the Day: Matthew 28:19 – 20 – *"Go ye therefore, and make disciples of all the nations, baptizing them into the name of the Father and of the Son and of the Holy Spirit: teaching them to observe all things whatsoever I commanded you: and lo, I am with you always, even unto the end of the world."*

The Great Commission. Given by Jesus to His Body of believers. Go. Make disciples. Baptize. Teach.

---

[45] OT Reading – Leviticus 18 - 19
[46] OT Reading – Leviticus 20 - 21

Today, let us focus on the last part – "*I am with you always, even unto the end of the world.*" Have you considered that Matthew starts in chapter 1 telling us that Jesus is to be "Immanuel" – God with us. And here he ends his redemptive biography of Jesus with His promise to be Immanuel always. He will never leave us nor forsake us. Always there – in good times and bad. Always there when we are doing right – and wrong.

Prayer: Jesus, thank You for the promise that we can hold to at all times. You are truly Immanuel in our lives. Knowing You are with me all the time gives peace and confidence.

February 16

Daily Bible Reading: Mark 1:1 – 22 [47]

Verse of the Day: Mark 1:1 – "*The beginning of the gospel of Jesus Christ, the Son of God.*"

Writing about three decades after the Resurrection, Mark gives us the second of the four redemptive biographies of Jesus Christ. Matthew showed us Jesus as a King, and now Mark will show us Jesus Christ the Servant.

In today's passage, we see the forerunner of the Servant, the baptism of the Servant, the temptation of the Servant, and the start of the mission of the Servant.

God takes on the form of a Servant to provide salvation to those who will believe. Over the next four weeks, we will observe the servant as He ministers to those around Him, and learn of His ministry to us today.

Prepare your heart and mind to receive the Servant. Let Him minister to you today.

Prayer: Father, help me to learn from the walk and ministry of Your Son then and today. May I be a servant to those around me, just as He was when He walked this earth. Amen.

---

[47] OT Reading – Leviticus 22 - 23

February 17

Daily Bible Reading: Mark 1:23 – 45 [48]

Verse of the Day: Mark 1:35 – *"And in the morning, a great while before day, he rose up and went out, and departed into a desert place, and there prayed."*

This is a great verse to remind me that I need to spend time each day in prayer with my Heavenly Father. The Greek word προσηυχετο is interesting. It is a verb set in the imperfect tense – this means that it is a continuing action. Jesus was in the habit of starting His day talking with the Father. It is the middle voice form meaning that the person is performing the action upon himself (reflexive action) or for his own benefit.

To help develop a likeness to Jesus in all areas of our life, we must meet often and alone with Him. We see for Jesus to do this with His Father, He had to get up early enough, far away enough, and stayed at it long enough. If He needed to do this – how much more do I need to do this today.

Prayer: *Father, I need to spend quality and quantity time talking and fellowshipping with You in Prayer. May it start now ---- Amen.*

February 18

Daily Bible Reading: Mark 2 [49]

Verse of the Day: Mark 2:17 – *"And when Jesus heard it, he saith unto them, They that are whole have no need of a physician, but they that are sick: I came not to call the righteous, but sinners."*

Jesus is here speaking to the Pharisees, who believed that they were righteous in God's sight, and was challenging their thoughts. The word righteous means one who is upright, virtuous, and keeping the commands of God. The Pharisees saw themselves as such. Jesus came to change sinners (those devoted to sin, wicked) not to condone what they were doing.

Jesus then (as well as today) demands repentance (a change of mind and will) that recognizes that one needs a Savior, and that Savior is Jesus Christ of Nazareth.

---

[48] OT Reading – Leviticus 24 - 25
[49] OT Reading – Leviticus 26 - 27

Prayer: Today Jesus, as I ponder the verse in our reading, help me to be aware that I am one who is in need of a Savior. As I have seen clearly from Your Word, You are that Savior promised from the book of Genesis throughout the whole Old Testament, and have come, died and rose again to remove my sin from me.

February 19

Daily Bible Reading: Mark 3:1 – 21[50]

Verse of the Day: Mark 3:9 – "*And he spake to his disciples, that a little boat should wait on him because of the crowd, lest they should throng him:*"

When I was growing up, I always pictured Jesus as a lonely Rabbi walking the countryside with 12 loyal followers. I understood that at times some others might have been with Him.

But, as I continued to study and grow in the Word, I became aware of the fact that as Jesus moved, there were large groups of people who moved with Him and gathered wherever He was. The Greek word in our verse above is οχλον and means a multitude of men who have flocked together in some place or a throng. In other words, He was not a lonely figure, but One who could not be missed wherever He went.

So, the question to consider, am I a true disciple or just one of the crowd?

Prayer: Jesus, may I be counted as one of Your faithful followers and not just one of the throng of those flocked together. Amen.

February 20

Daily Bible Reading: Mark 3:22 – 35[51]

Verse of the Day: Mark 3:28 – 29 – "*Verily I say unto you, All their sins shall be forgiven unto the sons of men, and their blasphemies wherewith soever they shall blaspheme: but whosoever shall blaspheme against the Holy Spirit hath never forgiveness, but is guilty of an eternal sin:*"

The Unpardonable Sin. People consistently worry about what this sin is, and whether they have committed it. One thing I have learned in my studies is this – If you are concerned over having committed it, you probably didn't.

---

[50] OT Reading – Numbers 1 - 2
[51] OT Reading – Numbers 3 - 4

So, what is the sin? Jesus says all sins are forgiven except blasphemy against the Holy Spirit. The word depicts continual action, perpetrated by the individual, and is a possibility if continued. What is it? It is consistently denying the truth brought to the individual by the Holy Spirit that Jesus is God.

Prayer: Holy Spirit, as I pause to pray today, I am thankful that I recognize the Lordship and Deity of God's Son – Jesus Christ. I place my trust in His Saving Grace. I renew my acceptance of His Person and Grace. Amen.

February 21

Daily Bible Reading: Mark 4:1 – 20[52]

Verse of the Day: Mark 4:17 – "*and they have no root in themselves, but endure for a while; then, when tribulation or persecution ariseth because of the word, straightway they stumble.*"

In today's passage, we read the Parable of the Sower (also in Matthew 13 and Luke 8). In this passage Jesus compares the message of the gospel as it works in the lives of four different types of people.

In our verse for the day above, Jesus is speaking of those who receive the truth as seed that falls upon rocky places. The seed does not go very deep, and when the troubles arise they fall away from anything to do with God. God is teaching in this parable that while we are focused on what fruit a person has, He is focused upon how deep their roots go. We watch the product, and He watches the process.

Prayer: Father, may the roots of Your truth go deep into my life. May I not only be concerned with producing fruit for You, but also developing deep, strong roots in Your love and grace. May I be firm in You. Amen.

February 22

Daily Bible Reading: Mark 4:21 – 41[53]

Verse of the Day: Mark 4:38 – "*And he himself was in the stern, asleep on the cushion: and they awake him, and say unto him, Teacher, carest thou not that we perish?*"

Have you ever been in this situation? All of life around you is in an uproar. You are being tossed and turned in all directions. You are sure that any moment will be the final one. And, then you look toward your

---

[52] OT Reading – Numbers 5 - 6
[53] OT Reading – Numbers 7

Lord. And He appears to be asleep. You cry out – Don't You care if I perish!?

Well, understand that going through this storm, Jesus could sleep because He had full trust in His Father. Did He care for the disciples? More than we can ever imagine. But, He was in full control of the situation and the outcome.

This same Jesus is the One who holds our situations and outcomes in His hand today. When it gets rough, trust the One who can grant the perfect outcome.

Prayer: Father, I often worry way too much. I show my lack of trust and faith – as recorded in Your Word, help my unbelief. Amen.

February 23

Daily Bible Reading: Mark 5:1 – 20[54]

Verse of the Day: Mark 5:19 – *"And he suffered him not, but saith unto him, Go to thy house unto thy friends, and tell them how great things the Lord hath done for thee, and how he had mercy on thee."*

I have felt many times that once Christ saved me, it would have been so much better if He took me to Heaven. All the struggles I could by-pass. But, in this healing of the Demon-possessed man gives us an insight in the reason we are left here.

When we have found the eternal promise and life given by the grace of God, our purpose in life takes on a brand new shade of meaning. We remain here to go and share what great things the Lord has done for us. We are to tell others about the mercy we have been granted, and that they too can receive this mercy. We are here today for the express purpose of telling others about Jesus and His saving grace and mercy.

Prayer: Jesus, help me to be Your hands, feet, and voice to others who need the wonderful solution to eternal doom. Amen.

February 24

Daily Bible Reading: Mark 5:21 – 43[55]

Verse of the Day: Mark 5:34 – *"And he said unto her, Daughter, thy faith hath made thee whole; go in peace, and be whole of thy plague."*

---

[54] OT Reading – Numbers 8 – 10
[55] OT Reading – Numbers 11 – 13

The Greek word πιστις, means trust or firm persuasion. The verb form then means to believe (see Mark 5:36). To have faith is to let go of our trust in ourselves and place that trust in someone or something else. Faith is only as good as the person or item that it is placed in. That is why the writers of the epistles often used the word πιστις to refer to what one believes, the content of our faith. This truth only comes from God's written Word (Romans 10:13 and Galatians 1:23).

So, the question to consider today is simply this – what am I placing my trust in? Myself? My bank account? My doctor? My family? Or, am I placing my faith in the Almighty, Eternal, All-loving God?

Prayer: God of Creation, Father of all, I stop today and reassert my faith in You and Your Son Jesus Christ. My faith is firm because You are firm and unchanging. Amen.

February 25

Daily Bible Reading: Mark 6:1 – 32[56]

Verse of the Day: Mark 6:31 – *"And he saith unto them, Come ye yourselves apart into a desert place, and rest a while. For there were many coming and going, and they had no leisure so much as to eat."*

R & R. Rest and relaxation. Renewal and restoration. However you want to say it, it is not a luxury, although we often consider it as such. Taking some time to be alone and rest is not a selfish thing. It is being Christlike.

Taking a day off each week, rewarding yourself with a relaxing, refreshing vacation is not being sinful or selfish. No, it is a spiritual thing to do. God designed us to take one day in seven to rest (the Sabbath). Focusing upon God during this time can recharge not only our physical batteries, but also our spiritual ones.

When have you taken a day to rest lately? When have you spent time focusing on God and refreshing yourself in Him? Take Christ's admonition to heart – "Come aside and rest a while."

Prayer: Jesus, You are my R & R. Amen.

---

[56] OT Reading – Numbers 14 – 15

February 26

Daily Bible Reading: Mark 6:33 – 56[57]

Verse of the Day: Mark 6:53 – 56 – *"And when they had crossed over, they came to the land unto Gennesaret, and moored to the shore. And when they were come out of the boat, straightway the people knew him, and ran round about that whole region, and began to carry about on their beds those that were sick, where they heard he was. And wheresoever he entered, into villages, or into cities, or into the country, they laid the sick in the marketplaces, and besought him that they might touch if it were but the border of his garment: and as many as touched him were made whole."*

Have you ever wondered why so many recognized Him and came to be healed? Look back to Mark 5:1 – 20 (February 23 reading) and reread the account of the healing of the demoniac. Because H e told others about Christ, they wanted what He could give. Obedience brings blessings.

Prayer: Jesus, may I develop the trust and faith to do what You tell me to. When I obey, great blessings for others and me are given. Many will find eternal life if I chose to obey.

February 27

Daily Bible Reading: Mark 7:1 – 13[58]

Verse of the Day: Mark 7:9 – *"And he said unto them, Full well do ye reject the commandment of God, that ye may keep your tradition."*

Jesus gives very condemning words to the Scribes and Pharisees in today's passage. He condemns them for placing greater emphasis upon the traditions that they had evolved from their study of the Scriptures than for the Scriptures themselves.

Can we be guilty of this today? Do we try too hard to hold on to our religious traditions and styles (worship, music, prayer, etc.) and lose the depth and beauty of what the Bible says to us. We must be sure that everything that we hold tightly to is God's Word and not how we think about them.

Stay in the Bible, learn it, memorize it, meditate upon it, apply it – and you will find that living God's way is better than any traditions or programs you may encounter.

---

[57] OT Reading – Numbers 16 – 17
[58] OT Reading – Numbers 18 – 20

Prayer: Father today, open my heart and eyes to Your Word. May I see it clearly. Amen.

February 28

Daily Bible Reading: Mark 7:14 – 37[59]

Verse of the Day: Mark 7:20 – *"And he said, That which proceedeth out of the man, that defileth the man."*

In our passage today, Jesus is dealing with the question of what defiles a man. What is it? Is it in the age-old philosophical question – is a man evil because of nature or nurture. Are we evil because of the world around us, or because we are born that way?

The Bible makes it clear (from Genesis to Revelation) that man does bad things, that he is evil because he is born that way. Our nature is what corrupts the nurture that we receive. In Genesis 3 we see where the perfect Adam and Eve become tainted with sin, and because of that, all mankind is born with this sin nature.

Where does evil begin? Not from what we learn, but from who we are. And, without a savior, we would all be doomed to an eternal separation from the true God of Creation.

Prayer: God of Creation, we are flawed from birth because of sin. We sin because we are sinners. We need Your Son as our Savior.

February 29

Daily Bible Reading: Your favorite passage of Scripture[60]

Verse of the Day: Revelation 4:11 – *"Worthy art thou, our Lord and our God, to receive the glory and the honor and the power: for thou didst create all things, and because of thy will they were, and were created."*

What a great and glorious doxology in the book of Revelation. Doxology literally means a study of praise. However, dictionaries usually define the term as expressions of praise to God, often associated with a hymn sung during Christian worship.

As we consider this verse of the day, notice that the 24 elders before the throne start with acknowledging the worth of God. He deserves our praise because of His glory, power and honor. We can proclaim praise to God because He is the great Creator, and we owe our very existence to

---

[59] OT Reading – Numbers 21 – 23
[60] OT Reading – Numbers 21 – 23

this One. They cast their crowns before Him in this passage because they surrender to His Lordship and Majesty. Can we do the same today?

Prayer: Worthy are You O God to receive my praise, my worship, my whole being today.

MARCH Spring Time New Promises

March. The month that the first day of Spring happens. After a long, cold winter we anticipate when the newness of life will come our way.

The dry, barren, empty, trees begin to bud. The grass begins to green up, and the flowers begin to poke up through the ground to establish a new life. I know that my wife begins in about January counting how many days until spring arrives. The barren becomes alive.

It is during March and April that we celebrate Easter. A reminder that the One who came to provide our salvation died, was buried, and rose again. From life to death to life – to establish us in the Father's family.

As we continue our reading of God's Word this year, let the life-giving words of God wash over you, warm your soul, and raise up the full force of His providing our salvation and adoption into God's Forever Family.

March 1

Daily Bible Reading: Mark 8[61]

Verse of the Day: Mark 8:15 – *"And he charged them, saying, Take heed, beware of the leaven of the Pharisees and the leaven of Herod."*

Jesus speaks to His disciples and warns them against ζυμης, leaven. Leaven is used to cause dough to rise – we call it yeast. A little pinch of yeast will quickly spread throughout the entire ball of dough.

In Scripture it can mean yeast (as in the Old Testament Passover where they were told to use only unleavened bread – bread without yeast), or it can be used metaphorically to stand for mental and moral corruption, viewed in its tendency to infect others.

Jesus is warning his disciples against the false teachings of the Pharisees that will infect them, and spread throughout the teachings of the church.

Prayer: Jesus, give me wisdom to see and reject the error that is so easily infecting our churches today. May I discern and hold to Your Truth and Your Truth – Jesus – only. Amen.

March 2

Daily Bible Reading: Mark 9:1 – 29[62]

Verse of the Day: Mark 9:28 – *"And when he was come into the house, his disciples asked him privately, How is it that we could not cast it out?"*

In our reading today, we go from the Mountaintop to the valley. From seeing the revelation of God's glory in Christ to the ineffective work of the disciples. Having watched Jesus as He released people from sickness and demonic holds, they were able to understand why they were so ineffectual at this time.

Jesus in reply stated that we must rely upon prayer (and some manuscripts add fasting) to prevail in particularly difficult circumstances. It is imperative that we, as disciples, understand that anything we do is only through the will and power of God. Prayer is our means of both requesting and hearing from God, while fasting helps to focus us on what we are seeking.

---

[61] OT Reading – Numbers 24 – 27
[62] OT Reading – Numbers 28 – 29

Prayer: Heavenly Father, let me never forget that all Power and work comes only by Your Will in our lives. Let us seek to focus upon You and what is Your purpose and plan. Amen.

March 3

Daily Bible Reading: Mark 9:30 – 50[63]

Verse of the Day: Mark 9:43 – *"And if thy hand cause thee to stumble, cut it off: it is good for thee to enter into life maimed, rather than having thy two hands to go into hell, into the unquenchable fire."*

Does Jesus mean for us to literally mutilate ourselves because of sin? Some religions teach this concept, but we can understand from all of Christ's teachings that his is an account of *hyperbole* (when more is said than literally meant). It is a form of exaggeration used to emphasize the point being made. It is making a superlative degree of implication.

Jesus wants us to understand that sin and Hell (Greek *gehenna*) are so hideous that one should take great lengths to avoid them. Avoiding sin can require drastic action on our part. Today, meditate upon the sin in my life, and how I must seek to avoid it at all costs.

Prayer: Heavenly Father, too often I do not see the utter hideousness of sin. I do not realize the depth of depravity and punishment that it can bring. Help me today to focus on Jesus and His ability to cleanse and restore. Amen.

March 4

Daily Bible Reading: Mark 10:1 – 31[64]

Verse of the Day: Mark 10:14 – *"But when Jesus saw it, he was moved with indignation, and said unto them, Suffer the little children to come unto me; forbid them not: for to such belongeth the kingdom of God."*

Are we guilty as the disciples of trying to make the way to Jesus complicated and for those who are what we would consider appropriate to come to Him? In the preceding verse, it states that Jesus was moved with indignation at them. The Greek word used here is made up of two words that mean "much grief."

We can make it hard for someone to come to Jesus by being in his or her way. We could do that by our actions or our words. We can set

---

[63] OT Reading – Numbers 30 – 31
[64] OT Reading – Numbers 32 – 33

standards that they could not meet, or we could simply not tell them about Him.

Today, watch whether we are standing between someone and Jesus, and seek to remove any hindrance from their way.

Prayer: Jesus, I do not want to cause You grief, help me to bring others to You. Amen.

March 5

Daily Bible Reading: Mark 10:32 – 52[65]

Verse of the Day: Mark 10:51 – *"And Jesus answered him, and said, What wilt thou that I should do unto thee? And the blind man said unto him, Rabboni, that I may receive my sight."*

I have often thought about this passage, and wondered why Jesus would ask a blind man what he wanted Him to do. Don't you think this would be obvious?

However, as I have pondered this over the years, I have come to the conclusion that Jesus was not seeking what the man wanted, He was wanting the man to ask for what he wanted. Jesus knew. Being a beggar, it was not unusual for them to call out to those passing by for mercy (wanting money). Jesus wanted this man to show his faith in Him that he would ask for the very thing he needed most. Sight. Jesus then gave it to him.

Today, when you pray to Jesus for something, be specific in the request that you make. He is waiting for you to ask.

Prayer: Jesus, I come to You in full assurance that You hear and answer. Amen

March 6

Daily Bible Reading: Mark 11:1 – 19[66]

Verse of the Day: Mark 11:17 – *"And he taught, and said unto them, Is it not written, My house shall be called a house of prayer for all the nations? but ye have made it a den of robbers."*

For those who want to think of Jesus as "gentle, meek and mild," the accounts of His cleansing the Temple (one at the start of His ministry and now at the close) create a problem. What we see in the account is

---

[65] OT Reading – Numbers 34 – 36
[66] OT Reading – Deuteronomy 1 – 2

not someone who is weak and mild, but One who is indignant and action oriented.

He quotes from two Old Testament prophets (Isaiah and Jeremiah), and shows how far the people had drifted from what God wanted. Are we guilty of this today? Maybe we are. Are we selling an inferior product to the world? We need to present the One who is the Truth, the Way, and the Life (John 14:6) for the world to see and desire.

Prayer: Father, I have been cheating others by giving them a poor view of Your Son by my words and actions. Cleanse me and use me today to show Him to others. Amen.

March 7

Daily Bible Reading: Mark 11:20 – 33[67]

Verse of the Day: Mark 11:21 – *"And Peter calling to remembrance saith unto him, Rabbi, behold, the fig tree which thou cursedst is withered away."*

Rabbi. In the New Testament times, the term Rabbi was a title of respect given to one who was learned and versed in the Mosaic Law. The title is from a Hebrew word that means "great," and is often translated as "Master." In the Aramaic (the language Jesus spoke), the word is Rabboni. This expresses an affectionate respect for the teacher. Both the disciples and the Jewish teachers of the Law called Him this.

Jesus cautioned His disciples from claiming this title for themselves, because there is only One true Master, the Lord Jesus Christ Himself. Today, let us pause and focus upon the One who is the true Master and Teacher. Ponder upon what He is teaching us through His Word.

Prayer: Glorious Rabbi, Teacher, Master, help me to find my understanding in You. The day may bring lessons and challenges, help me to turn to You for the knowledge and assistance I need. Amen.

March 8

Daily Bible Reading: Mark 12:1 – 27[68]

Verse of the Day: Mark 12:27 – *"He is not the God of the dead, but of the living: ye do greatly err."*

---

[67] OT Reading – Deuteronomy 3 – 4
[68] OT Reading – Deuteronomy 5 – 7

Jesus in this verse today gives us insight and reinforces the concept that a person continues throughout all eternity. The word He uses for death here, νεκρων, means separation, never annihilation or non-existence. It is referring to the separation of the spirit from the body. It is the concept of the body being dead and buried.

Man will continue to exist after he is buried. God is the God of the ζωντων, the living. A person may cease to exist bodily, but they will continue on in eternity forever and ever. We are not told exactly what the form the person will take, but the New Testament makes it clear that it will be a form that we will recognize one another (1 Corinthian 13:12; 15:44). The important point to consider is this, where will you spend eternity? You choose now where that will be.

Prayer: Eternal Father, I choose to spend my Eternity with You. I trust in Your provision for my destiny. I hold to You. Amen.

March 9

Daily Bible Reading: Mark 12:28 – 44[69]

Verse of the Day: Mark 12:29 – *"Jesus answered, The first is, Hear, O Israel; The Lord our God, the Lord is one: and thou shalt love the Lord thy God with all thy heart, and with all thy soul, and with all thy mind, and with all thy strength."*

The Scribes asked, "What commandment is the first of all?" Or, what is the most important commandment for us? Jesus never hesitated when He responded with the about statement. Knowing about God is an important pursuit in life. Knowing God is major importance, yet it is only half of the story.

We must not only know about God (the demons do and tremble, James 2:19), it is vital to know God, but the ultimate response to knowing God is to love Him. Love Him with every part of us. Today, meditate upon where God is in my life, and do I love Him in totality.

Prayer: Gracious God, it is my heart's desire to love You with all my totality. I fail so often, and I ask your forgiveness. Help me to turn my every thought, my life to loving You every moment of every day. Amen.

---

[69] OT Reading – Deuteronomy 8 – 10

March 10

Daily Bible Reading: Mark 13:1 – 13[70]

Verse of the Day: Mark 13:5 – *"And Jesus began to say unto them, Take heed that no man lead you astray."*

Chapter 13 of Mark is a section of Scripture that Jesus teaches on the end times (see Matthew 24 also). He instructs on the signs of the end times, the great tribulation, and His return.

He starts in this verse by saying that there will be those who will seek to deceive the believers from holding strong in their looking for Him. The last days will include religious deception, international conflicts, earthquakes, famines, and persecution of Christians.

The whole earth will be a place of chaos. However, Jesus reminds us in this section that the gospel will continue to spread. It will ultimately triumph in the return of the King. Don't lose heart, speak up and stand strong.

Prayer: Jesus, we look forward to Your return. To see You face to face is a heartfelt desire. Give me the courage to stand and speak to those who need Your Saving Grace. Amen

March 11

Daily Bible Reading: Mark 13:14 – 37[71]

Verse of the Day: Mark 13:33 – *"Take ye heed, watch and pray: for ye know not when the time is."*

This verse is in the present, active, imperative form in the Greek. That's a mouthful that means that it is of high importance. It means that it is taking place continuously right now (present), that I am to do it (active), as it is commanded by Jesus (imperative).

Taking heed means that I am to see and perceive my surroundings. To watch literally means to not be sleeping. To pray means to be in communication with God. Since we do not know when Jesus is coming back, we are to be in active anticipation and preparation for His return. That should make a major difference in how we live our lives each day. Constant vigilance in or watching for Him will help us to walk in the right way and live the right life.

---

[70] OT Reading – Deuteronomy 11 – 13
[71] OT Reading – Deuteronomy 14 – 16

Prayer: Coming King, I eagerly wait in anticipation of seeing You. I turn my thoughts and life to watching for Your return. I know that it may be years, or it could happen before I finish this sentence. Come. Amen.

March 12

Daily Bible Reading: Mark 14:1 – 25[72]

Verse of the Day: Mark 14:17 – *"And when it was evening he cometh with the twelve. And as they sat and were eating, Jesus said, Verily I say unto you, One of you shall betray me, even he that eateth with me. They began to be sorrowful, and to say unto him one by one, Is it I?"*

Imagine being at the table with the Lord that night. He says that one of them would betray Him. The question that they each asked is actually worded in the Greek as a negative question that would imply a negative answer. Each expected Him to say, No, not you. Yet, before the evening ends, Judas betrays with a kiss, Peter betrays with his denial of Jesus, and all of them had run away.

Don't we do the same today? We think, "Oh no, I would never betray Jesus." Yet, in our own ways we do exactly that. It is because of grace that we have the forgiveness and relationship we have.

Prayer, Jesus I praise You for Your marvelous Grace and Mercy. I live today because of what You have done in me. Amen.

March 13

Daily Bible Reading: Mark 14:26 – 50[73]

Verse of the Day: Mark 14:32 – *"And they come unto a place which was named Gethsemane: and he saith unto his disciples, Sit ye here, while I pray."*

In our passage today, we see Jesus demonstrating to us real prayer. We often delegate prayer to a rote nicety that we recite before lunch or at bedtime. Here we see the full impact of what true prayer is, the kind that Jesus modeled and taught.

Prayer is realistic, spontaneous, plain everyday communication with the Living God of Creation. It results in a relief of personal anxiety and gives us a calm assurance that God is in full control of all the circumstances in our life. What we have is a summary of His prayer; in verse 37 Jesus mentions them waiting one hour while He prayed. When

---

[72] OT Reading – Deuteronomy 17 – 19
[73] OT Reading – Deuteronomy 20 – 22

was the last time that a crisis or trial caused you to spend an hour in prayer with the Father? We are quick to send up flare prayers and move on. Let's take a lesson from Jesus today.

Prayer: Father, I come to You today and seek to spend time with You in Prayer....

March 14

Daily Bible Reading: Mark 14:51 – 72[74]

Verse of the Day: Mark 14:61 – *"But he held his peace, and answered nothing. Again the high priest asked him, and saith unto him, Art thou the Christ, the Son of the Blessed?"*

In a mock trial, the Sanhedrin (the religious ruling body of the Jews) seeks to condemn Jesus. False witnesses were called to give various evidence against Him. Over and over He was enticed to respond, yet He was silent before them (consider the prophecy of Isaiah in the Old Testament). Finally we see in this verse the High Priest directly asks Him if He is truly the promised Messiah, the Son of God. Jesus will not lie, nor reject Himself, and responds to the High Priest. "And Jesus said, I am: and ye shall see the Son of man sitting at the right hand of Power, and coming with the clouds of heaven." (Mark 14:62).

Jesus knew full well what that proclamation would lead to. He proclaims Himself as the promised Messiah.

Prayer: Jesus, Son of the Most High God, Savior, Redeemer, Creator, Restorer, may I give You the full measure of Praise today. Amen.

March 15

Daily Bible Reading: Mark 15:1 – 26[75]

Verse of the Day: Mark 15:25 – *"And it was the third hour, and they crucified him."*

9:00 am in the morning. And on a hill outside of the city of Jerusalem, the Roman soldiers crucified Jesus. Mark's gospel is terse and to the point. No long descriptions. Just the stated fact.

Mark's gospel appears to be written to a Roman readership. They wanted the facts, short and sweet. Also, they were totally familiar with

---

[74] OT Reading – Deuteronomy 23 – 25
[75] OT Reading – Deuteronomy 26 – 27

the horrors and extreme torture that this system of execution provided. They did not need to have it described.

How often today do we consider the life of Jesus, and maybe like the Romans feel that we totally understand it? We pass over the full impact of what happened, on the cross and in the eternal realm. The King of Creation was murdered by His creatures. Why? To bring us into full fellowship with the Father.

Prayer: Jesus, as I contemplate Your death today, may I feel the fullness of what it cost and what a gift I have received from You. Amen.

March 16

Daily Bible Reading: Mark 15:27 – 47[76]

Verse of the Day: Mark 15:37 – *"And Jesus uttered a loud voice, and gave up the ghost."*

It was on the Cross. One awful terrifying moment. Jesus Christ, the eternal Son of God took all of my sins upon Himself and satisfied the righteous demand of the Father. Yours, too. And at that moment He completely, instantaneously, and forever cleared away the debt that we had. Our sin is not only forgiven but taken away. Our being slaves to the sin nature is broken. Set free. Set free from sin's penalty. Set free from sin's power. And, one day we will be set free from the very presence of sin. What a wonderful Savior. His death was complete. It left nothing undone to be finished. Our pardon was sealed with His blood. Our position was established in Heaven with the Father. One moment in time. One moment was all that was needed for the Son of God to restore what sin had destroyed. I am His, and He is mine.

Prayer, Jesus, O how I love You. How I owe You my very soul. I cannot comprehend all that You have done, but thank You! Amen.

March 17

Daily Bible Reading: Mark 16[77]

Verse of the Day: Mark 16:4 – *"and looking up, they see that the stone is rolled back: for it was exceeding great."*

Very early on Sunday morning, the women had prepared and were on their way to the Tomb to anoint the body and finish the burial proceedings. They discussed about how they would get the stone rolled

---

[76] OT Reading – Deuteronomy 28
[77] OT Reading – Deuteronomy 29 – 30

back from the entrance. It was huge and heavy. As they come into view of the Tomb they see it. The Stone is rolled away and the entrance is standing open. They will shortly find out that He is not there, not among the dead but with the living. He had arose.

When God is involved anything can happen. He guided the stone from the sling of David between the eyes of Goliath. He leveled the walls of Jericho. He divided the Red Sea into two massive walls of water.

When we believe that the situation is impossible, don't count God out. He changes things.

Prayer: Thank You God! Amen.

March 18

Daily Bible Reading: Luke 1:1 – 23[78]

Verse of the Day: Luke 1:1 – 4 – *"Forasmuch as many have taken in hand to draw up a narrative concerning those matters which have been fulfilled among us, even as they delivered them unto us, who from the beginning were eyewitnesses and ministers of the word, it seemed good to me also, having traced the course of all things accurately from the first, to write unto thee in order, most excellent Theophilus; that thou mightest know the certainty concerning the things wherein thou wast instructed."*

Today we begin a 50 day study in the Gospel of Luke. Luke, a doctor, wrote this letter with the Greeks in mind. He covers the coming, seeking, and saving Savior. He gives us a historical look at Jesus and His ministry. Written around 59 to 63 A.D., to a man named Theophilus, it is the only Gospel with a sequel. Luke continues the history in the book of Acts.

Prayer: Jesus, we seek to see your life and ministry through the historical writings of Luke. Father, open our eyes that we may see Him and his purpose of coming, seeking, and saving.

March 19

Daily Bible Reading: Luke 1:24 – 56[79]

Verse of the Day: Luke 1:38 – *"And Mary said, Behold, the handmaid of the Lord; be it unto me according to thy word. And the angel departed from her."*

---

[78] OT Reading – Deuteronomy 31 – 32
[79] OT Reading – Deuteronomy 33 – 34

What must it have been like for Mary on that day long ago? The Angel Gabriel shows up and tells her that he has news that will change her life forever. She appeared fearful over what was happening so Gabriel tells her "Fear not, Mary: for thou hast found favor with God." (Luke 1: 30). Can you even begin to imagine the thoughts that must have been going through her young, teenage mind?

She may have been stunned, confused, puzzled, and surprised, yet never do we see her saying "No way. I won't do that." She submitted to the will of God and we have salvation available today by her submission and obedience. How can God use you?

Prayer: Father, I am Your servant. I bow to Your Will and seek to be used by You today. I may not know right now what it will require, but I am willing to allow You to utilize Me for Your honor and glory. Amen.

March 20

Daily Bible Reading: Luke 1:57 – 80[80]

Verse of the Day: Luke 1:67 – "*And his father Zacharias was filled with the Holy Spirit, and prophesied, saying,*"

In this set of verses today, we find the "Benedictus" or the song of Zacharias. The title "Benedictus" comes from the first word in the Latin translation of this passage. We see it translated into English as blessed from the Greek word ευλογητος.

God's Spirit came to Zacharias allowing him to announce the promise of God. Zacharias was part of the priestly line, but God here uses him as a prophet. There are three types of prophecy in the Bible: 1) foretelling future events; 2) forthtelling the Word of God; and, 3) praising God. This prophecy of Zacharias under the inspiration of the Holy Spirit contains all three forms.

Prayer: Spirit of the Almighty God, open my mind, my heart, and my eyes to see the wonder of Your great plan You have revealed in Your Holy Scriptures. I praise You for You plan that allows me to be restored to You and Your family. Alleluia. Amen.

---

[80] OT Reading – Joshua 1 – 3

March 21

Daily Bible Reading: Luke 2:1 – 24[81]

Verse of the Day: Luke 2:6 – *"And it came to pass, while they were there, the days were fulfilled that she should be delivered."*

We are guilty of relegating the second chapter of Luke to the Christmas season. We hardly read it other than Christmas Eve or Day. What a great mistake that is. This passage contains "the greatest story every told."

It is too important, too magnificent, to encouraging to be only a Christmas tradition. Today, read the verse of the Daily Bible Reading out loud. Muse over what it meant for the Creator of the Universe to step down from His Throne and wrap Himself in the flesh of a helpless little baby. To make His residence here. To become like us so that we can become like Him. This section of Scripture deserves our praise as we accept the challenge to adore Him today. Now. Completely. Without hesitation.

Prayer: Jesus, I pause to bow before You in pure adoration and worship. What You did by coming as a baby and growing into the Man who would die for me, provide my restoration and redemption to the Father. All glory to You.

March 22

Daily Bible Reading: Luke 2:25 – 52[82]

Verse of the Day: Luke 2:52 – *"And Jesus advanced in wisdom and stature, and in favor with God and men."*

This is a very informative verse about Jesus as a human being. It states that He developed from a baby into a man in the very same way that every other human being does. When we take apart the different words (from the Greek) we see a picture of how He grew up.

The word advanced in this verse is in an imperfect, active, indicative form. This means that it is a continuing action that happens, and that the word is a simple statement of fact. He did not come as a baby with full capacities as a human, but went through the process just as we do.

---

[81] OT Reading – Joshua 4 – 6
[82] OT Reading – Joshua 7 – 8

He grew in wisdom (the mental ability or intelligence), stature (age and height), and favor (the goodwill with others) on a steady basis. He knows what we go through at any stage.

Prayer: Jesus, I know that You understand all that I go through each day, both as You watch me and experientially Yourself. Amen.

March 23

Daily Bible Reading: Luke 3[83]

Verse of the Day: Luke 3:7 – *"He said therefore to the multitudes that went out to be baptized of him, Ye offspring of vipers, who warned you to flee from the wrath to come?"*

Βαπτισθηναι. Baptizo, the Greek word that we transliterate as baptize creates a lot of discussion in Christian circles. Consider some thoughts from the Greek word itself.

The Greek word was not a religious word to begin with. It was used in everyday language. It meant to immerse, or submerge (of vessels sunk); it also meant to cleanse by dipping or submerging, to wash, to make clean with water, to wash one's self, to bathe.

The Jews were used to Gentiles being baptized into Judaism, but John's baptism was new to them. It symbolized renouncing their old life and preparing their hearts to receive the coming Messiah. Later, we see that baptism showed that a person had repented and accepted Jesus Christ as their Savior.

Prayer: May I be totally immersed in my relationship with Jesus today and forever.

March 24

Daily Bible Reading: Luke 4:1 – 32[84]

Verse of the Day: Luke 4:1 – 2 – *"And Jesus, full of the Holy Spirit, returned from the Jordan, and was led in the Spirit in the wilderness during forty days, being tempted of the devil. And he did eat nothing in those days: and when they were completed, he hungered."*

The Temptation of Jesus Christ. Matthew, Mark, and Luke all include this in their redemptive biographies of Jesus. Consider this, Matthew wrote about Jesus as a King, Mark wrote about Him as a servant, and

---

[83] OT Reading – Joshua 9 – 10
[84] OT Reading – Joshua 11 – 13

Luke wrote about Him as the Perfect Man. John wrote about Him being Deity. Muse over the reasons why they included or left out this account.

Jesus as the Last Adam (1 Corinthians 15:45) would go on to be the Great High Priest (Hebrews 4:15) who has been tempted just as we are. One big difference, He does not fail the test as we are prone to do. Therefore, He understands what we face, and demonstrates that through God's Word we can pass the test also.

Prayer: Fill my mind and heart with Your Word, O God. Amen.

March 25

Daily Bible Reading: Luke 4:33 – 44[85]

Verse of the Day: Luke 4:38 – 39 – "*And he rose up from the synagogue, and entered into the house of Simon. And Simon's wife's mother was holden with a great fever; and they besought him for her. And he stood over her, and rebuked the fever; and it left her: and immediately she rose up and ministered unto them.*"

As I was pondering this account in Mark, I became aware of an important point in it. I have always focused on the importance of Jesus' healing ministry here. I have also saw that the Apostles had lives like ours, they worked, they married, they had the same everyday occurrences.

What struck me in reading this account again and meditating on it was that she "*immediately she rose up and ministered unto them.*" How often does God work in our lives and we don't do anything in response? How should we respond to His blessing?

Prayer: Father, forgive me for the many blessings I have received and taken them so lightly. I praise You for Your care. Amen.

March 26

Daily Bible Reading: Luke 5:1 – 16[86]

Verse of the Day: Luke 5:15 – 16 – "*But so much the more went abroad the report concerning him: and great multitudes came together to hear, and to be healed of their infirmities. But he withdrew himself in the deserts, and prayed.*"

---

[85] OT Reading – Joshua 14 – 15
[86] OT Reading – Joshua 16 – 18

Ever feel overwhelmed? Feel like you are being cornered and unable to escape? Everyone is crowding you and needing you? Feeling anxious and it seems more than you can handle?

Sometimes we must do what Jesus did. He is the God-man, and yet there were times that He physically needed space. He understood (after all He made man in the first place) His physical needs (and ours).

What did He do? He spent some quiet moments with the Father. What makes us believe that we can handle everything ourselves without going to the Father, when even Jesus sought to meet His needs in the Father?

Prayer: Jesus, may I learn from Your example, may I take small moments of quiet to commune with the Father each day. Amen.

March 27

Daily Bible Reading: Luke 5:17 – 39[87]

Verse of the Day: Luke 5:37 – " *And no man putteth new wine into old wine-skins; else the new wine will burst the skins, and itself will be spilled, and the skins will perish.* "

We spend a lot of time in our religious circles holding on to traditions and struggling over any change that we might face in presenting the message of Salvation through Jesus Christ.

I was meditating on this verse and saw something in it to consider. Jesus is making a point that we must be concerned with what is the main thing, and not be hung up on the secondary items.

The wine in this passage is the main thing. It is what is important. It stands for the gospel, timeless and ageless. The wineskins are the secondary, structure, methods, traditions, etc. We need to keep our focus on the main thing and use whatever secondary things can make it successful. Keep the main thing the main thing.

Prayer: Father, help me keep the main thing the main thing every day. Amen.

---

[87] OT Reading – Joshua 19 – 20

March 28

Daily Bible Reading: Luke 6:1 – 26[88]

Verse of the Day: Luke 6:26 – *"Woe unto you, when all men shall speak well of you! for in the same manner did their fathers to the false prophets."*

We, as Christians, often believe that because we are believers that people should like us and what we believe. However, even from early in His ministry, Jesus makes it clear that the world is no friend of grace. He gives this warning to us in what we call the Beatitudes. We read them (here and in Matthew 5) and look at the promises and see what wonderful things we can receive (being satisfied, gaining the Kingdom, comforted, filled) and miss some of the poignant considerations that Jesus gives.

We will not be liked by all. In fact, the world in general will tolerate at best and persecute at worst. Those who walk in the faith will find that we must be focused on God and not the reactions of those around us.

Prayer: Father, as I seek to walk in Your way, I will find those who like me and those who don't. I will not succumb to popular opinion, but to Your approval. Amen.

March 29

Daily Bible Reading: Luke 6:27 – 49[89]

Verse of the Day: Luke 6:37 – *"And judge not, and ye shall not be judged: and condemn not, and ye shall not be condemned: release, and ye shall be released:"*

If you are like me, you have blown it this week. In fact, I can't remember a day that when I am honest that I didn't blow it. Sorry, but I am human (just as you are).

And, I have found that Satan smiles whenever we blow it. Especially if we allow ourselves to become discouraged and quit. That's it. Throw in the towel. Quit. I blew it so that's it.

No it's not. I know, I've felt this way, too. However, when I remember that the enemy hates love and forgiveness, I know where those thoughts come from. God offers forgiveness, grace, mercy, and restoration. Not only for us, but also for anyone who will receive it.

---

[88] OT Reading – Joshua 21 – 22
[89] OT Reading – Joshua 23 – 24

So, let's give this to others we come in contact with (and ourselves if we need it).

Prayer: Father, I thank You for Your grace, mercy, love, forgiveness, and restoration. Amen.

March 30

Daily Bible Reading: Luke 7:1 – 30[90]

Verse of the Day: Luke 7:9 – 10 – "*And when Jesus heard these things, he marvelled at him, and turned and said unto the multitude that followed him, I say unto you, I have not found so great faith, no, not in Israel. And they that were sent, returning to the house, found the servant whole.*"

This is one of the only two places in the New Testament that says that Jesus marveled. In Mark 6:6, he marveled at the unbelief of those in His hometown. Here, He marvels at the faith of a Gentile.

Think about the contrast. Those who were of Israel didn't believe Him, the Centurion believed. Do we who know Him lack trusting faith in His ability to meet our day-to-day needs? Do we lack the belief system that trusts Him to accomplish what only He can do? Do we need to re-evaluate our trust and faith. Pause today, and seek to have Jesus "marvel" at us in the right way.

Prayer: Jesus, I believe, help my unbelief. I ask You to strengthen my faith in You and Your ability to uphold me today. Amen.

March 31

Daily Bible Reading: Luke 7:31 – 50[91]

Verse of the Day: Luke 7:48 – 50 – "*And he said unto her, Thy sins are forgiven. And they that sat at meat with him began to say within themselves, Who is this that even forgiveth sins? And he said unto the woman, Thy faith hath saved thee; go in peace.*"

As we close out this month, let us pause and consider the question presented in this passage. "*Who is this that even forgiveth sins?*" We are studying the redemptive biographies of Jesus called the Gospels. They begin to paint the picture for us to see this God-man and His life and purpose.

---

[90] OT Reading – Judges 1 – 2
[91] OT Reading – Judges 3 – 5

Who is He? What would you say? C. S. Lewis gave us only three choices, liar, lunatic, or Lord. Did He know He was not God, but led us on? Liar. Did He have a disillusionment thinking He was something He was not? Lunatic. Or, is He really the Eternal Son of God, Creator, Redeemer, Restorer? What do you believe? Make sure you get the answer right, your future depends on it.

Prayer: Jesus, I believe! You are the Son of God. You are my only hope and future. Amen.

APRIL Showers of Blessings

We often hear the proverbial saying that April showers bring May flowers. The old joke goes – "If April showers bring May flowers, then what does May flowers bring?" the silly answer – "Pilgrims."

We laugh at a joke like that because of the freshness that Spring brings into our lives. Spending time in God's Word daily draws us closer to our God. It refreshes our souls.

As we watch the trees green up, the flowers begin to bud, the grass come out of dormancy, all because of the refreshing rain that waters and feeds the earth, we can consider how God's Word does the same in our souls. Without the needed rain showers, the earth dries up, there is a drought of what is needed to produce the plant life. Eventually even the animal kingdom is affected. In our lives, not spending time in God's Word brings a dryness, a drought that eventually affects everything about us.

Continue this month to water your soul with the refreshing showers of blessing gleaned from God's precious Word.

April 1

Daily Bible Reading: Luke 8:1 – 21[92]

Verse of the Day: Luke 8:11 – *"Now the parable is this: The seed is the word of God."*

In our reading today we muse over the Parable of the Sower. This is very appropriate for this season of the year. Farmers and gardeners everywhere are preparing the soil for the planting of flowers and vegetables.

Jesus uses visual images that His listeners were very familiar with. Some has suggested that maybe there was a farmer nearby actually sowing seed as He spoke this parable. His disciples asked Him to explain the parable's meaning to them.

Often in our reading of God's Word, we seek the meaning of a passage, coming to God in prayer and comparing the passage with other parts of the Bible helps us to glean the meaning that God has in the section of Scripture. Spend some time today re-reading this passage to fully understand the message of Jesus to us today.

Prayer: Father, open my eyes that I may see the wonder and beauty of Your Word to me. Give me an open mind and heart to receive it.

April 2

Daily Bible Reading: Luke 8:22 – 56[93]

Verse of the Day: Luke 8:24 – *"And they came to him, and awoke him, saying, Master, master, we perish. And he awoke, and rebuked the wind and the raging of the water: and they ceased, and there was a calm."*

Storms. They are so unpredictable. They can crop up in a moment. They can be violent or not so much. They all have one thing in common; they can be very disturbing and troublesome.

Sometimes, the storms of our life can be so overwhelming that we feel that we are in a sinking boat. We face some storms that may shake our faith in whether God is really concerned with us. Does He really care?

In our passage today, the disciples had Jesus in the boat in the storm with them, and they are terrified by the storm. They wake Him and accuse Him of not caring. Yet, remember that He was in the same boat in

---

[92] OT Reading – Judges 6 – 7
[93] OT Reading – Judges 8 – 9

the same storm, and He would see them through. He will see you through also.

Prayer: Jesus, strengthen my trust in You.

April 3

Daily Bible Reading: Luke 9:1 – 36[94]

Verse of the Day: Luke 9:13 – *"But he said unto them, Give ye them to eat. And they said, We have no more than five loaves and two fishes; except we should go and buy food for all this people."*

All four writers include this feeding of the people in their accounts. When God tells us something four times, it means we need to take deep notice of it. In John (6:6) we are told He told them what we have in our verse above to test them.

They understood the situation, they looked at the possibility (the boy's lunch) and they saw nothing but impossibilities. They tried to account for all possible solutions, but they missed the most obvious one. It was the obvious One. They came with a problem, their solutions would not solve the problem, they gave all the negative responses, and missed that they were talking to the One who would be able to solve the problem. How often do we do that in our lives today?

Prayer: Jesus, here is my problem, I trust You to provide the solution. Amen.

April 4

Daily Bible Reading: Luke 9:37 – 62[95]

Verse of the Day: Luke 9:43 – 45 – *"And they were all astonished at the majesty of God. But while all were marvelling at all the things which he did, he said unto his disciples, Let these words sink into your ears: for the Son of man shall be delivered up into the hands of men. But they understood not this saying, and it was concealed from them, that they should not perceive it; and they were afraid to ask him about this saying."*

Even at an early point in time, while He was popular among the many, Jesus told His followers that He would face betrayal and death. At this point in time, they were unable to understand or believe it.

---

[94] OT Reading – Judges 10 – 11
[95] OT Reading – Judges 12 – 14

Jesus was not taken by surprise with the Cross. It was for that very purpose that He came. Without the Cross we would not have forgiveness. Without the Cross we would be eternally condemned. It is the Cross that brings the crown of forgiveness and restoration to the Father.

Prayer: Jesus, I praise You for Your steadfast plan that bought me back. Amen.

April 5

Daily Bible Reading: Luke 10:1 – 24[96]

Verse of the Day: Luke 10:20 – *"Nevertheless in this rejoice not, that the spirits are subject unto you; but rejoice that your names are written in heaven."*

Jesus had sent out the seventy disciples (35 teams of two) to spread the word throughout the region. He had bestowed upon them His authority to protect them and have power over demons.

When they return excited about the fact that even demonic spirits cowered before them, Jesus reminds them that more important than this share of His authority was the fact that their names were written down in Heaven. They were God's children. He knew their names. He had them inscribed in the Book of Life (Rev. 17:8).

Our greatest blessing is not what we receive, not what we are able to do, but that we are eternally secure in our relationship with the Father.

Prayer: Father, thank You for making me one of Your children. Amen.

April 6

Daily Bible Reading: Luke 10:25 – 42[97]

Verse of the Day: Luke 10:33 – *"But a certain Samaritan, as he journeyed, came where he was: and when he saw him, he was moved with compassion,"*

In this parable, Jesus used specifically one who would often be thought of as a "bad guy" in Israelite conversation. He draws out irony by contrasting the "bad" Samaritan with the "good" Levite and Priest.

It is a reminder to us that God notices the unnoticed. In Jesus' day, women were often unnoticed or considered. There were many social groups that the Jews considered not worth considering. Gentiles,

---

[96] OT Reading – Judges 15 – 17
[97] OT Reading – Judges 18 – 19

shepherds, Samaritans, the poor, lepers, tax collectors and sinners. Yet Jesus took time to notice those who did what was good, and was available to save to the uttermost those who come to Him in repentance and belief.

Prayer: Father, what a blessing that in a world of many "superstars," you notice those of us who are the unnoticeable. I seek to serve You in my little part of the world, not to be seen, but to serve. Thank You. Amen.

April 7

Daily Bible Reading: Luke 11:1 – 28[98]

Verse of the Day: Luke 11:3 – *"Give us day by day our daily bread."*

The Greek word for daily here is επιουσιον and is only used twice in the New Testament and is not found in any Greek literature before this time. The other place in the New Testament that it is found is Matthews account in Matthew 6:11.

It is a compound word that means that which gives us substance and the coming day. The point that Jesus is making in His model prayer is that we acknowledge and understand that we are dependent upon God for our daily needs.

One reason that Jesus had taught that it is hard for a rich man to enter God's kingdom (Luke 18:25) is that they will often depend upon their wealth to provide, and not recognize that it is from God that all blessings and need fulfillment comes.

Prayer: Jesus, I acknowledge today that You are the Provider of all my needs today, tomorrow and forever. Thank You. Amen.

April 8

Daily Bible Reading: Luke 11:29 – 54[99]

Verse of the Day: Luke 11:33 – *"No man, when he hath lighted a lamp, putteth it in a cellar, neither under the bushel, but on the stand, that they which enter in may see the light."*

This little light of mine,

I'm gonna let it shine.

This little light of mine,

---

[98] OT Reading – Judges 20 – 21
[99] OT Reading – Ruth

I'm gonna let it shine,

Let it shine, let it shine, Let it shine.

Remember singing this as a child? Using your pointer finger as a candle. What a fun and enjoyable little song. (It can get stuck in your head).

That's what Jesus is telling us in our verse today. Let our lives become lights to the world, pointing them to Him, the Savior, for all to come to Him. Today, become a candle in your sphere of influence.

Prayer: Jesus, may I reflect Your Light for all the world to see and follow. Amen.

April 9

Daily Bible Reading: Luke 12:1 – 34[100]

Verse of the Day: Luke 12:20 – *"But God said unto him, Thou foolish one, this night is thy soul required of thee; and the things which thou hast prepared, whose shall they be?"*

Αφρων. The Greek word translated "foolish one" carries with it the meaning of one without reason senseless, foolish, stupid, without reflection or intelligence, one who is acting rashly. Pretty heavy condemnation coming from Jesus.

In this parable of the rich fool, Jesus is reminding us that each person has a God-shaped vacuum in their heart that is searching for something to fill it. This vacuum can't provide peace until God invades it and fills it.

In your life, do you struggle with contentment? Are you constantly looking for something to provide peace and security? Only God can do this, let Him invade you and fill you to the brim.

Prayer: Gracious Father, invade my being, my presence with Your Being, Your Presence. Let it overflow and provide contentment.

April 10

Daily Bible Reading: Luke 12:35 – 59[101]

Verse of the Day: Luke 12:54 – 56 – *"And he said to the multitudes also, When ye see a cloud rising in the west, straightway ye say, There*

---

[100] OT Reading – 1 Samuel 1 – 3
[101] OT Reading – 1 Samuel 4 – 6

cometh a shower; and so it cometh to pass. And when ye see a south wind blowing, ye say, There will be a scorching heat; and it cometh to pass. Ye hypocrites, ye know how to interpret the face of the earth and the heaven; but how is it that ye know not how to interpret this time?"

We pay a lot of attention to the weather forecasts. We plan events and then watch and pray for good weather. Jesus in these verses above is challenging His followers that they need to pay as much attention to the events of history happening around them as they do to the weather.

They had fulfillment of prophecy happening all around them in Jesus, and yet they were missing it. Do we pay as much attention to what the Scriptures are teaching us as we do to the weather?

Prayer: Give me eyes to discern the events around me in light of Your Word. Amen.

April 11

Daily Bible Reading: Luke 13:1 – 21[102]

Verse of the Day: Luke 13:15 – *"But the Lord answered him, and said, Ye hypocrites, doth not each one of you on the sabbath loose his ox or his ass from the stall, and lead him away to watering?"*

The Greek word υποκριται, appears frequently in the synoptic Gospels of Matthew, Mark, and Luke, means an actor, stage player, a dissembler, pretender, hypocrite, basically, one who plays a part. This is a person who either pretends to be something they are not, or disguises who they really are. This word is only used by Jesus in the Scriptures.

Jesus is God and can see the inner being of a person. The real motives and heart of the person. We tend to judge by the exterior, He judges by the heart. Like the adage, "you can't judge a book by its cover."

When He looks at me, what does He really see?

Prayer: Father, may I be on the outside what I am on the inside. More importantly, may I be Your child inside and out. Amen.

April 12

Daily Bible Reading: Luke 13:22 – 35[103]

Verse of the Day: Luke 13:23 – 24 – *"And one said unto him, Lord, are they few that are saved? And he said unto them, Strive to enter in by*

---

[102] OT Reading – 1 Samuel 7 – 9
[103] OT Reading – 1 Samuel 10 – 12

the narrow door: for many, I say unto you, shall seek to enter in, and shall not be able."

Jesus is very straightforward in responding to questions from serious seekers. In this case, Luke records a question from a person after Jesus had been teaching about how many would be saved.

The response basically states that we must be saved on God's terms, not our own. Many will miss salvation because they seek to achieve it on their terms, their own way.

Yes, Christianity is narrow-minded, because the only way that Jesus states that one can be saved and enter into the presence of God is through Him. Any other way we chose will result in our failure to enter into God's presence.

Prayer: Father, today I seek to be sure that my only hope and way into God's Presence is through You and You alone. Nothing to the cross I bring, Just to You I cling. Amen.

April 13

Daily Bible Reading: Luke 14:1 – 24[104]

Verse of the Day: Luke 14:11 – *"For everyone that exalteth himself shall be humbled; and he that humbleth himself shall be exalted."*

Stay real. It doesn't matter how many honors, how many degrees, what position you hold, just be real. Get rid of any ideas of the special privileges, the rewards you should have, or the accolades and pats on the back you should have. We should serve out of love for God and only for His approval.

He has so many unseen ways of rewarding us for our service to Him. If we do our service to impress others, we will always hunger for glory and approval. All glory belongs to God and Him alone.

If we are trying to impress others, the approval we receive from them will probably be the only reward we will receive. God never shares His glory with others (Isa. 42:8).

Prayer: Father, all Glory and Honor belongs to You and You alone. I will not seek to take any credit that belongs to You today. May others see only You through me. Amen.

---

[104] OT Reading – 1 Samuel 13 – 14

April 14

Daily Bible Reading: Luke 14:25 – 35[105]

Verse of the Day: Luke 14:26 – *"If any man cometh unto me, and hateth not his own father, and mother, and wife, and children, and brethren, and sisters, yea, and his own life also, he cannot be my disciple."*

Wow, strong words from Jesus. Does He mean I must literally "hate" my parents and family? He is the One who wrote in the Ten Commandments that we are to honor our fathers and mothers.

What He is telling us is that true discipleship is giving Christ first place in our lives. In Jesus' day (and in some cultures today even) to follow Jesus results in being rejected, persecuted, or even killed by their family or friends. If a person feared the disapproval and/or rejection by their family, they would never become a follower of Him.

Today, consider if our concerns for how others view us is greater than our desire to follow Him at all costs, do we need to get our hearts right with Him?

Prayer: Holy Spirit search me today. Amen.

April 15

Daily Bible Reading: Luke 15:1 – 10[106]

Verse of the Day: Luke 15:1 – 3 – *"Now all the publicans and sinners were drawing near unto him to hear him. And both the Pharisees and the scribes murmured, saying, This man receiveth sinners, and eateth with them. And he spake unto them this parable, saying,"*

Todays' reading contains two parables leading up to the Parable of the Lost Son. All three parables go together to deliver the response of Jesus to the murmuring of the Scribes and Pharisees.

As we read these today, and the Parable of the Lost Son tomorrow, look at how Jesus narrows down the concern and care of God. He starts out with 1 out of 100, then goes to 1 out of 10, and ends with 1. He is drawing the attention to the important fact that God while caring about the whole world, cares about the individual. We too, should care and be concerned with all those around us, and the individual next to us.

Prayer: Father, help me to see the world and the individual through Your eyes. Amen.

---

[105] OT Reading – 1 Samuel 15 – 16
[106] OT Reading – 1 Samuel 17 – 18

April 16

Daily Bible Reading: Luke 15:11 – 32[107]

Verse of the Day: Luke 15:20 – *"And he arose, and came to his father. But while he was yet afar off, his father saw him, and was moved with compassion, and ran, and fell on his neck, and kissed him."*

A well-known parable to many. The account of the Prodigal Son. We can become so familiar with the account that we miss the depth and beauty of the story.

The son chooses to go out his own way, and the father allows it (consider the account of Adam and Eve). Freedom to choose. And we as mankind generally choose our own way and not the way of the Father. Yet, we find in this account that the father was waiting daily for the son's return. The parable shows us the compassion of the father in his running to meet the boy and kissed him. This shows us the compassion of the Heavenly Father who is waiting for our return. He will immediately accept the sinner who returns to the Father.

Prayer: Father, You are a good, good Father. You love us and accept us when we come back to You. Amen.

April 17

Daily Bible Reading: Luke 16:1 – 18[108]

Verse of the Day: Luke 16:17 – *"But it is easier for heaven and earth to pass away, than for one tittle of the law to fall."*

We so often try to minimize what God has given us in His written word. We pick and choose what we think is important and what can be ignored. If we got together, we probably would find that our lists of what is important and what can be ignored would be different.

Jesus was making a strong point to the Pharisees that all of God's Word is exactly that. The Word of God. We must be careful in what we want to trivialize in the Scriptures. He uses the extreme of the smallest letter in the Hebrew alphabet is just as important as the largest. So, what we might consider a minor point in the Scriptures is very important and will remain forever.

Today, ponder what you think about the Bible and its importance to life.

---

[107] OT Reading – 1 Samuel 19 – 21
[108] OT Reading – 1 Samuel 22 – 24

Prayer: May I observe the importance of Your Word in my life today, Heavenly Father.

April 18

Daily Bible Reading: Luke 16:19 – 31[109]

Verse of the Day: Luke 16:31 – *"And he said unto him, If they hear not Moses and the prophets, neither will they be persuaded, if one rise from the dead."*

Many call this the Parable of the Rich Man and Lazarus. I don't believe it is a parable because Jesus gives us a name of a person. This may have been a recent event of these two men dying that the people were aware of.

He gives a glimpse into the spiritual world of events following the death of a person. We see that Paradise and the place of torment are two distinct real places. The gulf tells us that a person makes his or her choice of where they spend eternity here and now, not after death. That is why it is important that we receive Jesus Christ now, and that we share this with others so they can make their choice.

Today, who can you share the message of salvation with? Don't delay, they may not have tomorrow to make a choice.

Prayer: Holy Spirit, give me insight and wisdom to speak to others about Christ. Amen.

April 19

Daily Bible Reading: Luke 17:1 – 19[110]

Verse of the Day: Luke 17:1 – *"And he said unto his disciples, It is impossible but that occasions of stumbling should come; but woe unto him, through whom they come!"*

Jesus here in this verse uses a Greek word σκανδαλα that is a noun that means stumbling block. The term was used to speak about the spring of a trap that would trigger its snapping shut. In the New Testament, it generally referred to anything that would hinder someone from doing what is right. He said that it was inevitable that we would face these stumbling blocks, and He condemns those who create them. He goes on in the following verse to say that death by drowning would be preferable to causing a believer to stumble.

---

[109] OT Reading – 1 Samuel 25 – 26
[110] OT Reading – 1 Samuel 27 – 29

Today, let us muse over what stumbling blocks happen, and check ourselves that we are not causing others to stumble in their walk with Christ.

Prayer: Heavenly Father, it is my heart's desire to help others walk like Christ. If I in any way cause others to stumble in their walk, show me, forgive me, help me not to do this. Amen.

April 20

Daily Bible Reading: Luke 17:20 – 37[111]

Verse of the Day: Luke 17:26 – *"And as it came to pass in the days of Noah, even so shall it be also in the days of the Son of man."*

When Jesus was asked about when the Kingdom of God would come (meaning the Day of the Lord), Jesus goes into statements about this event. Many have tried to attach dates and eras to these events. A very important statement in this passage is our verse today.

The people in the days of Noah (see Gen. 6:5-13) paid very little attention to God and faced His judgment because of that. Jesus says that it will be the same preceding the return of the King.

As we look at the world around us, does it recognize God? Is there a concern for the things of God? Or, is it much like the "days of Noah?"

Prayer: Jesus, as we consider Your words today, let us muse over the way our world (and ourselves) meet the description that You give. Help us to focus upon God and His ways. Help us to be ready to meet Your return. Amen.

April 21

Daily Bible Reading: Luke 18:1 – 17[112]

Verse of the Day: Luke 18:13 – *"But the publican, standing afar off, would not lift up so much as his eyes unto heaven, but smote his breast, saying, God, be thou merciful to me a sinner."*

The Greek word used here in the verb form, ιλασθητι, is used as a verb only one other time in the New Testament. This is in Hebrews 2:17 where it speaks of how Christ made reconciliation between God and man possible on the Cross. The verb means to be favorably inclined or to reconcile.

---

[111] OT Reading – 1 Samuel 30 – 31
[112] OT Reading – 2 Samuel 1– 3

The noun form of this word is found in 1 John 2:2; 4:10, and in both places Jesus is called the propitiation for our sins. He appeased God on the Cross. The tax collector here was asking God for reconciliation. We can have this reconciliation today through Jesus Christ.

Prayer: Jesus, today I thank You for what You so willingly went through that I might be favorably viewed by the Father, that I am reconciled to Him. My sins have found Your mercy, they are removed, and I can stand before You clean and whole. Amen.

April 22

Daily Bible Reading: Luke 18:18 – 43[113]

Verse of the Day: Luke 18:22 – *"And when Jesus heard it, he said unto him, One thing thou lackest yet: sell all that thou hast, and distribute unto the poor, and thou shalt have treasure in heaven: and come, follow me."*

On Malow's Hierarchy of Needs, the second place goes to Safety. As human beings, we seek to have safety as one of the most important needs of our lives. We often find it hard to let go of our treasures because we fear for their safety.

I find it hard to give to God my house, car, children, spouse, jobs, wealth, dreams, even my life out of fear. Yet, anything that is not committed to God is not truly safe. With God, all that we give to Him is completely safe. If He is in control of them we do not have to fear. We are released from worry and fear. Are you worried or fearful about something, then turn it completely over to God and watch the worry and fear melt away.

Prayer; Heavenly Father, today I give over to You that which I am worried about, what causes me fear. I thank You for Your peace.

April 23

Daily Bible Reading: Luke 19:1 – 28[114]

Verse of the Day: Luke 19:9 – 10 – *"And Jesus said unto him, To-day is salvation come to this house, forasmuch as he also is a son of Abraham. For the Son of man came to seek and to save that which was lost."*

The biblical account of Zacchaeus, a story often taught in Sunday School. We have a children's song about this "wee little man."

---

[113] OT Reading – 2 Samuel 4– 6
[114] OT Reading – 2 Samuel 7– 9

The focus we are considering today is about a tax-collector (sinner) that was curious about this Jesus of Nazareth. He climbed a tree to get a look at this one who was causing such a stir. Jesus starts the interaction when He looks up and speaks to Zacchaeus. He is doing what He says in our verse today, seeking the lost.

Maybe today God will place someone in our path that is curious. That Jesus is seeking. When God opens these doors, do we share about Him? Because, not only does He seek, He saves. Maybe He will use us to lead someone to Him.

Prayer; Jesus, give me eyes to see Your open doors to share with others. Amen.

April 24

Daily Bible Reading: Luke 19:29 – 48[115]

Verse of the Day: Luke 19:45 – *"And he entered into the temple, and began to cast out them that sold, saying unto them, It is written, And my house shall be a house of prayer: but ye have made it a den of robbers."*

This section of Scriptures where Jesus enters into Jerusalem begins the final section of Luke's writing. He displays anger at what was going on. The merchants that were in the court of the Gentiles were selling sacrificial animals at exorbitant prices. Moneychangers were making excessive profit. This holy place of worship had become a site for taking advantage of the people. Instead of turning people to God in worship, they were causing hardship and misery.

Today, do we sometimes place hardships on others that keep them from focusing upon God? How do you think Jesus feels about this? What would He say today?

Prayer: Holy Spirit, keep me from being a burden or hindrance to someone's worship of the Father. Make me a channel of praise today. Amen and Amen.

April 25

Daily Bible Reading: Luke 20:1 – 26[116]

Verse of the Day: Luke 20:21 – *"And they asked him, saying, Teacher, we know that thou sayest and teachest rightly, and acceptest not the person of any, but of a truth teachest the way of God:"*

---

[115] OT Reading – 2 Samuel 10– 12
[116] OT Reading – 2 Samuel 13– 14

Flattery. In our verse today, we can think that these who came to ask Him a question thought very highly of Him and His teaching. However, if we read the preceding verse, "And they watched him, and sent forth spies, who feigned themselves to be righteous, that they might take hold of his speech, so as to deliver him up to the rule and to the authority of the governor." Jesus knowing their hearts in questioning Him responded in a way "that they were not able to take hold of the saying before the people: and they marvelled at his answer, and held their peace" (20:26).

People today seek to trap us with our words, that is why it is imperative that we know and use the Scriptures. They are always correct, no matter what the world says.

Prayer: May I speak what is in Your Word today at all times. Amen.

April 26

Daily Bible Reading: Luke 20:27 – 47[117]

Verse of the Day: Luke 20:46 – 47 – *"Beware of the scribes, who desire to walk in long robes, and love salutations in the marketplaces, and chief seats in the synagogues, and chief places at feasts; who devour widows' houses, and for a pretence make long prayers: these shall receive greater condemnation."*

Jesus is speaking against those who are religious authorities that walk in unrestrained pride. As believers we should walk in humility.

Humble. Consider these four points about being humble. First, when we are humble we are meek, not weak. Second, being humble is active, not passive. Third, when we are humble we see others, not ourselves. And finally, it comes from a good self-image not a poor one.

Today, seek to walk humbly before God and man. Receive His praise and not His condemnation.

Prayer: Jesus, give me the power to walk humbly. To be meek, active in Your service, seeing others in their needs. Give me a heart to walk in Your footsteps today. Amen.

---

[117] OT Reading – 2 Samuel 15– 16

April 27

Daily Bible Reading: Luke 21:1 – 9[118]

Verse of the Day: Luke 21:1 – 4 – *"And he looked up, and saw the rich men that were casting their gifts into the treasury. And he saw a certain poor widow casting in thither two mites. And he said, Of a truth I say unto you, This poor widow cast in more than they all: for all these did of their superfluity cast in unto the gifts; but she of her want did cast in all the living that she had."*

When it comes to giving to God, Jesus teaches us that it is not so much how much we give (this can lead to pride and a works based thought of salvation), but what we have left. Do we give out of abundance or sacrificially? The rich paraded their giving, while the widow gave from her meager supply because she loved God and worshipped Him with her giving.

How do I give? From my abundance or as a sacrifice of praise to God?

Prayer: God, lead me to give to You in full worship and love for all that You have done for me. May what I give reflect a heart overflowing with praise. You say You love a cheerful giver, may I be such a one today.

April 28

Daily Bible Reading: Luke 21:20 – 38[119]

Verse of the Day: Luke 21:37 – 38 – *"And every day he was teaching in the temple; and every night he went out, and lodged in the mount that is called Olivet. And all the people came early in the morning to him in the temple, to hear him."*

Early morning meditation upon the words of Jesus. I personally have sought to start each day by first spending time in God's Word. I understand that this does not often work for others, and the important point is to spend time every day with Jesus in His Word.

By starting my day in the Word, I have found it helps to set the tone for my day, to focus my thoughts on God from the first, and to direct my steps throughout the day. When I get out of this habit, I find that I stray from the walk I should have.

---

[118] OT Reading – 2 Samuel 17– 18
[119] OT Reading – 2 Samuel 19– 20

What works best? Consistency. Daily spend time alone with Jesus in His Word. You won't regret it.

Prayer: Jesus, I value my time with You. I look forward to hearing You speak. Amen.

April 29

Daily Bible Reading: Luke 22:1 – 30[120]

Verse of the Day: Luke 22:1 – *"Now the feast of unleavened bread drew nigh, which is called the Passover."*

This verse begins the passion narrative of the writer Luke. It depicts to us the events of the death, burial and resurrection of Jesus Christ.

The Feast of Unleavened Bread took place immediately after the Feast of the Passover (Ex. 12:1 – 20; Deut. 16:1 – 8). They were often thought of as one. The Feast of the Passover commemorated the night of the tenth plague on Egypt. The night the death angel passed over the houses of Israel that had the blood on the doorways. The firstborn of the Egyptians died on this night. The Feast of Unleavened Bread (Ex. 12; Lev. 23:5, 6) was a celebration in remembrance of the Exodus. Many Jewish pilgrims travelled to Jerusalem to celebrate these feasts each year. These feasts carry many earthly pictures of the things about to take place in Jesus' life.

Prayer: Father, thank You for the provision that we have for reconciliation through the Passion of Jesus. Amen.

April 30

Daily Bible Reading: Luke 22:31 – 53[121]

Verse of the Day: Luke 22:31 – 32 – *"Simon, Simon, behold, Satan asked to have you, that he might sift you as wheat: but I made supplication for thee, that thy faith fail not; and do thou, when once thou hast turned again, establish thy brethren."*

In this passage in the Greek we see some interesting thoughts concerning the word "you." In the first usage, it is in the second person plural referring to all of the disciples. Satan had asked permission to trouble all of the disciples (remember him asking to trouble Job in the Old Testament). But in the latter usage is in the second person singular meaning that they refer to Peter especially.

---

[120] OT Reading – 2 Samuel 21– 22
[121] OT Reading – 2 Samuel 23– 24

What do we see? First, Satan needs to ask permission to tempt us. Second, notice that he wants to trouble all believers. Third, we see that Jesus restored Peter before he had actually denied Him. So, when we face temptations (and failures) know that they are temporary to prepare us for triumphant service to Christ.

Prayer: Jesus, thank You for praying for me before I fall, and the restoration You can give.

MAY Flowers of Promise From God

May. The month that we see the beauty of the earth displayed in the flowers, trees, birds, and movement into warm weather.

The cold dead days of winter have moved behind us. The hot weather is still before us. It is during this time we find refreshing breezes that entice us to move around outside. We are reminded that the dead looking trees, grass, and shrubs come back into life. The earth resurrects to life from what could appear to be the end of life in those trees, etc.

We start the month with the account of the crucifixion as recorded by the writer Luke. We see the resurrection of our Lord, and His special instructions to His disciples. This historical, biographical redemption account about Jesus will resume in the Book of Acts, also written by Dr. Luke.

We will continue in the month by turning to the accounts penned by the Apostle John. He writes to show us that Jesus was God, is God, and will be God. Let us continue our time with Jesus each day as we go through this month.

May 1

Daily Bible Reading: Luke 22:54 – 71[122]

Verse of the Day: Luke 22:60 – 62 – "*But Peter said, Man, I know not what thou sayest. And immediately, while he yet spake, the cock crew. And the Lord turned, and looked upon Peter. And Peter remembered the word of the Lord, how that he said unto him, Before the cock crow this day thou shalt deny me thrice. And he went out, and wept bitterly.*"

Our last reading shows Christ predicting the betrayal of Peter. In our reading today we see that even with his boldness, Peter succumbed to the seduction and deception of Satan. Satan attacked him where he least expected it, in his strength. Peter was bold and courageous, yet while warming himself at the enemies fire, Peter lost his strength. He failed Jesus.

This is our story. Often in our strength we fail our precious Savior. Why? Because we are no match for the wiles and schemes of the Devil. If we fail, let us do as Peter did, return in repentance and tears.

Prayer: Jesus, I fail you more than I want to admit. I come to You seeking Your strength and forgiveness. Restore me to Your servant. Amen.

May 2

Daily Bible Reading: Luke 23:1 – 26[123]

Verse of the Day: Luke 23:18 – "*But they cried out all together, saying, Away with this man, and release unto us Barabbas:*"

Luke wants us to see that not only the Jewish leaders, but the populace called for the death of Jesus. The people preferred a murderer, a seditious man in the place of Jesus. How could this have been? Surely, I would have spoke differently that day. Would I?

It is a blessing that Jesus was sent to the Cross. Without the sacrificial death of Christ, I would still be in my sins today (and, by the way, so would you). The substitution of Jesus for this noted murderer was no fluke; it foreshadowed the substitutionary death of Jesus for all mankind. Jesus went to the Cross to be my substitute. He went to be yours. What a blessing that Jesus not only died to spare Barabbas that day, He died to spare you and me today.

---

[122] OT Reading – 1 Kings 1 – 2
[123] OT Reading – 1 Kings 3 – 5

Prayer: Father, thank You that You had a plan and means that I could be forgiven, changed, and restored. I am Barabbas. And I am overwhelmed at Your Love and Grace.

May 3

Daily Bible Reading: Luke 23:27 – 38[124]

Verse of the Day: Luke 23:35 – *"And the people stood beholding. And the rulers also scoffed at him, saying, He saved others; let him save himself, if this is the Christ of God, his chosen."*

In ignorance of God's Grand Plan, even the religious rulers of the Jews taunted Jesus as He was dying on the Cross. They mocked Him by saying that He saved others (He would forgive sins as He healed and restored people), so they challenged Him to come down from the Cross. They equated the power of saving Himself with the power to save others. Yet, in God's Grand Plan, His willingly sacrificing Himself actually provided the power to save others.

If Jesus accepted the challenge and came off the Cross (and He had the power to do that) we would be the losers. If He saved Himself, we would all be lost and without any hope for eternity. Forgiveness and restoration comes only by His death. No other way.

Prayer: Jesus, thank You that You did not come down from the Cross, but fulfilled the requirement to bring me back to the Father.

May 4

Daily Bible Reading: Luke 23:39 – 56[125]

Verse of the Day: Luke 23:43 – *"And he said unto him, Verily I say unto thee, To-day shalt thou be with me in Paradise."*

Paradise. Παραδεισω. The word in the Greek literally means a "garden" or "park." The part of Hades, which was thought by the Jews to be the abode of the souls of the pious until the resurrection: but some understand this to be a heavenly paradise. Jesus may have alluded to it in His account of Lazarus going to Abraham's bosom in Luke 16:19 – 31. The word in the Greek translation of the Old Testament used this word for the Garden of Eden.

When He spoke these words to the thief on the Cross, it was a message of comfort and acceptance. Jesus actually did for this thief what

---

[124] OT Reading – 1 Kings 6 – 7
[125] OT Reading – 1 Kings 8 – 9

the Rulers were calling for Him to do for Himself. The day of the Crucifixion gives many physical pictures of what was taking place spiritually.

Prayer: Heavenly Father, You have provided for me to be brought back to You by being bought back by what Your Son did for me upon the Cross. I worship You. Amen.

May 5

Daily Bible Reading: Luke 24:1 – 35[126]

Verse of the Day: Luke 24:13 – *"And behold, two of them were going that very day to a village named Emmaus, which was threescore furlongs from Jerusalem."*

Emmaus, (εμμαους) the village to which the two disciples were going when our Lord appeared to them on the way, on the day of His resurrection. Luke makes its distance from Jerusalem, sixty stadia, or 7.5 miles (12 km); and the historian Josephus mentions "a village called Emmaus" at the same distance.

Jesus suddenly comes alongside of them, and after inquiring about their conversation, begins to open up the Scriptures to show that the Christ must die and rise again. And, it was through the use of the Scriptures that Jesus opened their hearts and spirits to the truth.

Today, we need to remember that this is God's method of bringing people to Himself. His Word (written) will open hearts to His Word (living, Jesus). Use it.

Prayer: Father, may I use Your Word to introduce Your Word to those around me.

May 6

Daily Bible Reading: Luke 24:36 – 53[127]

Verse of the Day: Luke 24:49 – *"And behold, I send forth the promise of my Father upon you: but tarry ye in the city, until ye be clothed with power from on high."*

In the Old Testament, the Holy Spirit came upon a person to accomplish God's work, and then would depart. However, the prophets Joel (2:28) and Jeremiah (31:31-33) spoke of a future day when the Holy

---

[126] OT Reading – 1 Kings 10 – 11
[127] OT Reading – 1 Kings 12 – 13

Spirit of God would come and stay with His people. This would be fulfilled on the Day of Pentecost when the Holy Spirit would baptize the believers, and stay with them. Peter referred to this as the beginning (Acts 11:15) because from that moment on, whenever a person received Jesus Christ as their Lord and Master, they received the Holy Ghost as a promise of God's salvation fulfillment in their lives. He would come into their life and stay until they were changed before God in Heaven. What a great promise for them, and even more for us today.

Prayer: Holy Spirit, I am so glad that You live in me, may I release and let You have the control of my life every moment. Amen.

May 7

Daily Bible Reading: John 1:1 – 28[128]

Verse of the Day: John 1:1 – *"In the beginning was the Word, and the Word was with God, and the Word was God."*

In three of John's five books in the Bible (John 1:1; 1 John 1:1; and Rev. 19:13), we find John using the Greek word λογος. This word speaks of the principle or creative energy that generated the universe. The Gnostics of John's day studied this principle, and held strong beliefs that it was what was the foundation of all things.

Still John was battling the Gnostic heresy in the first-century church; he started by explaining that the foundation of all Creation was the Creator God, or Jesus Christ. Jesus embodied all of the Godhead. He was God. He was not a part of Creation as a man would be. He is the revealer of God, and God Himself.

Jesus Christ came in the form of flesh (1:14) to reveal the One True God. He was, is, and always will be God.

Prayer: Jesus, You are the express image of God because You are God. Amen.

May 8

Daily Bible Reading: John 1:29 – 51[129]

Verse of the Day: John 1:41 – *"He findeth first his own brother Simon, and saith unto him, We have found the Messiah (which is, being interpreted, Christ)."*

---

[128] OT Reading – 1 Kings 14 – 15
[129] OT Reading – 1 Kings 16 – 18

Here is the first picture of a person leading another person to accept Jesus. Did Andrew have a great theological understanding of who Jesus was? Did he have all the answers? No. He had just met Jesus himself.

We don't need to read people a long list of rules; we don't need to instruct them in the great truths of Christianity. Our job is not to clean the fish, simply fish. Just fish.

It is not our responsibility to get a person saved, that's God's job. Our job is to introduce them to the Savior. We seek to present what He has done for us, and to encourage their relationship to Christ. So, today, get out your fishing gear, and fish. Share what He has done for you, and lead them to see Jesus.

Prayer: Jesus, I so often try to make coming to You so complicated. I am glad that it is simple, otherwise I would never have come.

May 9

Daily Bible Reading: John 2[130]

Verse of the Day: John 2:11 – *"This beginning of his signs did Jesus in Cana of Galilee, and manifested his glory; and his disciples believed on him."*

In the Gospel of John, John calls His miracles, signs. John writes his redemptive biography showing us that Jesus is God. His signs that he records point to His Deity and Messiahship. John records seven signs (the concept of completeness) look for them as we go through our study.

Each of the signs that John chooses (remember that he states in 20:30-31 that Jesus did many other signs than those recorded) is to show forth His deity and power.

This sign of changing water into wine showed forth His power over nature. Consider the attribute and power each following sign displays.

Prayer: Jesus, I am so glad that there is overwhelming evidence that You are the Christ, the Son of the Living God. I place my trust in You, assured You are who You say You are.

---

[130] OT Reading – 1 Kings 19 – 20

May 10

Daily Bible Reading: John 3:1 – 21[131]

Verse of the Day: John 3:16 – *"For God so loved the world, that he gave his only begotten Son, that whosoever believeth on him should not perish, but have eternal life."*

Today's reading includes one of the most well-known verses in the Bible. John 3:16, we see it at ball games, billboards, on cars and trucks, virtually everywhere. This is the "Gospel in a Nutshell," as it has been called.

We see that it embodies the love of God, not for a select few, but for everyone. He offers His love to every one and anyone who will come and take it.

That's the important point, it is there for anyone, but is only effective for those who will come and receive. There is not a single nationality, race, culture, gender, or language that is restricted from His love. Only our lack of receiving, or rejecting, His love separates us from Him.

Prayer: Heavenly Father, I praise You today for the vastness and availability of Your love. May I never take it for granted. Amen.

May 11

Daily Bible Reading: John 3:22 – 36[132]

Verse of the Day: John 3:36 – *"He that believeth on the Son hath eternal life; but he that obeyeth not the Son shall not see life, but the wrath of God abideth on him."*

In our verse today, the word translated hath (Greek εχει) is in the present tense. That means that the one who believes has at that moment eternal life. It is not something that will be gained in the future, but at this very moment they have it.

Likewise, the word translated abideth (Greek μενει) is also in the present tense. That means that the one who refuses to believe upon Jesus Christ has the wrath of God already abiding on them as a present reality.

Whether we have eternal life, or eternal wrath is our choice. God freely offers life, we must choose to take it or leave it. Whichever choice we make is our present reality. I chose Christ, have you?

---

[131] OT Reading – 1 Kings 21 – 22
[132] OT Reading – 2 Kings 1 – 3

Prayer: Jesus, I have chosen to receive You as my Lord and Savior. I am glad that I have at this moment eternal life – and I have it forever.

May 12

Daily Bible Reading: John 4:1 – 30[133]

Verse of the Day: John 4:23 – 24 – *"But the hour cometh, and now is, when the true worshippers shall worship the Father in spirit and truth' for such doth the Father seek to be his worshippers. God is a Spirit: and they that worship him must worship in spirit and truth."*

God seeks our worship. He looks for the praise of His people... that wondrous worship of the redeemed children. He desires to inhabit our hearts, our lives, our houses of worship, and this happens when we praise Him (Psa.22:3).

We must beware that our worship times do not become rote minutes of repetitive meditations allowed to become meaningless responses. Worship is becoming a lost art, a missing jewel in the lives of so many Christians. We go through the motions without focusing upon the one who seeks and deserves our full attention.

Prayer: Heavenly Father, today help me pause and focus upon the only One worthy of praise, You. Focus my attention upon You and You alone. May I truly worship today. Amen.

May 13

Daily Bible Reading: John 4:31 – 54[134]

Verse of the Day: John 4:54 – *"This is again the second sign that Jesus did, having come out of Judaea into Galilee."*

The account of the healing of the Nobleman's son. In our verse today, we see that this is the second of seven signs (miracles) that Jesus did. This does not mean that this is the second miracle He performed, it is the second one that John records. Earlier (May 9) we saw where these signs that John chooses are to show forth His deity and power. The first one recorded showed His power over nature. Today we see that Jesus had power over distance (and disease). Jesus did not even go to where the boy was, He spoke and the lad was healed. Jesus is not physically beside us today, but just as this sign reveals, distance is no obstacle to the

---

[133] OT Reading – 2 Kings 4 – 5
[134] OT Reading – 2 Kings 6 – 8

God-man. So, no matter what I am facing today, Jesus is able to achieve His purpose in our lives.

Prayer: Heavenly Father, I often fear that because You are not right here physically with me that the struggles I face are insurmountable. But, distance is never a problem to You. Amen.

May 14

Daily Bible Reading: John 5:1 – 24[135]

Verse of the Day: John 5:6 – *"When Jesus saw him lying, and knew that he had been now a long time in that case, he saith unto him, Wouldest thou be made whole?"*

In our reading today, we see the account of a man who had been sick for 38 years. We are not told whether this was from birth or later, all we know is that he was unable to walk. Jesus sees him lying beside the Pool of Bethesda, which was purported to have healing properties when the waters were stirred by an angel, and knows how long he has been there.

In our verse today, the first question that Jesus asks this man is, "Do you want to get well?" Sounds like a silly question, doesn't it? But the point Jesus was making was that we must desire with our hearts what Jesus has to offer. Do you want your sins forgiven? Really? Then we must tell Jesus this, ask Him to forgive and cleanse us. And, as He did with this man, He will do it.

Prayer: Jesus I come to You today and ask that You will do - _____ for me. Amen.

May 15

Daily Bible Reading: John 5:25 – 47[136]

Verse of the Day: John 5:31 – *"If I bear witness of myself, my witness is not true."*

The Greek word translated witness (μαρτυρω) can also mean to give testimony. In Jewish law, one could not give testimony about themselves. Truth, or validity of a point had to come from two or three witnesses (Deut. 17:7; 19:15).

---

[135] OT Reading – 2 Kings 9 – 11
[136] OT Reading – 2 Kings 12 – 14

Jesus' statements about Himself would not validate His claims to who He was. He needed witness of another. John the Baptist was a witness that could be called forth. He lists the Father in verse 37, and the Scriptures as witnesses to who He is. The love of God was demonstrated through Christ and witnessed to the validity of His teachings.

Jesus is believed as the Son of God, not because He said so, but by the various witnesses of His life, the Scriptures, and those who were with Him

Prayer: Jesus, I know that You are the Son of God, the evidence is strong and overwhelming. I worship You today. Amen.

May 16

Daily Bible Reading: John 6:1 – 21[137]

Verse of the Day: John 6:9 – *"There is a lad here, who hath five barley loaves, and two fishes: but what are these among so many?"*

Have you ever heard the statement that little is much when it is the hands of the Master? This account of the feeding of the five thousand gives us a physical picture of the ability of Jesus to meet our needs.

Five thousand men (besides the women and children) needed to be fed. The disciples were totally at wit's end trying to figure out how to feed them. Andrew brings forward a young lad with five barley loaves and two small fish. Doesn't sound like it would feed the disciples, let alone the rest. Yet, in the hands of the Master, the disciples, the men, the women, the children were all fed (I am sure to their satisfaction), and there were twelve wicker baskets full left over. With Jesus, what little I have is more than enough.

Prayer: Jesus, I come with what I have. Often it seems meager and insufficient. Yet as I trust You with it, You can make it supply more than what I could ever need. Amen.

May 17

Daily Bible Reading: John 6:22 – 44[138]

Verse of the Day: John 6:39 – *"And this is the will of him that sent me, that of all that which he hath given me I should lose nothing, but should raise it up at the last day."*

---

[137] OT Reading – 2 Kings 15 – 17
[138] OT Reading – 2 Kings 18 – 19

This verse brings us great encouragement. It reminds us that our salvation is resting entirely upon God's strength, not our own. My safety and my protection are based upon Christ's power and the Father's firm grip, not on my own. I am so thankful; I can be so weak, unsure, so wavering with the circumstances around me. He is forever steady. No one, not even Satan can break the connection between Jesus and me. How can I say that, am I boasting? In a way, I am. I am boasting in the death, burial, and resurrection of my Savior. He was perfect, His death purchased me, and I can rest assured in His provision. He finished the work on the Cross once and forever. And that finished work holds me for all eternity.

Prayer: Jesus, I praise You today. I worship You for the great finished work, that You supplied my salvation, my adoption into the family of God. Hallelujah, what a Savior. Amen.

May 18

Daily Bible Reading: John 6:45 – 71[139]

Verse of the Day: John 6:66 – *"Upon this many of his disciples went back, and walked no more with him."*

This is an interesting verse. Because Jesus had fed them, they wanted to "walk" with Him (the concept built into the word disciple used here). When Jesus brought it from the physical into the spiritual realm, they did not want to believe in Him as the Messiah, they were not willing to "walk" in all of His teachings. Because of this, many of them left. Hey, it is alright if He is feeding me and meeting my needs, but to commit to Him? No way.

These who left were not believers in Christ, they were only there for the benefits. Today, are there people in our churches who fit this description? Are they willing to "walk" in His way, or do they just want His freebies? Which one are you?

Prayer: Father, search my heart and help me to fully surrender to Jesus, to "walk" in His teachings in their entirety. Help me to not be one who only comes to Him for the benefits, but because He has the words of eternal life.

---

[139] OT Reading – 2 Kings 20 – 22

May 19

Daily Bible Reading: John 7:1 – 31[140]

Verse of the Day: John 7:30 – *"They sought therefore to take him: and no man laid his hand on him, because his hour was not yet come."*

John in this verse does not provide what may have been the immediate physical reason that they couldn't take Him. He had proclaimed publically that He was of divine origin. The religious leaders sought to arrest Him.

John gives us a glimpse of the Divine reason they couldn't take Him. We get a glimpse into the truth that God is Sovereign and He has control over the timing of all events. He alone sets the time. What a glorious picture for us today. God is still the same, and as He decreed that no one could touch Jesus without His consent, we can be assured of the same protection on us today. All events that happen to us are not coincidences, they are "God-instances." Trust Him.

Prayer: Father, I thank You for Your watchcare and protection over me. I can rest assured that no matter what is happening around me, I trust Your control. Amen.

May 20

Daily Bible Reading: John 7:32 – 53[141]

Verse of the Day: John 7:37 – *"Now on the last day, the great day of the feast, Jesus stood and cried, saying, If any man thirst, let him come unto me and drink."*

On each day of this feast, the people came with Palm branches and marched around the great Altar. A priest would bring a pitcher of water from the Pool of Siloam and pour it on the altar as an offering. It was to commemorate the water flowing from the rock when Moses struck it in the wilderness. On the last day, the people would march around the altar 7 times to commemorate what happened at Jericho.

Many believe that it was at the precise moment that the priest was pouring the water on the altar that Jesus' voice rang out with the words in our verse today. Jesus is the One who provides for the spiritual thirst of man, and He provides abundantly.

---

[140] OT Reading – 2 Kings 23 – 25
[141] OT Reading – 1 Chronicles 1 – 2

Prayer: Jesus, today I come to You as the provider of the Living Water. You give me daily water from Your Word, and You live in me eternally providing for my thirst. I praise You for Your provision and care. Amen.

May 21

Daily Bible Reading: John 8:1 – 20[142]

Verse of the Day: John 8:5 – *"Now in the law Moses commanded us to stone such: what then sayest thou of her?"*

We live in a profundity of people who will quote the Scriptures to make their point. The problem? Often they will correctly quote a part of the Scriptures without maintaining the correct meaning of the passage. They are the Pharisees and teachers of the law in our culture. Paul in I Timothy 2:15 warns us that we need to be diligent in our study of the Word of God, so that we are "handling aright the word of truth."

If we need to study the Bible to handle the Word correctly, that warns us that it can be misused. Satan misused Scripture in his temptation of Christ at the beginning of His ministry. The Scribes, Pharisees, and teachers of the law in Jesus' day would misuse it. Tomorrow, let us consider the way to see the proper use of a verse of Scripture.

Prayer: Holy Spirit, guide my study in the sacred Scriptures so that I can be one who uses God's Word properly. Guard me from error. I thank You that You will do this in my life.

May 22

Daily Bible Reading: John 8:21 – 36[143]

Verse of the Day: John 8:31 – 32 – *"Jesus therefore said to those Jews that had believed him, If ye abide in my word, then are ye truly my disciples; and ye shall know the truth, and the truth shall make you free."*

Yesterday we saw that one can misuse Scripture, especially when trying to prove a point. So, what can we do to detect this misuse?

First, always check out what a person quotes. Did they quote it correctly? To see the proper use of a passage, first, gain a good overview of the Bible in its entirety. Then look at the book the passage is located in, what is the main theme of that book. Narrow down to the chapter of the passage, and again what is the main theme in that passage. Finally, look at the verses surrounding the passage, see how they all fit together.

---

[142] OT Reading – 1 Chronicles 3 – 5
[143] OT Reading – 1 Chronicles 6 – 7

If we take time to check out what is said, we will quickly learn to discern the proper use of the Word.

Prayer: Holy Spirit, thank You for Your helping me to understand the Word of God.

May 23

Daily Bible Reading: John 8:37 – 59[144]

Verse of the Day: John 8:58 – *"Jesus said unto them, Verily, verily, I say unto you, Before Abraham was born, I am."*

εγω ειμι. This is the Greek words used as "I am." The use of these words in the Greek denotes self-identity in self-sufficiency. It is the words used in the Septuagint (the Greek translation of the Old Testament) in Exodus 3:6, 14, which is translated "I AM WHO I AM." This is the covenant name of God as given to Moses.

Jesus here was claiming to be the everlasting, self-existent God of the Universe. Some try to say that Jesus never claimed to be God, but we find many instances that He plainly spoke of His divinity. Not sure, read the next verse in this section, "They took up stones therefore to cast at him..." They understood what He said. They were going to stone Him for blasphemy.

Prayer: Heavenly Father, as I study the life of Jesus, I see so plainly Who He is, and that He is the Eternal Son of God, God incarnate, the One through Who we come to You. Amen.

May 24

Daily Bible Reading: John 9:1 – 23[145]

Verse of the Day: John 9:1 – *"And as he passed by, he saw a man blind from his birth."*

John 9 has an interesting account of a man born blind. In this, God is teaching us to see people as He sees them.

In verse 2 the disciples saw this one as a theological discussion. What was the sin that caused this condition? His or his parents? They didn't stop to help, only discuss him. The man's neighbors and friends saw him only as a beggar in verse 8. Later, in verse 22 the Pharisees saw him as a tool to be used against Jesus.

---

[144] OT Reading – 1 Chronicles 8 – 10
[145] OT Reading – 1 Chronicles 11 – 13

None of these saw this one as Jesus saw him. A discussion, beggar, or tool, yet when we read this account we see Jesus sees a MAN.

How often do we miss out being like Christ with the people we see around us? We look at everything except that they are a person who will spend eternity somewhere.

Prayer: God give me the eyes and heart of Jesus. Let me see people as He sees them. I want to be like Him and reach out to those who are eternal beings in need of you. Amen.

May 25

Daily Bible Reading: John 9:24 – 41[146]

Verse of the Day: John 9:28 – 29 – *"And they reviled him, and said, Thou art his disciple; but we are disciples of Moses. We know that God hath spoken unto Moses: but as for this man, we know not whence he is."*

When our spiritual blindness is finally removed, we should not be surprised if we encounter resistance. When we begin to share the account of our journey from spiritual blindness to faith in Jesus, we are bound to find those who will resist the truth. What is sad is that often this resistance comes from other religious folks.

The issue is that religious folks are uncomfortable around bona fide believers whose lives have been changed by their relationship with Christ.

Prayer: Father, today as I consider my life, do I share with others what Christ has done for me? Open my eyes to see the ones around me who need to hear this message of truth. Father, help me not allow myself to be silenced because of the truth inside of me. I must speak, I must obey and follow You. Amen.

May 26

Daily Bible Reading: John 10:1 – 21[147]

Verse of the Day: John 10:6 – *"This parable spake Jesus unto them: but they understood not what things they were which he spake unto them."*

The Greek word used here (παροιμιαν) is used by John in his writings, the other three use the word παραβολη, while they are similar, their meanings have a slight difference. In John's use of the first term, it carries

---

[146] OT Reading – 1 Chronicles 14 – 16
[147] OT Reading – 1 Chronicles 17 – 19

the idea of an analogy or figure of speech. The other word carries the meaning of a earthly story with a heavenly meaning.

The important part here is that those listening did not understand the illustration or figure of speech that Jesus applied to this conversation. Sin had so hardened their hearts that they were incapable of understanding. We must beware that we do not allow sin to harden our hearts to God's voice.

Prayer: Heavenly Father, may I confess my sin today, I do not want my heart to become hard against Your Voice. I long to hear and obey You. Help me to walk in the right way, to listen for Your voice and to obey it always.

May 27

Daily Bible Reading: John 10:22 – 42[148]

Verse of the Day: John 10:28 – *"and I give unto them eternal life; and they shall never perish, and no one shall snatch them out of my hand."*

Some times people wonder where the idea of Eternal Security comes from. Here is one place where we understand that it comes from Jesus Himself. This is a marvelous and wonderful promise from the One who cannot lie. The word eternal used here means without end. The life that Jesus gives us at the moment of salvation never ends. He promises that we will never be destroyed. And, that there is nothing that can snatch us out of His hand, His protection and provision.

I don't know about you, but I find this promise one that gives me confidence to live my life in wonder and praise to God. I can trust it. I can find encouragement when I fail. I can look forward to a forever with the One who loves me so much.

Prayer: God, thank You for the great promises in Your Word. I can trust You to keep them, and I will praise You forever. Amen.

May 28

Daily Bible Reading: John 11:1 – 17[149]

Verse of the Day: John 11:1 – *"Now a certain man was sick, Lazarus of Bethany, of the village of Mary and her sister Martha."*

---

[148] OT Reading – 1 Chronicles 20 – 22
[149] OT Reading – 1 Chronicles 23 – 25

Today and tomorrow we will muse over the powerful illustration of Jesus' power over death. The account of Jesus raising Lazarus from the dead is powerful and encouraging.

In today's reading, we see the death of Jesus' friend Lazarus. Jesus was a family friend, and had visited them in their home. They sent word to Jesus that Lazarus was very ill. They knew that Jesus was the only One who could heal their brother. As we read the account, it appears almost cruel on His part to stay and wait to go.

He arrives on the fourth day, in their belief system the soul hovered over the body for three days and then departed. So, all would know that Lazarus was dead.

If the account ended here, we would see Jesus as cruel and uncaring. Tomorrow, we will see the power of this One.

Prayer: Jesus, Your time is always right.

May 29

Daily Bible Reading: John 11:18 – 46[150]

Verse of the Day: John 11:25 – *"Jesus said unto her, I am the resurrection, and the life: he that believeth on me, though he die, yet shall he live;"*

We left Lazarus dead in yesterday's reading. Today we see the power of Jesus over death.

To our view, death is final. But, in the view of Jesus, death does not have the final word, if we are believers and live in Christ. Jesus is the Lord of all life and has the power over death and life. He can raise the dead to life.

When He made the promise we read two days ago, we see that He has the power to make that promise. He said that we can have eternal life, and He has the ability to give us that life.

I don't know about you, but I can put my trust in One who has done what He has promised in the past. I can trust Him with my life now and forever.

Prayer: Jesus, I am trusting You with my present life, knowing that as Your child I have received eternal life. I praise You! Amen.

---

[150] OT Reading – 1 Chronicles 26 – 27

May 30

Daily Bible Reading: John 11:47 – 57[151]

Verse of the Day: John 11:50 – *"nor do ye take account that it is expedient for you that one man should die for the people, and that the whole nation perish not."*

Caiaphas was the High Priest of that year makes a statement to the gathered group of Pharisees and chief priests. In his opinion, it would be better that Jesus die than take the chance of plunging the nation into destruction because of insurrection. John in our passages today tells us that by the virtue of Caiaphas' office that he was unconsciously proclaiming a message from God.

Caiaphas was a prophet unknown to himself or those around them. God often uses people when they least expect it. Sometimes God will use us even when we are unaware of Him doing it. Today, watch and see if God uses you unexpectedly. Pray that He will.

Prayer: Heavenly Father, I seek You to use me even when I am unaware of it today. You are able to make everything that I do count for the Kingdom. Make it so today, dear Lord. I pray this in Your Son's Name, Amen.

May 31

Daily Bible Reading: John 12:1 – 19[152]

Verse of the Day: John 12:19 – *"The Pharisees therefore said among themselves, Behold how ye prevail nothing; lo, the world is gone after him."*

As we witness the evil design growing in the readings of today, we see Jesus anointed in Bethany, and we read of the chief priests plotting to put Lazarus to death. They could not accept that Jesus could do what He did. They wanted to rid the world of the evidence of the power of the Son of God. They saw the people placing their faith in Jesus, and they could not be a part of it. Then, the unthinkable, Jesus comes into Jerusalem in a triumphal parade.

The hatred begins to grow. The popularity of Jesus is expanding and these religious leaders could not accept who He was. They saw the world turning to Him. And we move into the final week before His crucifixion.

---

[151] OT Reading – 1 Chronicles 28 – 29
[152] OT Reading – 2 Chronicles 1 – 3

Prayer; Father open my eyes to how You are working today. May I seek to join with You, even when it seems opposite to what I have held dear in my life. Amen

JUNE Summer Promises of Continued Blessing

June. The beginning of summer. The time when we begin to look forward to the garden to produce. The promise of tomatoes and other great vegetables make us look forward with anticipation. We can almost taste the goodness of the freshness of these vegetables.

Summer promises us of continued blessings from God. In our readings this month we will see the final week of the Crucifixion, the death, burial, and resurrection of Jesus. We will muse over the restoration of Peter as we conclude the book of John.

The continued blessing will flow as we start reading in the book of Acts. This is a book of transition. We move from Jesus' physical presence to the inhabiting of the Holy Spirit. We move from a small group in Jerusalem to a large group. We see God change the Jewish sect of the Way into a multinational church. And we will see God use Peter and the introduction of the Apostle Paul.

Blessings. Let us muse over the many blessings that God gives us today. He is the same yesterday, today and tomorrow (Hebrews 13:8)

June 1

Daily Bible Reading: John 12:20 – 50[153]

Verse of the Day: John 12:37 – *"But though he had done so many signs before them, yet they believed not on him:"*

I have heard many people say that if they had been alive when Jesus walked the earth and watched all the miracles, they would have no problem believing in Him and having a bold witness. Yet, this verse in today's reading tells us that those who did see the many things He did still did not believe in Him.

These people had full opportunity to observe Jesus, yet they lacked belief. They may have witnessed the miracles; they may have even received a miracle, yet they did not put their faith in Him.

We can spend all of our time examining the evidence; the Bible accounts, accounts from friends and others, and still lack the grace that He so freely offers. Faith in faith accomplishes nothing. Faith in Christ alone will see us through.

Prayer: Jesus, I believe, help my lack of faith. I seek Your grace and mercy today. Fill me. Use me.

June 2

Daily Bible Reading: John 13:1 – 17[154]

Verse of the Day: John 13:10 – *"Jesus saith to him, He that is bathed needeth not save to wash his feet, but is clean every whit: and ye are clean, but not all."*

In our account today, Jesus uses two different Greek words to discuss washing (νιψασθαι), and bathed (λελουμενος). The first word used is in reference to washing the extremities such as the hands and feet. The second refers to an "all-over" bath.

According to social custom of the day, if a person had a bath, they only needed to wash their hands and feet before a meal.

Jesus here is showing that if a person had been cleansed by the Spirit and the Word, they only needed to cleanse themselves from their daily contact with the world. If we have been saved, all our sins are forgiven and we only need to come and keep short accounts of confession with God.

---

[153] OT Reading – 2 Chronicles 4 – 6
[154] OT Reading – 2 Chronicles 7 – 9

Prayer: Father, today I come confessing _____, cleanse me and make me clean by Your forgiveness and grace. Amen.

June 3

Daily Bible Reading: John 13:18 – 38[155]

Verse of the Day: John 13:34 – *"A new commandment I give unto you, that ye love one another; even as I have loved you, that ye also love one another."*

The command to love was not new. Moses said in Lev. 19:18, "thou shalt love thy neighbor as thyself." The word in the Greek used here for new carries the meaning of being of a new kind, unprecedented, novel, uncommon, unheard of in substance.

Jesus did not change the command; He gave it a new standard to be measured by. Moses said we use our love for ourselves as the standard of love for those around us. Jesus said that the new standard was not ourselves, but Him. In yesterday's readings we saw the way that Jesus loved His disciples. He provided the example. Can we say that we truly love others in the same way that He loved?

Prayer: Jesus, today I am asking for a heart and spirit to love all those around me as You have loved. I tend to pick and choose who I love, You offer love to all. May I learn to see others through Your heart of love. Amen.

June 4

Daily Bible Reading: John 14[156]

Verse of the Day: John 14:1 – *"Let not your heart be troubled: believe in God, believe also in me.*

Believe. Πιστευετε. The word for believe literally means to place one's trust in someone else. In the KJV we find it used 248 times, in the book of John we can find it over 90 times alone. What is important is not that we believe, but that our belief is in the right person. We can believe that the Bible accounts of Jesus are true, but we must believe in Him.

In our verse today, the first use of the word is in the present, active, indicative form. It is a simple statement of fact. At that moment they

---

[155] OT Reading – 2 Chronicles 10 – 12
[156] OT Reading – 2 Chronicles 13 – 16

believed in God. The second use is in the present, active, imperative form. It is a command. At that moment they are commanded to believe in Him.

Do we just have a factual belief in Christ, or do we have a personal relational belief in Him?

Prayer: Jesus, I seek to know not only about You, but to know You in a personal relationship. Not facts, but personal familiarity.

June 5

Daily Bible Reading: John 15[157]

Verse of the Day: John 15:1 – *"I am the true vine, and my Father is the husbandman."*

The Greek word αμπελος, can be used to describe a single vine or the entire vineyard. Either way it causes us to see an image of a corporate dependence on God. The word used here for true (αληθινη) is emphatic so that we understand what is real. Jesus wants us to see that when we are connected to Him, we have that which has not only the name and resemblance, but the real nature corresponding to Him, in every respect corresponding to the idea signified by Him, real, true genuine.

When we are connected to the Vine, we are seen as being as He is by the Vinedresser (the Father). What a blessing, when we are connected to the Son, we are being changed into His image and likeness. What a responsibility that places upon us. If we are not being like Christ, we need to be sure that we are connected to Him.

Prayer: Jesus, I want to be connected, to gain sustenance, to be like You, to bring forth the fruit that You are looking for from me.

June 6

Daily Bible Reading: John 16:1 – 15[158]

Verse of the Day: John 16:8 – 11 – *"And he, when he is come, will convict the world in respect of sin, and of righteousness, and of judgment: of sin, because they believe not on me; of righteousness, because I go to the Father, and ye behold me no more; of judgment, because the prince of this world hath been judged."*

---

[157] OT Reading – 2 Chronicles 17 – 19
[158] OT Reading – 2 Chronicles 20 – 22

The word "convict" means to reprove or correct. The coming Holy Spirit would reprove/correct the world in three areas: sin, righteousness, and judgment.

Notice in this passage, sin is singular not plural. It is not the things we do, it is the foundation of who we are. Receiving the full pardon made by Christ is the only cure for the disease of sin. The Spirit would provide the correct understanding that righteousness (of Christ) is what each person needs. And finally, that there is no neutral ground, either we are a child of God or a child of the devil.

Prayer: Holy Spirit, today help me to see Your glorious work that Christ has sent You to do in the world. I praise You for Your vocation.

June 7

Daily Bible Reading: John 16:16 – 33[159]

Verse of the Day: John 16:33 – *"These things have I spoken unto you, that in me ye may have peace. In the world ye have tribulation: but be of good cheer; I have overcome the world."*

We live in a day when so many preach a "gospel" of happiness and ease. They seek to entice people into their churches and organizations by proclaiming a message that God will make us healthy, happy, and rich. In fact, many will say if you are sick, struggling, or in need that you are not getting what God has promised. They try to spiritualize or explain away verses like the one we read today.

Jesus told us that we are going to face pressures, afflictions, and/or distress. The Greek translated "be of good cheer" literally means to be confident and have courage. In who? In Jesus. No matter what you are going through today, He has given the ultimate victory. Just hold on and trust.

Prayer: Jesus, I trust in You. My confidence is in You and You alone, no matter what. Help me to trust Your Heart and Hand in this today.

June 8

Daily Bible Reading: John 17[160]

Verse of the Day: John 17:20 – *"Neither for these only do I pray, but for them also that believe on me through their word;"*

---

[159] OT Reading – 2 Chronicles 23 – 25
[160] OT Reading – 2 Chronicles 26 – 28

In this prayer of Jesus, often times referred to as His "High Priestly Prayer," Jesus first prays for Himself, then His disciples around Him (v.9), and finally starting at verse 20 for all who will follow. This part of the prayer is for you and me today.

He prays specifically for two things in regard to us, our unity in the Body (vv.20-23), and our glory in the future (vv.24-26).

He starts by praying for our unity that the world would then see the reality of Jesus' love. The world finds it hard to understand Jesus' love for them when they do not see us loving one another. He has commanded us to love each other as He loves us. Do we really show the love of Christ by our actions today? Do we make the world want what we have?

Prayer: Jesus, I know that You included me in Your prayer that day, and now I need to allow You to work in me to show Your Love.

June 9

Daily Bible Reading: John 18:1 - 23[161]

Verse of the Day: John 18:4 – 6 – *"Jesus therefore, knowing all the things that were coming upon him, went forth, and saith unto them, Whom seek ye? They answered him, Jesus of Nazareth. Jesus saith unto them, I am he. And Judas also, who betrayed him, was standing with them. When therefore he said unto them, I am he, they went backward, and fell to the ground."*

This passage found in John's Gospel shows us that Jesus did not die as a victim at the hands of man. Jesus, the Christ, was in control of all that took place. He was not overpowered, not caught by surprise, He could have escaped this ordeal.

In a brief instant, Jesus unveiled His majesty. His statement of deity "I AM" manifested His glory that literally cast the soldiers to the ground. He went voluntarily to the Cross for you and me.

Prayer: Lord Jesus, I praise and thank You that You went to the Cross to pay my debt and because You did, I can be forgiven before the Father. May Your Name be praised. Amen.

---

[161] OT Reading – 2 Chronicles 29 – 31

June 10

Daily Bible Reading: John 18:24 - 40[162]

Verse of the Day: John 18:38 – *"Pilate saith unto him, What is truth? And when he had said this, he went out again unto the Jews, and saith unto them, I find no crime in him."*

"What is truth?" This statement has been described as being a cynical denial to the concept of knowing truth, a quip that it is impossible to know absolute truth, or as a desire to know what no one had been able to explain to Pilate.

People today are seeking truth. They may say that it is impossible to know absolute truth, or that absolute truth does not exist (by the way, making that absolute statement negates the idea being spoken). Yet, deep down, people are looking for truth. They desire that they might find what is really true in a world that often exposes only the fallacies around them. John 14:6 reminds us that Jesus is "The Way, the Truth, and the Life."

Prayer: Holy Spirit, help me to guide others in the way of finding Truth. Help me help them discover Jesus, the One and Only Truth in the universe. Show me, lead me, guide me. Amen.

June 11

Daily Bible Reading: John 19:1 - 22[163]

Verse of the Day: John 19:12 – *"Upon this Pilate sought to release him: but the Jews cried out, saying, If thou release this man, thou art not Caesar's friend: every one that maketh himself a king speaketh against Caesar."*

Pilate three times (18:38; 19:4, 6) stated that he found no fault in Jesus worthy of death. In reality, Jesus was the sinless, perfect sacrifice that would meet the requirement to purchase our redemption.

In our verse today, the Jewish leaders seeing that they were not getting anywhere with Pilate on their religious grounds, twisted the accusation into a political one. This in turn pushed Pilate into a corner, did he stand for what was right, or what was politically expedient.

As Christians today, we are finding that the world around us often misrepresents the issues so that we are in a position of either standing on truth, or caving into the pressure around us.

---

[162] OT Reading – 2 Chronicles 32 – 33
[163] OT Reading – 2 Chronicles 34 – 36

Prayer: Spirit of the Living God, give me the strength to stand for the right today. Amen.

June 12

Daily Bible Reading: John 19:23 - 42[164]

Verse of the Day: John 19:30 – *"When Jesus therefore had received the vinegar, he said, It is finished: and he bowed his head, and gave up his spirit."*

Τετελεσται. When Jesus died on the Cross, He poured out His life blood once and for all to provide our redemption. He cried out "IT IS FINISHED." The Greek term used here has it's root in the word that means completed, finished, the end.

When Jesus spoke this word on the Cross, He was proclaiming that the sacrifice of the Lamb of God was finished, over, complete, once for all. Man need ever offer another sacrifice for the atonement of sin. It is complete. It is done. It is accomplished.

Religion tells us what we need to do to appease God, Christianity tells us that it has been done.

Prayer: Glorious Father, I praise You that my sacrifice to atone for my sin is complete and finished by the work of Your Son upon the Cross. I can come before You because of Him.

June 13

Daily Bible Reading: John 20[165]

Verse of the Day: John 20:31 – *" but these are written, that ye may believe that Jesus is the Christ, the Son of God; and that believing ye may have life in his name."*

John in each of the five books that he wrote in the Scriptures takes the time to disclose the purpose for them.

In 1st John he gives it in 5:13, "These things have I written unto you, that ye may know that ye have eternal life, *even* unto you that believe on the name of the Son of God." In 2nd John it is found in verse 7, "For many deceivers are gone forth into the world, *even* they that confess not that Jesus Christ cometh in the flesh. This is the deceiver and the antichrist." And 3rd John has it in verse 11, "Beloved, imitate not that which is evil,

---

[164] OT Reading – Ezra 1 – 2
[165] OT Reading – Ezra 3 – 5

but that which is good. He that doeth good is of God: he that doeth evil hath not seen God." The Book of Revelation gives us his purpose in 1:19, "Write therefore the things which thou sawest, and the things which are, and the things which shall come to pass hereafter."

Prayer: God show us Your Purpose for us.

June 14

Daily Bible Reading: John 21[166]

Verse of the Day: John 21:25 – "*And there are also many other things which Jesus did, the which if they should be written every one, I suppose that even the world itself would not contain the books that should be written.*"

It is so easy to lose sight of the fact that the four gospel accounts are factual, yet they are not exhaustive about the Lord Jesus Christ.

When you consider that John starts his gospel in eternity past, and ends his Book of Revelation in eternity future, we can see the truth of this verse.

God in the Person of Jesus has, is and will do more than anyone could comprehend and write about. If all there was to know about God is in the book we call the Bible, we would have a small God indeed. Look around you today to see the many blessings and works of God going on in just this moment. And then praise Him for His vast care.

Prayer: Jesus, You are beyond my full comprehension, yet You have made much known by Your living here on Earth. Amen.

June 15

Daily Bible Reading: Acts 1[167]

Verse of the Day: Acts 1:15 – "*And in these days Peter stood up in the midst of the brethren, and said (and there was a multitude of persons gathered together, about a hundred and twenty).*"

We begin our time in the Book of Acts. Considered the History Book of the first-century church, it is a book of transitions. If you want to know how the church should be modeled and operate, use the epistles. This tells us how it transitioned into what it is.

---

[166] OT Reading – Ezra 6 – 8
[167] OT Reading – Ezra 9 – 10

It is a transition from Jesus being bodily here to the leading of the Holy Spirit. It is a transition from a Jewish sect into the international body. It is the transition from a small group of fearful people into a major bold movement of God.

As we read this together, see the Hand of God as He leads using the marching orders given in Acts 1:8.

Prayer: Spirit, guide me to become more of the bold courageous witness that we find in this group of believers. Amen.

June 16

Daily Bible Reading: Acts 2:1 – 13[168]

Verse of the Day: Acts 2:13 – *"But others mocking said, They are filled with new wine."*

We sometimes are fearful about sharing Jesus with those around us because of many reasons. One reason is that we are afraid some will make fun of us. No one likes being the brunt of someone else's amusement.

In our verse today, we see that on the Day of Pentecost, the disciples were made the mocking accusations of many. Yet, the very thing that they were accused of was not a reality. They were not filled with wine, they were filled with the Holy Spirit. And, being filled with the power from on high that John the Baptist and Jesus both predicted (as well as the Old Testament Scriptures), they were sharing the message of Jesus boldly in the very place where He had been crucified.

Today, let us put aside our fears and be willing to stand and deliver the truth of the only way of salvation. Trust in Jesus Christ.

Prayer: Holy Spirit, dwelling in me, help me to be bold and share the Good News today.

June 17

Daily Bible Reading: Acts 2:14 – 47[169]

Verse of the Day: Acts 2:42 – *"And they continued stedfastly in the apostles' teaching and fellowship, in the breaking of bread and the prayers."*

---

[168] OT Reading – Nehemiah 1 – 3
[169] OT Reading – Nehemiah 4 – 6

How good the depth of a church is measured by the quality of the worship and instruction they are committed to. As believers, this must be at the top of our list to be aware of. How broad our church is, is determined by our commitment to fellowship and evangelism. We must keep reaching out to those around us who are in need, both in the church and outside of it.

Jesus told us to love God and to love people (Mark 12:30, 31). Love is an action verb. It is only really seen by the outward actions that we display. We can do actions without love, but we cannot love without actions.

Today, seek out ways that you can demonstrate the love of God to those around you. All of them.

Prayer: Holy Spirit, fill me with the love of God, so that I can show others this love. Amen.

June 18

Daily Bible Reading: Acts 3[170]

Verse of the Day: Acts 3:1 – *"Now Peter and John were going up into the temple at the hour of prayer, being the ninth hour."*

The early disciples were Jews who had been raised in the ways of Judaism. They continued to follow the Jewish traditions of the day. They did this not for their being accepted by God, but to provide a clear opportunity to witness about Jesus. Each day there were two prayer times, each of them followed the two daily sacrifices. One was in the morning, and the other was in the evening. The reference to it being the ninth hour means this was about 3 pm.

The beggar chose this location at the Beautiful Gate because it served as the front door into the Temple. People going to worship would be confronted by the cries of this man's need. To assuage their guilt, they would need to respond. Peter's response not only brought healing to the man, but an opportunity to tell others about Jesus. Look for ways to communicate about Jesus today.

Prayer: Father, open doors of opportunity.

---

[170] OT Reading – Nehemiah 7 – 8

June 19

Daily Bible Reading: Acts 4:1 – 22[171]

Verse of the Day: Acts 4:8a – *"Then Peter, filled with the Holy Spirit, said unto them..."*

The Greek word πλησθεις is used to describe the filling of anything from a boat to a sponge. It was a common term in their language, and Luke uses it here to describe how the Holy Spirit will influence a person's life. Luke uses this phrase eight times in his books. In every instance he showed that the filling of the Holy Spirit gave power to speak or preach for God. So, in his writings, Luke associated the filling of the Holy Spirit to the prophetic ministry. The giving of the ability to reveal or explain the Word of God.

Today, as you seek God's Spirit in your life, look for Him to give you the ability to share the good news with those around you. The ability to apply the Word of God in every circumstance in which you find yourself.

Prayer: Holy Spirit, fill me, use me, lead me, guide me. Show me the people in which You want me to invest God's Word in today.

June 20

Daily Bible Reading: Acts 4:23 – 37[172]

Verse of the Day: Acts 4:31 – *"And when they had prayed, the place was shaken wherein they were gathered together; and they were all filled with the Holy Spirit, and they spake the word of God with boldness."*

After Peter and John were released, we see their companions' response. It was one of praise, song, and prayer. It was not a planned or orchestrated service, it was a spontaneous outburst. They had been so intense in their time of interceding for the apostles, that when God responded in answer, they responded in full emotional release.

Once again, we see Luke recording that they were filled with the Holy Spirit. And again, we see him equating the outcome of this filling with being bold in the witness of the word of God. Do we seek God to fill us with His Spirit, and then want to just use it for our own emotional fulfillment? He fills us to serve and to share.

---

[171] OT Reading – Nehemiah 9 – 11
[172] OT Reading – Nehemiah 12 – 13

Prayer: Spirit, fill me with Your presence. Again, may I be filled to serve You in my life today.

June 21

Daily Bible Reading: Acts 5:1 – 16[173]

Verse of the Day: Acts 5:12a – *"And by the hands of the apostles were many signs and wonders wrought among the people..."*

At the start of the New Testament church, they did not have the completed Word of God to validate their message. God gave the apostle's the ability to perform miracles on a regular basis to validate their message.

Luke says that they performed signs; this is supernatural events that pointed to a warning, instruction, or encouragement from God. He also speaks of wonders, these were the responses to the signs. Jesus spoke about this in Matt. 12:38,39).

Today, we have the complete validated teaching of God in the Bible. Sometimes God still performs miracles, not to validate His Word, but to accommodate His plan. Look for the signs and wonders, but trust in the infallible Word of God.

Prayer: God, speak to me through Your Word. Let me speak to others through the revealed truth in Your Word. Amen.

June 22

Daily Bible Reading: Acts 5:17 – 42[174]

Verse of the Day: Acts 5:29 – *"But Peter and the apostles answered and said, We must obey God rather than men.'"*

This verse has been pulled out of context and misused. Some have refused to pay taxes and quoted this as the reason. Yet, Jesus instructed His followers to render unto Caesar that which belongs to Caesar (Matt. 22:21).

However, when the authorities go in direct contradiction of the Word of God, then we are charged to obey the Author of all Authority, God Himself. We are to submit to governmental authority because God established the order of things. When we submit to government, we are submitting to God.

---

[173] OT Reading – Esther 1 - 3
[174] OT Reading – Esther 4 - 6

We are living in times that often challenge us to go against God and His Word. If God commands it, no one can change it. We must obey God rather than others.

Prayer: Father, give us the wisdom to know Your commands, and the courage to stand for them before men. Amen.

June 23

Daily Bible Reading: Acts 6[175]

Verse of the Day: Acts 6:1 – *"Now in these days, when the number of the disciples was multiplying, there arose a murmuring of the Grecian Jews against the Hebrews, because their widows were neglected in the daily ministration."*

So often we can become so busy, so overwhelmed in the hectic, breakneck schedules that we keep that we overlook some of the more important things. The idea of the tyranny of the urgent can cause us to look after the most pressing areas without considering the most important.

My schedule can get booked up fast with the many needs around me, that I fail to see the most important things. One of the single, simple, sometimes silent things that I can quickly overlook is that of helping. Helping those who may not be able to normally catch my attention because I am so busy.

Prayer: Father, today give me eyes, ears, and a heart to watch for those who need a helping hand. Those who You have placed around me to allow me to be You before them.

June 24

Daily Bible Reading: Acts 7:1 – 19[176]

Verse of the Day: Acts 7:1 – *"And the high priest said, Are these things so?"*

At the end of yesterday's readings, Stephen, one of the seven men chosen to fulfill the need of the church (some believe these were the first deacons), had been arrested and accused of blasphemy. Today, we pick up with the Sanhedrin's trial.

The high priest (presumably Caiaphas) starts the preceding with a question (or a challenge) to Stephen about the validity of what he was

---

[175] OT Reading – Esther 7 – 10
[176] OT Reading – Job 1 – 3

teaching. In today's reading through the next two days, we see the response that was given in boldness before the assembled group.

Stephen doesn't start with the resurrection; he goes back to the beginning that they would all be in agreement with, and then proceeds to bring them up to the very present time. It is a good reminder to us that often to present the message, we need to start with where they are, and then bring them up to where they need to be.

Prayer: Spirit, give me wisdom in sharing.

June 25

Daily Bible Reading: Acts 7:20 – 43[177]

Verse of the Day: Acts 7:39 – *"...to whom our fathers would not be obedient, but thrust him from them, and turned back in their hearts unto Egypt..."*

Continuing in his lesson before the Sanhedrin, Stephen starts with Moses in today's reading. This is one who the leaders of the Sanhedrin would associate with. He gives them a continuing history lesson to refresh their memory on the background leading up to Jesus.

He tells them that Moses prophesized that Jesus would come (Deut. 18:15), and that even then, the people would not obey God. They desired Egypt (a picture of the world) over top of following God. They went so far as making Aaron construct an idol to worship. God allowed the nation to follow their folly, but He punished them for it.

Stephen is building his case that they have been witnesses of God's plan, and yet they rejected it.

Prayer, Father, give me eyes to see and follow Your plan and purposes today. Amen.

June 26

Daily Bible Reading: Acts 7:44 – 60[178]

Verse of the Day: Acts 7:57 – 58 – *"But they cried out with a loud voice, and stopped their ears, and rushed upon him with one accord; and they cast him out of the city, and stoned him: and the witnesses laid down their garments at the feet of a young man named Saul."*

---

[177] OT Reading – Job 4 – 6
[178] OT Reading – Job 7 – 9

The Sanhedrin finally reached a point of anger at Stephen. He had accused them of being like their ancestors, rejecting God and His prophets. He equated their rejection of Jesus with the rejection of God in the Old Testament. In their anger, they decided to kill Stephen. In a way, they were fulfilling what Stephen had just talked about.

In this account today, we see that standing strong for the Lord can be costly. Yet, it can influence others. Many believe that this account with Stephen was the opening crack into the life of Saul, preparing him to meet Jesus on the road to Damascus.

Prayer: Father, may I stay consistent in my witness for You. I never know who is watching. In Jesus' name, Amen.

June 27

Daily Bible Reading: Acts 8:1 – 25[179]

Verse of the Day: Acts 8:1b – *"And there arose on that day a great persecution against the church which was in Jerusalem; and they were all scattered abroad throughout the regions of Judaea and Samaria, except the apostles."*

In chapters 8 – 12 we see a time of dynamic growth. During this period of around 12 years the church grew and spread out from Jerusalem to Judea and to Samaria.

Some have wondered why God would allow a great persecution to come against the church in Jerusalem. I believe in reading and studying that part of the reason was that they were not obeying Him. In Acts 1:8, He had instructed them on what they were to do, and here years later they had focused on Jerusalem and had not gone out as He had commanded them. This verse tells us that He scattered them to do what He had called them to do.

Prayer: Father, help me to determine if why I am facing these struggles is that I am not following Your plan and purpose for my life. Help me to see and correct my ways. Amen.

June 28

Daily Bible Reading: Acts 8:26 – 40[180]

Verse of the Day: Acts 8:32 – *"Now the passage of the scripture which he was reading was this, He was led as a sheep to the slaughter;*

---

[179] OT Reading – Job 10 – 12
[180] OT Reading – Job 13 – 15

And   as   a   lamb   before   his   shearer   is   dumb,
So he openeth not his mouth..."

αμνος. The New Testament writers often referred to Jesus as being the lamb or the Lamb of God. This was drawn from the Old Testament pictures about the sacrificial lamb.

In the minds of the Jewish hearers, the use of the Lamb of God would bring to mind the account of the Passover lamb (consider Ex. 12). The prophets gave the pictures of sacrificial lambs in their prophecies (i.e., Isa. 53:7). The Law gave the instructions on how the sacrifices and the lambs were to be handled (Lev. 14:12, 21, 24; Num. 6:12). The pictures and prophecies in the Old Testament were given to help them (and us) see that the coming Messiah would not be a philosopher nor a teacher of morals. He would come to do what we cannot do for ourselves, take away our sin.

Prayer: Jesus, thank You that You came to be my sacrifice, my substitute, my Lamb. Amen.

June 29

Daily Bible Reading: Acts 9:1 – 22[181]

Verse of the Day: Acts 9:20 – *"And straightway in the synagogues he proclaimed Jesus, that he is the Son of God."*

The church's greatest human enemy becomes the church's greatest evangelist.

God has a purpose and a plan, and we can never outguess who or what He will use to accomplish His plan. Throughout the Old Testament we find God using pagan, heathen nations to correct and discipline His people the Jews. In the New Testament we find Him using Saul, one who was bound and determined to destroy the church.

As we go through our day, look for ways that God unexpectedly uses people, places, and possibilities that we may not have considered to accomplish His will. Sometimes, in the most surprising way He will show up.

Prayer: Father, give me eyes to see You at work in my life and those around me. When it seems that things are the darkest, give me the faith to trust You. And help me look continually for the way that you will show up. Amen.

---

[181] OT Reading – Job 16 – 18

June 30

Daily Bible Reading: Acts 9:23 – 43[182]

Verse of the Day: Acts 9:31a – *"So the church throughout all Judaea and Galilee and Samaria had peace..."*

For a brief period of time, Rome under the rule of Caligula was immersed in the concept of emperor Worship. Because of this, the nation of Rome was heavily persecuting the Jewish nation. Since Rome was creating so much tension in the nation of the Jews, they did not have the time or inclination to continue persecuting the church. However, at the end of the reign of Caligula, this all changed.

Sometimes in our lives we find ourselves in a tranquil period. However, if we are doing what God has called us to do, we can be assured that trouble will find us. One has said that we are either in trouble, just out of trouble, or the phone is about to ring.

Trust God that He has everything under control, whether it is peaceful or in turmoil.

Prayer: Father, help me to continue to trust and follow all the time. Peaceful times can make me lax, call me to do your will. Amen.

---

[182] OT Reading – Job 19 – 20

JULY Warmth of God's Goodness

July, where I live it is one of the hot summer months. The days get hotter and hotter. The humidity rises, and we seek shelter – shade, air-conditioning, pools, and seashores, anything that will help to release the uncomfortable feeling of the three H's – hazy, hot, and humid.

As I ponder over the warmth that we experience each day, I am reminded of the goodness of our blessed God. He provides for us throughout all seasons, cool, cold, warm, and hot. We progress through Fall, Winter, Spring, and Summer each year. We are promised that "While the earth remaineth, seedtime and harvest, and cold and heat, and summer and winter, and day and night shall not cease" in Genesis 8:25.

In turn, we can be assured that the promises of God are true and faithful. We will spend this month in the Book of Acts. We will move from the inclusion of Gentiles into the church to the first chapter of Paul's letter to the church at Rome. We will travel with Paul on three missionary journeys and his time in prison. Shipwreck and beatings are not able to stop the forward movement of God and His Church.

July 1

Daily Bible Reading: Acts 10:1 – 23[183]

Verse of the Day: Acts 10:15 – 16 – "*And a voice came unto him again the second time, What God hath cleansed, make not thou common. And this was done thrice: and straightway the vessel was received up into heaven.*"

God was about to make a major shift in Peter's thinking. In our reading today, Peter was hungry and while waiting for the meal, he fell into a trance. This trance was repeated three times and each time God challenged Peter with the statement, "What God hath cleansed, make not thou common."

While Peter at first may have been musing over God's change of dietary restrictions, he would soon learn that this had a deeper significance. From this point on, the early church (made up of Jews) could not longer look at Gentiles as unclean. God was breaking down Peter's prejudices. What people group do we have a prejudice about?

Prayer: Heavenly Father, change my heart to see all people as You see them. Amen.

July 2

Daily Bible Reading: Acts 10:24 – 48[184]

Verse of the Day: Acts 10:34 – "*And Peter opened his mouth, and said, Of a truth I perceive that God is no respecter of persons:*"

Continuing with the thought presented yesterday, we see again the emphasis upon the fact that God does not show partiality. To the mind of the Jews, they saw themselves as "God's Chosen" and those all others were rejected. Now in the Church, God was teaching that through Jesus' shed blood all are accepted if they trust in Him.

In Matthew 28:19, Jesus told them that every kind of person from every nation was welcome to come into the kingdom of God. The only requirement... repentance of sin and placing one's faith in Jesus Christ. There is no room in God's Kingdom for rejection of anyone for any other reason than rejecting Jesus.

Prayer: Jesus, You shed Your Blood for every person who has ever lived. You are offering to everyone Your forgiveness and redemption if

---

[183] OT Reading – Job 21 – 22
[184] OT Reading – Job 23 – 25

they will only take it. Help me to be one who shares with everyone I come in contact with. Amen.

July 3

Daily Bible Reading: Acts 11[185]

Verse of the Day: Acts 11:26 – " *and when he had found him, he brought him unto Antioch. And it came to pass, that even for a whole year they were gathered together with the church, and taught much people; and that the disciples were called Christians first in Antioch.*"

Historians tell us that this designation of "Christian", or "little Christ" was probably a term of ridicule given to the believers because of their worship of Jesus. The historian Josephus called them "the tribe of Christians." Tacitus, a Roman historian, referred to them as Christians because they belonged to Christ.

Originally the believers called themselves "The Way." But later they began to wear the name "Christian" as a badge of honor even though it had been a taunting ridicule.

Prayer: Father, man has tried so often to ridicule and mock those who believe in Your Son, Jesus. We are no different today, so help us to wear our belief in Jesus in a way that others will see Him in us. May we be "Little Christs" to all we come in contact with. Amen.

July 4

Daily Bible Reading: Acts 12[186]

Verse of the Day: Acts 12:24 – *"But the word of God grew and multiplied."*

Today we celebrate Independence Day in America. We have a day of fun, food, fellowship, and fireworks. We celebrate the fact that we are a free people. However, it seems almost daily these freedoms are eroding. Our nation was founded upon the Judeo-Christian ethics presented in the Bible. The Founding Fathers held the Bible in high esteem and quoted from it frequently.

In our reading today, Peter has been set free from prison in a miraculous way. Herod had started a movement to eradicate the leaders and followers of this group. He placed himself up almost as a god to be worshipped. However, Herod died a painful and horrible death, while

---

[185] OT Reading – Job 26 – 28
[186] OT Reading – Job 29 – 30

the church of God grew and multiplied. No matter how it looks today, the ultimate victory will always be God's. Trust Him.

Prayer: Glorious God of Freedom, we thank You for Your promise of the ultimate victory over sin, Satan, and the world. Amen.

July 5

Daily Bible Reading: Acts 13:1 - 23[187]

Verse of the Day: Acts 13:15 – *"And after the reading of the law and the prophets the rulers of the synagogue sent unto them, saying, Brethren, if ye have any word of exhortation for the people, say on."*

The word in the Greek translated as exhortation in today's verse means to comfort and encourage. That is one thing that as believers we need to be doing for one another. When the world sees the criticism and division in our churches why would they want what we have. After all, the world does this daily.

Being a part of God's family means that we are above verbal put-downs, sarcastic jabs, harsh judgments, or critical comments. We need to be the epitome of encouragement, the cornerstone of comfort, servants of solace, and the resources of refreshment. If we cannot feel this comfort and encouragement from our brothers and sisters in Christ, where can we?

Prayer: Holy Spirit, work in my heart today to seek ways that I can encourage, comfort, and refresh my fellow believers. May I be an extension of You to those around me. Amen.

July 6

Daily Bible Reading: Acts 13:24 - 52[188]

Verse of the Day: Acts 13:47 – *"For so hath the Lord commanded us, saying I have set thee for a light of the Gentiles, That thou shouldest be for salvation unto the uttermost part of the earth."*

In this verse from today's reading, we see Paul and Barnabus quoting from the Old Testament. They are quoting from Isaiah 49:6. In this section of Isaiah (chapters 49-53), Isaiah paints a picture of the Suffering Servant, the Messiah, or as we know Him, Jesus Christ.

Even in the Old Testament Scriptures, God had disclosed that His salvation was and would be for all nations. That shows that when Jesus

---

[187] OT Reading – Job 31 – 32
[188] OT Reading – Job 33 – 34

gave the Church its "marching orders" in Acts 1:8 it was not a change or a new direction. His plan has always been for anyone who would accept it.

We are called today to share this message of Jesus Christ with everyone and anyone who will listen.

Prayer: Jesus, may I accept and submit to Your Call to share the good news to all. Amen.

July 7

Daily Bible Reading: Acts 14[189]

Verse of the Day: Acts 14:15 – *"and saying, Sirs, why do ye these things? We also are men of like passions with you, and bring you good tidings, that ye should turn from these vain things unto a living God, who made the heaven and the earth and the sea, and all that in them is:"*

In Lystra and Derbe, Paul and Barnabus came into a new circumstance. Having faced opposition in so many places that they had travelled, here they are being exalted as gods. They went from being cursed to being worshipped. They handled it correctly. They realized who they were, and that only God was to be worshipped.

As human beings we must be careful to not take for ourselves any of the honor and glory that belongs to God. Worship Jesus and hide behind Him in all that we do.

Prayer: Jesus, help me to maintain my proper place in this life. I am a sinner saved by grace, and You only are to be glorified and praised. May all the words and works I do simply reflect You to this world. Amen.

July 8

Daily Bible Reading: Acts 15:1 – 21[190]

Verse of the Day: Acts 15:11 – *"But we believe that we shall be saved through the grace of the Lord Jesus, in like manner as they."*

Grace (χαριτος), we sing about it and talk about it, yet we often do not find the full dynamic of this word. It is probably the equivalent of the Hebrew word *chesed* in the Old Testament. In the Old Testament, it means lovingkindness, and is often used by the Psalmists to describe the character of God. In the New Testament, it means that which gives joy or that which is a free gift.

---

[189] OT Reading – Job 35 – 37
[190] OT Reading – Job 38 – 39

It stands out to us, because it is Paul's favorite word for God's free gift of salvation. In today's reading we see Peter use it in the same way before the Jerusalem Council. These are the last recorded words of Peter in the book of Acts. The emphasis will now shift from Peter to Paul. Yet, we see that it is all about the free gift of God's salvation, grace.

Prayer: Father, we pause and thank you today for this free gift. Your grace is what has provided our relationship restoration and forgiveness. May we never stop praising You.

July 9

Daily Bible Reading: Acts 15:22 – 41[191]

Verse of the Day: Acts 15:39 – "*And there arose a sharp contention, so that they parted asunder one from the other, and Barnabas took Mark with him, and sailed away unto Cyprus:*"

Even in the first church, and among none other than Paul and Barnabus, the possibility of a heated argument (the Greek word here used is the base of our word paroxysm), so great was the disagreement that Paul and Barnabus separated from each other. Luke does not assign blame for the disagreement.

Sometimes Christians will disagree heartily over some issues. The lesson we can take from this is, it is probably best for believers to separate instead of getting the whole church involved. Each went the way that God directed them and were used by Him.

Are there fellow Christians that you are ardently in disagreement with? Perhaps, instead of entangling the whole Body in this case, it would be best to step away and allow God to handle it.

Prayer: God, give insight in relationships.

July 10

Daily Bible Reading: Acts 16:1 – 15[192]

Verse of the Day: Acts 16:6 – 7 – "*And they went through the region of Phrygia and Galatia, having been forbidden of the Holy Spirit to speak the word in Asia; and when they were come over against Mysia, they assayed to go into Bithynia; and the Spirit of Jesus suffered them not:*"

---

[191] OT Reading – Job 40 – 42
[192] OT Reading – Psalm 1 – 3

The Holy Spirit had shut the door on Paul's southwesterly move and his northern path. So, Paul was seeking God where he should go when he was given the Macedonian vision. He knew this was the way, and went there.

Often in my life I have been presented with a decision of a direction to go in God's service. During such times, I pray sincerely for God to "shut the door" if this was not His will. And, I can truthfully say that many times He has slammed that door shut. I know that when He closes the door, He has another avenue for me to take. I like the old quote from the *Sound of Music*, "When God closes a door, somewhere He opens a window."

Prayer, Father help me see the closed door as Your directing me to something better in You.

July 11

Daily Bible Reading: Acts 16:16 – 40[193]

Verse of the Day: Acts 16:25 – *"But about midnight Paul and Silas were praying and singing hymns unto God, and the prisoners were listening to them;"*

We never know what effect we might have on those around us. Paul and Silas, beaten and chained in prison at Philippi were about to have a major effect.

This account reminds me how important it is that I understand that I daily make a choice about my attitude. It can cripple me or give me a boost to go forward. It will either fuel my fire or assault my hope. However, my attitude does not only affect me, it will affect those around me.

Paul and Silas singing hymns to God and praying affected the other prisoners, and eventually would lead to the salvation of the jailer and his family.

What does my attitude say to those around me?

Prayer: Father, encourage me to always have an attitude that shows You to others.

---

[193] OT Reading – Psalm 4 – 6

July 12

Daily Bible Reading: Acts 17:1 – 15[194]

Verse of the Day: Acts 17:11 – *"Now these were more noble than those in Thessalonica, in that they received the word with all readiness of mind, examining the scriptures daily, whether these things were so."*

Being is more important than doing in the Scriptures. Doing is part of our challenge by Jesus, but He always emphasizes that what we do is measured by who we are. In our account today, the Berean believers were spoken of as being a nobler people because they spent time in the Word of God.

God is saying that these people were able to do what they needed to do by being what they were supposed to be. And how did they have the character to be what they were to be? By spending time in God's Word.

Want true Christian character in your life? How much time do you spend in His Word?

Prayer: Holy Father, I want to be like Your Son. I know I need to be in Your Word, encourage me and keep me in the Bible. I long to be an image of Jesus. Amen.

July 13

Daily Bible Reading: Acts 17:16 – 34[195]

Verse of the Day: Acts 17:18 – *"And certain also of the Epicurean and Stoic philosophers encountered him. And some said, What would this babbler say? others, He seemeth to be a setter forth of strange gods: because he preached Jesus and the resurrection."*

The philosophers in Athens spent time discussing various views from their own personal worldviews. The Epicureans and Stoics were from schools of philosophy that were popular in that day. The followers of Epicurus believed that chief end of life was pleasure and happiness and that if gods existed they were not involved in human affairs. The Stoics were followers of Zeno. They were pantheists and that the universe was ruled by an Absolute Purpose and Will. The perfection of virtue was if a person could be unmoved by circumstances and change. It was a philosophy of arrogance and self-will. Can we see these philosophical basics in life today?

---

[194] OT Reading – Psalm 7 – 9
[195] OT Reading – Psalm 10 – 12

Prayer, Spirit of God, protect my heart and mind from the false philosophies of today. May I walk only in the Biblical Worldview You give.

July 14

Daily Bible Reading: Acts 18[196]

Verse of the Day: Acts 18:3 – *"and because he was of the same trade, he abode with them, and they wrought; for by their trade they were tentmakers."*

Tentmakers. When Paul went to Corinth we find that he connected with Aquila and Priscilla who had come here because the Jews were sent out from Rome by the Emperor. Aquila and Paul both made their living by tentmaking.

All young Jewish lads, even the Rabbinical students were required to learn a trade to support themselves. Paul often supported himself entirely from the trade he had learned. Even today, many groups refer to bi-vocational ministers as tentmakers.

All of God's people, believers, are called to be "tentmakers" in the sense that we 24/7 are called to be a witness for Jesus in our lives. How is your trade going?

Prayer: Jesus, may I serve You wherever I am called to work. All I do with my hands, mind, and heart are ministries for You each day.

July 15

Daily Bible Reading: Acts 19:1 – 20[197]

Verse of the Day: Acts 19:15 – *"And the evil spirit answered and said unto them, Jesus I know, and Paul I know; but who are ye?"*

This is an interesting account in the Book of Acts. In that day the use of magical names in incantations was commonplace. Jewish mystics enjoyed prestige because they claimed to know the sacred name of God and use it to release the full power of God.

In our account today, 7 sons of a Jewish priest were exorcists, and they grabbed hold of Jesus' name to use in their incantations. When they sought to use this incantation against a real demon in a man, this demon spoke out, attacked them, and then sent them running. They learned a

---

[196] OT Reading – Psalm 13 – 16
[197] OT Reading – Psalm 17 – 18

vital lesson for us even today, it is not enough to know the name of Jesus; we must know Him personally.

Prayer: Jesus, I know a lot about You. I am in awe of You. I praise You. But, I realize that this is worthless unless I know You personally. Check my heart, may I know not only about You, but may I know You personally. Cleanse me, draw me close, I trust You for my eternity.

July 16

Daily Bible Reading: Acts 19:21 – 41[198]

Verse of the Day: Acts 19:40 – *"For indeed we are in danger to be accused concerning this day's riot, there being no cause for it: and as touching it we shall not be able to give account of this concourse."*

Someone once remarked that everywhere that Paul went he either evoked a revival or a riot. There was no middle ground. You loved him or you hated him. However, it was not Paul personally that caused this, it was the message that he brought. The Gospel of Jesus Christ.

If we seek to live like the first century church did, we will also be placed in this situation. If we speak the truth of God's Word, we will find that in general people will either welcome us or want us gone. We will either comfort or convict. We will bring restoration or cause division. So, let us think, how am I looked at in my part of the world.

Prayer: Jesus, I want to be a true witness for You. Help me not to be offensive personally, but if Your Truth is offensive, may I be willing to face whatever may come from it. Amen.

July 17

Daily Bible Reading: Acts 20:1 – 16[199]

Verse of the Day: Acts 20:7 – *"And upon the first day of the week, when we were gathered together to break bread, Paul discoursed with them, intending to depart on the morrow; and prolonged his speech until midnight."*

This account of Eutychus falling asleep and then falling out of the window takes place in Troas. Paul was teaching them that evening before he would depart to go to Jerusalem to deliver the offering that the people of Gentile churches had provided for the suffering there.

---

[198] OT Reading – Psalm 19 – 21
[199] OT Reading – Psalm 22 – 24

The Jewish believers still celebrated their Sabbath on Saturday, but the Gentile believers met to celebrate the resurrection of Jesus from the grave each week. In Hebrews 4:8 – 10, we are reminded that Christ finished His work on the first day of the week and it is our Sabbath (rest).

Prayer: Jesus, may I remember that the reason we devote the first day of the week to You is because You have finished the work of our rest. Amen.

July 18

Daily Bible Reading: Acts 20:17 – 38[200]

Verse of the Day: Acts 20:22 – *"And now, behold, I go bound in the spirit unto Jerusalem, not knowing the things that shall befall me there:"*

Paul is telling the Ephesian elders that he is going to Jerusalem. He admits to them that he has no idea what may happen to him there, yet as he goes on to explain he is strictly following the Holy Spirit. In reality, that is what this Christian life is all about. Going... yet not knowing. That is being all in, trusting completely, totally surrendered. I need to check my stance. Am I all in?

In verse 24, Paul goes on to say, "But I hold not my life of any account as dear unto myself, so that I may accomplish my course, and the ministry which I received from the Lord Jesus, to testify the gospel of the grace of God."

Prayer: Grace giving God, may I be in total submission to Your Will and mission. May I follow Paul's example and not count my life and plans more important than Yours. May I too be able to finish the course and ministry You give to me. All is Yours. Amen.

July 19

Daily Bible Reading: Acts 21:1 – 14[201]

Verse of the Day: Acts 21:1 – *"And when it came to pass that we were parted from them and had set sail, we came with a straight course unto Cos, and the next day unto Rhodes, and from thence unto Patara:"*

"That we parted from them" in the Greek can also be rendered, "after tearing ourselves away from them." We see over and over again the heart of Paul for those that he ministered to. His love and concern for them ran deep, and is visible in his interactions.

---

[200] OT Reading – Psalm 25 – 27
[201] OT Reading – Psalm 28 – 30

It must have been hard and difficult for Paul. He over and over again would develop friends and family among those he ministered to, only to leave them to follow God's leading to proclaim the Gospel. We can be thankful that God allows us to remain where we are to do the same. The question is, "Are we doing it?"

Prayer: Holy God, we are often trying to find out Your Will for our lives while we are living in the center of it. Father, we thank You that You will use us where we are, and move us when You need to. May I spend my days serving where You have placed me. Amen.

July 20

Daily Bible Reading: Acts 21:15 – 40[202]

Verse of the Day: Acts 21:39 – 40 – *"But Paul said, I am a Jew, of Tarsus in Cilicia, a citizen of no mean city: and I beseech thee, give me leave to speak unto the people. And when he had given him leave, Paul, standing on the stairs, beckoned with the hand unto the people; and when there was made a great silence, he spake unto them in the Hebrew language, saying,"*

As we read in today's passage, the city of Jerusalem rose up in an uproar over Paul. They literally started a riot, and it was so bad that the Roman commander brought troops to quell this violent disturbance. The people were beating Paul with the intent to kill him because of his teaching about Christ.

Yet, we see Paul's heart and compassion for his fellow Israelites. After all they had just done to him, his number one desire was to speak to them about salvation. Could we do the same?

Prayer: Jesus, may I so have Your heart like Paul did, that even when mistreated and attacked I want to see all men come to salvation. Give me Your heart. Amen.

July 21

Daily Bible Reading: Acts 22[203]

Verse of the Day: Acts 22:3 – 4 – *"I am a Jew, born in Tarsus of Cilicia, but brought up in this city, at the feet of Gamaliel, instructed according to the strict manner of the law of our fathers, being zealous for*

---

[202] OT Reading – Psalm 31 – 33
[203] OT Reading – Psalm 34 – 35

God, even as ye all are this day: and I persecuted this Way unto the death, binding and delivering into prisons both men and women."

People may attack our doctrinal beliefs, our church, and our stance on issues. They may not seek to hear what we have to say about truth. They may not want to hear about Jesus, but one thing they can't deny is the fact that our lives have been changed.

The best method of evangelism is simply sharing our testimony. This may be about what we have gone from in our past, or it may be about what God has kept us from. We all have a testimony, and no one can dispute that.

Prayer: Savior, I come to You today asking You to place someone in my path that I can share my testimony with. You have changed me, and kept me, and now I need to tell others what a great Savior and Lord You are. Amen.

July 22

Daily Bible Reading: Acts 23:1 – 11[204]

Verse of the Day: Acts 23:11 – *"And the night following the Lord stood by him, and said, Be of good cheer: for as thou hast testified concerning me at Jerusalem, so must thou bear witness also at Rome."*

Paul's friends had all warned him not to go to Jerusalem. Agabus had prophesied that Paul would be bound in Jerusalem. Paul knew that God wanted him to go there.

Yet, as the events played out, perhaps Paul began to question his decision. He had written to the Roman believers of his desire to come to them. Now, it appeared that he was facing his possible demise.

Yet, he was under the Sovereign care of God, Paul's chains in Jerusalem would take him to Rome. He would have his opportunity to spread the Gospel again.

Prayer: Sovereign God, I often cannot see how I can accomplish what You have called me to do. I must learn to trust Your Heart when I cannot see Your Hand. You can bring about Your glory in ways that I cannot imagine. Amen.

---

[204] OT Reading – Psalm 36 – 37

July 23

Daily Bible Reading: Acts 23:12 – 35[205]

Verse of the Day: Acts 23:14 – *"And they came to the chief priests and the elders, and said, We have bound ourselves under a great curse, to taste nothing until we have killed Paul."*

I dare say that I have not been so much of a threat to the kingdom of darkness as Paul was. More than 40 Jews bound themselves under an oath to kill Paul. They came to the religious leaders and shared their plans. They requested them to get the Roman commander to bring Paul to them for a hearing.

Paul's nephew heard of these plans and brought them to Paul. Paul had the boy taken to the Commander, who then took the threat so seriously that he used almost half of the garrison under him to transport Paul out of the city at night.

As we think on this account, we can see that God's Hand was set to deliver Paul to Rome. Nothing or no one would hinder His plan.

Prayer: Father, may I place myself totally in Your Hand for Your Plan. Use me. Amen.

July 24

Daily Bible Reading: Acts 24[206]

Verse of the Day: Acts 24:16 – *"Herein I also exercise myself to have a conscience void of offence toward God and men always."*

What a great thought for us to seek. The importance of a clear, free from blame conscience is undervalued today. We must beware, when we continue to allow the little things that are not right to be accepted, we harden our conscience. We lose the ability to be blameless before others and before God.

Paul says he exercised himself, and anyone who follows an exercise regimen knows that it takes willpower and work to accomplish it. God has forgiven us, we are clean before Him because of the blood of Christ, but are we truly exercising our will to be blameless before Him? I rest in Christ's provision, but I also have the balancing need to seek to grow in the grace and knowledge of Jesus (2 Peter 3:18).

---

[205] OT Reading – Psalm 38 – 40
[206] OT Reading – Psalm 41 – 43

Prayer, Gracious Heavenly Father, I seek to have a clear, blameless conscience before You. I will fail, but with Your help I will seek to walk in Your path and follow my example, Jesus Christ. May what I do be for His Glory. Amen.

July 25

Daily Bible Reading: Acts 25[207]

Verse of the Day: Acts 25:11 – *"If then I am a wrong-doer, and have committed anything worthy of death, I refuse not to die; but if none of those things is true whereof these accuse me, no man can give me up unto them. I appeal unto Caesar."*

The Roman Empire was the ruling power (on earth) in Paul's day. Paul was born a Roman citizen. Being a citizen carried certain rights, responsibilities, and status. When it suited his needs, Paul would use his citizenship status to frustrate his enemies. Other times he would use his status of a Jew trained under the great Gamaliel.

We are citizens of Heaven. We have gained this privilege by receiving Jesus Christ as our Lord and Savior. We should use our status as children and citizens of the King rightly. He has sent us as ambassadors for Him. Let us stand proud and strong in His commission today.

Prayer: Sovereign King of Creation, as Your child and citizen, I bow humbly before You and You alone. I am sent to be Your Ambassador, may I humbly stand in this commission. Amen.

July 26

Daily Bible Reading: Acts 26[208]

Verse of the Day: Acts 26:16 – *"But arise, and stand upon thy feet: for to this end have I appeared unto thee, to appoint thee a minister and a witness both of the things wherein thou hast seen me, and of the things wherein I will appear unto thee;"*

In Acts 26, Paul shows us how to witness to others. A witness simply tells what they have experienced or seen. It is a word about the greatest Hope in all the world.

Paul starts with his pre-Christ life, then describes what happened at his conversion, and then shares about his life after conversion. Really, any of us should be able to do the same thing. And when we do, a person

---

[207] OT Reading – Psalm 44 – 46
[208] OT Reading – Psalm 47 – 49

can't argue about what was, and now is. It is simple and easy to talk about what God has done for us.

And the results, we leave them up to God. Even Paul did not lead everyone to accept Christ. Verse 28 states, "And Agrippa *said* unto Paul, With but little persuasion thou wouldest fain make me a Christian."

Prayer, Father give me boldness to speak.

July 27

Daily Bible Reading: Acts 27:1 – 25[209]

Verse of the Day: Acts 27:21 – 22 – "*And when they had been long without food, then Paul stood forth in the midst of them, and said, Sirs, ye should have hearkened unto me, and not have set sail from Crete, and have gotten this injury and loss. And now I exhort you to be of good cheer; for there shall be no loss of life among you, but only of the ship.*"

Can you imagine the Apostle Paul saying, "I told you so." The very thing that he had warned the sailors about was now taking place. And they were all in great throes of fear. Paul stands up and says, "I told you so."

But, he doesn't use it against them, he is reminding them so that when he now tells them the good news that they will all survive, they will believe and listen to him.

We must continually warn others about the destiny outside of Jesus, and then use it to share with them the truth of salvation through Christ.

Prayer: Father, help me to warn others about the end of those who reject Christ, but in love, let me tell them how to avoid this end.

July 28

Daily Bible Reading: Acts 27:26 – 44[210]

Verse of the Day: Acts 27:33 – 34 – "*And while the day was coming on, Paul besought them all to take some food, saying, This day is the fourteenth day that ye wait and continue fasting, having taken nothing. Wherefore I beseech you to take some food: for this is for your safety: for there shall not a hair perish from the head of any of you.*"

Yesterday, we spoke about Paul saying, "I told you so." Today, we see that as they are soon to become shipwrecked, that Paul encourages

---

[209] OT Reading – Psalm 50 – 52
[210] OT Reading – Psalm 53 – 55

them. These sailors were blessed because of Paul and didn't know it. God had planned for Paul to go to Rome, and His plan will not fail. And, because Paul needed to be safe, they would be too.

Still, they would all have to go through the consequences to arrive safely at the other side. Sometimes in our lives, we must go through the consequences of other's choices before we can arrive safely in God's plan. Trust Him.

Prayer: Jesus, I find that sometimes I am the victim of other's choices. Yet, I can trust You to accomplish Your plan and will for me. Amen.

July 29

Daily Bible Reading: Acts 28:1 – 15[211]

Verse of the Day: Acts 28:14 – *"where we found brethren, and were entreated to tarry with them seven days: and so we came to Rome."*

The Apostle and those with him were washed ashore on the island of Malta in the Mediterranean Sea. After a very short ministry on that island, Paul and the others were able to continue on their journey until, as we read today, they arrived safely in Rome.

One thing I take from these passages is that God may have a plan for us, He may make that plan clear to us, yet the way He accomplishes that plan may not be what we had anticipated.

God had told Paul that he would be able to go to Rome. God provided the means through Paul's imprisonment and subsequent trials. And now, Paul will be able to reach those in Caesar's household.

Prayer: Gracious God, I get impatient when I do not see things working out the way that they should. Help me to be open to You to see the methods and means that You will use.

July 30

Daily Bible Reading: Acts 28:16 – 31[212]

Verse of the Day: Acts 28:30 – 31 – *"And he abode two whole years in his own hired dwelling, and received all that went in unto him, preaching the kingdom of God, and teaching the things concerning the Lord Jesus Christ with all boldness, none forbidding him."*

---

[211] OT Reading – Psalm 56 – 58
[212] OT Reading – Psalm 59 – 61

What a way to conclude the book of Acts. After all that Paul had been through, he made it to Rome. While under arrest, no one came to bring charges against him. So for two years he was allowed to stay in a dwelling that he rented. This gave him total freedom to proclaim Jesus and the Kingdom of God.

The last words in this book speak of him being bold in what he said, and that no one stopped him. The plan of God came to a conclusion. We know from other books in the New Testament that ultimately Paul was rearrested, tried and executed. But this part of God's plan spread the gospel right in the heart of the Roman government and city.

Prayer: Jesus, may I speak with all boldness about You and the Kingdom. I do not face what Paul did, I am blessed. Thank You. Amen.

July 31

Daily Bible Reading: Romans 1[213]

Verse of the Day: Romans 1:7 – *"to all that are in Rome, beloved of God, called to be saints: Grace to you and peace from God our Father and the Lord Jesus Christ."*

We end this month in the beginning of the letter from Paul to the Roman believers. This is considered a prime example of a first century legal treatise. Paul was trained by Gamaliel in all Jewish education. And he was well versed in the Greco-Roman thought patterns. He was the perfect choice of God for ministry to Gentiles.

In our readings this next month we will see Paul present a case for the Gospel doctrinally, nationally, and practically. He will deal with faith, hope, and love.

In this letter, Paul works through the doctrine of God, humanity, and sin. All necessary for a proper understanding of salvation from God's wrath to our peace with Him.

Prayer: Spirit, as I read this letter, guide me, instruct me, and provide me with a mind, will, heart, and determination to live in His Victory.

---

[213] OT Reading – Psalm 62 – 64

AUGUST Rest Assured God's Greatness

The lazy, hazy, crazy days of summer are well under way. We swelter under the heat and complain. We seek the cooler days of Autumn and long for the enjoyment that we can have in the cooling breezes and beautiful colors.

But, we must beware that in our haste to wish for the next season we do not miss the beauty that God gives now. In the days of summer, we need to seek rest. I am not talking about lying in a hammock, or stretching out on the beach, I am talking about resting in the greatness of our God.

This month we will travel through the writings of Paul to the churches at Rome and Corinth. We will see the greatness of God displayed in full majesty in the polemic[214] words to the Roman believers. We can see the greatness of God in Paul's corrections to the Corinthians. Join me as we see the display from the pen of Paul of God's Majestic Being.

---

[214] Polemic = **a** piece of writing or a speech in which a person argues forcefully for or against someone or something

August 1

Daily Bible Reading: Romans 2[215]

Verse of the Day: Romans 2:1 – *"Wherefore thou art without excuse, O man, whosoever thou art that judgest: for wherein thou judgest another, thou condemnest thyself; for thou that judgest dost practise the same things."*

The passage today hits on a very hard subject. This is a horrible form of pride, holding a harsh, abusive, almost militant attitude that comes out in judging others.

If I grasp the whole truth of the forgiveness of God for me, I should be one of the most accepting of people around me. By accepting a person does not mean that I accept their lifestyle, issues, etc. It means that as a part of the body of Christ, if I can learn to be winsome and forgiving, I can lead others to find the ultimate truth to life, the Lord Jesus Christ.

Today, I will seek to guide those that I come in contact with to the One who will not only forgive, accept, and love them, but who will also make a difference in their life.

Prayer: Jesus, let me see others as You see them and love them to You. Amen.

August 2

Daily Bible Reading: Romans 3[216]

Verse of the Day: Romans 3:23 – *"for all have sinned, and fall short of the glory of God;"*

We are probably very familiar with this verse today. It is part of the Romans Road to salvation many have used for ages to help lead a person to a saving knowledge of Jesus Christ.

The term used here for fall short can be translated to fail, be destitute, to lack, or to be inferior. It is the Middle Voice in the Greek, and that means that the subject is performing an action upon himself (reflexive action). It is in the Indicative Mood, or is simply a statement of fact.

In other words, we miss the mark of attaining the glory of God by our own actions. In even simpler terms as Paul is building his case, we don't have to do anything to be in this situation. How are you doing

---

[215] OT Reading – Psalm 65 – 67
[216] OT Reading – Psalm 68 – 69

today? Have you come to Jesus and received the free gift that He has for you?

Prayer: Heavenly Father, I surrender to You. I have missed the mark so often, and I have no one to blame but myself. I submit to You today.

August 3

Daily Bible Reading: Romans 4[217]

Verse of the Day: Romans 4:3 – *"For what saith the scripture? And Abraham believed God, and it was reckoned unto him for righteousness."*

Some want to teach that the means of salvation in the Old Testament was different from the New Testament. Even in Paul's time, this was what some thought. In our verse today, Paul quotes from Genesis 15:6 to refute this erroneous idea,

If we study the surrounding material of this quote, God had made a promise to Abraham, and Abraham simply trusted God to fulfill it. In other words, he believed God.

Abraham didn't have to obey some law, follow some rule, take part in some ritual, or do any other kind of task to achieve his relationship to God. He simply believed God. Because of his trust, God credited righteousness to his account. Abraham was saved by faith through grace just as we must do.

Prayer: Gracious God, You are the same yesterday, today, and forever. I am so glad that You stay constant and I can trust in You. Amen.

August 4

Daily Bible Reading: Romans 5[218]

Verse of the Day: Romans 5:18 – *"So then as through one trespass the judgment came unto all men to condemnation; even so through one act of righteousness the free gift came unto all men to justification of life."*

The Greek word for justification (δικαιωσιν) is from the base word that means to acquit or declare righteous. It is a legal term used in the first century that meant a very favorable verdict.

The picture that Paul is painting here is one of a courtroom with God as the judge. He is sitting in judgment determining who had faithfully kept the Law. Paul's writing up to this has shown that no one is capable, nor has kept all the Law. We begin to understand that the Law was not given

---

[217] OT Reading – Psalm 70 – 72
[218] OT Reading – Psalm 73 – 74

to justify us, but to expose our sin. When we believe in Jesus, God imputes His righteousness in place of our sinfulness. Thus, we are justified by faith through grace.

Prayer, Gracious Judge of all mankind, I am so thankful that You provided for my forgiveness and justification through Your Son Jesus. By myself I stand condemned, in His Blood I stand redeemed. Hallelujah. Amen.

August 5

Daily Bible Reading: Romans 6[219]

Verse of the Day: Romans 6:23 – *"For the wages of sin is death; but the free gift of God is eternal life in Christ Jesus our Lord.*

Earned wages versus free gift. Actually the term free gift is redundant. If it costs something, it is neither free nor a gift. The passage above helps us to see that eternal life is given to us without any work or purchase on our part. It is a gift.

The phrase eternal life is used 42 times in the New Testament, the majority meaning a gift we receive at the moment of our belief in the gospel. However, 11 times it is used as something to be attained. We can see from this that eternal life is not static. It is a growing, dynamic, and expanding relationship with Jesus Christ. When we live in obedience, we realize a full enjoyment of God's gift of eternal life.

Prayer: Jesus, as I seek to be in obedience to Your Word, I grow in understanding of the marvelous gift You have given me in eternal life. My growing closer to You brings out more grace and more enjoyment as I walk through this world. I didn't earn it, but I love it.

August 6

Daily Bible Reading: Romans 7[220]

Verse of the Day: Romans 7:7 – *"What shall we say then? Is the law sin? God forbid. Howbeit, I had not known sin, except through the law: for I had not known coveting, except the law had said, Thou shalt not covet:"*

Beginning at this point to the end of the chapter, Paul uses his personal example and experience to answer the question as to whether the Law is sin.

---

[219] OT Reading – Psalm 75 – 77
[220] OT Reading – Psalm 78

He tells us that without the Law, there would be no sin (verse 8). This starts his dialog dealing with the question. The truth of the matter is, that the morality that is espoused by the Law is in existence. God is the ultimate expression of this morality. We would not know that we were living contrary to His moral standards if it were not for the Law. We now know we are in sin because the Law exposes our sin.

Prayer: Holy Spirit, as I study God's Word bring to light the sin that is in my life. Help me to see my great need of a Savior, and to see that Savior, Jesus Christ. I want to walk in His way and be like Him today. Amen.

August 7

Daily Bible Reading: Romans 8:1 – 18[221]

Verse of the Day: Romans 8:2 – *"For the law of the Spirit of life in Christ Jesus made me free from the law of sin and of death."*

The Greek term used for law in this passage means an inward principle that works with the regularity of a law. It designates the standard of the life of a person. Paul in his writing points out three such laws.

First is the "law of sin" which we often call the operation of the flesh. It is what causes us to sin. Then he spoke of "the law of the Spirit of life in Christ Jesus" that frees us from the bondage to the "law of sin and death."

When we are governed in our daily life by the Holy Spirit, we can and should have victory over "the law of sin." The Spirit living in us provides what we need to rise above the law that would seek to destroy us. It comes from our relationship with Jesus Christ.

Prayer: Holy Spirit, it is my desire and earnest prayer that You would lead me in the path that allows "the law of the Spirit of life in Christ Jesus" to free me from "the law of sin."

August 8

Daily Bible Reading: Romans 8:19 – 39[222]

Verse of the Day: Romans 8:29 – 30 – *"For whom he foreknew, he also foreordained to be conformed to the image of his Son, that he might be the firstborn among many brethren: and whom he foreordained, them he also called: and whom he called, them he also justified: and whom he justified, them he also glorified."*

---

[221] OT Reading – Psalm 79 – 81
[222] OT Reading – Psalm 82 – 84

The word "foreknew" in the Greek means to know beforehand. God knew beforehand who would accept Him and who would reject Him. In this foreknowledge, God foreordained these believers to be made into the likeness of His Son.

One of the exciting things about this passage is that all the verbs (foreordained, conformed, called, justified, and glorified) all are in the past tense. God from His Eternal perspective sees all things as completed. I am already glorified in the mind of God.

Prayer: Lord, may I live my life aware of my stand before You. Thank You that my glorification is all in Your hands, and that You are the One who completes it all for me. Amen.

August 9

Daily Bible Reading: Romans 9[223]

Verse of the Day: Romans 9:13 – *"Even as it is written, Jacob I loved, but Esau I hated."*

This is a quote from the Old Testament prophet Malachi (1:2,3). In both places many find it hard to understand. What can help is to realize that Malachi (and in turn, Paul) are using a Hebrew idiom. *Idiom* comes from a Greek word that means "personal". *Idiom* originally meant "speech peculiar or proper to a people or country." These days we use *idiom* for a specialized vocabulary or an expression that isn't obvious, like *kick the bucket*, which means "die." If you're studying a foreign language, idioms are the hardest phrases to translate.

The Hebrew idiom here is where the opposite is used but to a lesser degree. It is a form of comparison. God loved Jacob so much that it made His feelings for Esau to look like hatred. God did provide for Esau, but not in line with the promises.

Prayer: Loving Father, I can take Your gracious plan and privilege for granted. Help me to remember that Your Love for me is so great You would sacrifice Your Son for me.

August 10

Daily Bible Reading: Romans 10[224]

Verse of the Day: Romans 10:12 – 13 – *"For there is no distinction between Jew and Greek: for the same Lord is Lord of all, and is rich unto*

---

[223] OT Reading – Psalm 85 – 87
[224] OT Reading – Psalm 88 – 89

all that call upon him: for, Whosoever shall call upon the name of the Lord shall be saved."

Fellow believers, it will do us well to grasp and understand these verse from today's reading. The two divisions that Paul uses here, Jew and Greek, in the Jewish mind encompass all people.

Paul is reminding the Roman believers that God does not distinguish between nationalities, races, or cultures. To Him, there is only one division, those who believe and are saved and those who reject and remain condemned. The beautiful part of this division is that anyone who comes to God, He will not reject.

Prayer: God of all Salvation, as our reading today challenges us, we need to be telling people about the Gospel and giving them the chance to believe and become a part of Your family. May I be challenged by the words of Paul to make it a vital part of my lifestyle to tell others about Christ. Amen.

August 11

Daily Bible Reading: Romans 11:1 – 21[225]

Verse of the Day: Romans 11:3 – 5 – *"Lord, they have killed thy prophets, they have digged down thine altars; and I am left alone, and they seek my life. But what saith the answer of God unto him? I have left for myself seven thousand men, who have not bowed the knee to Baal. Even so then at this present time also there is a remnant according to the election of grace."*

Paul goes back to 1 Kings 19:18 to use Elijah as an example in today's reading. Some possibly felt that all of Israel had rejected Jesus, just as we may believe that there are no Christians around us. Elijah felt all alone, yet God encourages him by telling him that He still had 7,000 believers in that day.

Today, we need to take stands for what is morally and biblically true, even when we feel all alone. God is with us, and He has an army that will stand for the truth.

Prayer: Lord of All, remind me when I find that I am wavering in my stand that You have an army of believers that will stand strong. Give me the courage to stand for You and Your Word at all times in all places. Amen.

---

[225] OT Reading – Psalm 90 – 92

August 12

Daily Bible Reading: Romans 11:22 – 36[226]

Verse of the Day: Romans 11:25 – *"For I would not, brethren, have you ignorant of this mystery, lest ye be wise in your own conceits, that a hardening in part hath befallen Israel, until the fulness of the Gentiles be come in;"*

Paul here speaks of a "mystery" (Greek μυστηριον). He often uses this word in his writings (26 of the 27 times it is used by Paul, the last time is in the Book of Revelation). They are not meaning something incomprehensible, the word pictures something that was hidden and has now been revealed. Many religious groups have secret meanings and beliefs that only the initiated can know. Paul speaks instead of a secret that has been revealed for all to see.

Here in this passage, the mystery is that Israel has been temporarily and partially hardened against the Gospel, but God has not rejected the Nation. God is not finished with Israel yet.

Prayer: God of Israel, help me to remember Your love for Your Chosen Nation, and that that same Love is bestowed upon me. Thank You that You are not finished with us yet.

August 13

Daily Bible Reading: Romans 12[227]

Verse of the Day: Romans 12:1 – 2 – *"I beseech you therefore, brethren, by the mercies of God, to present your bodies a living sacrifice, holy, acceptable to God, which is your spiritual service. And be not fashioned according to this world: but be ye transformed by the renewing of your mind, that ye may prove what is the good and acceptable and perfect will of God."*

Romans 12 starts a few chapters that deal with the Christian Life. Paul describes a Christian in these passages.

In Chapter 12 he challenges us to be living sacrifices, holy and acceptable to God. In the verses above he tells us to transform our minds by renewing them in God. He also calls us to serve God with the Spiritual Gifts that we have been given. Beginning in verse 9 of our reading, Paul tells us that we need to behave like a Christian. Take inventory, how are we doing?

---

[226] OT Reading – Psalm 93 – 95
[227] OT Reading – Psalm 96 – 98

Prayer: Holy Spirit, transform my thoughts so that I can live a life that is pleasing to God. As I seek to utilize the gifts You have given me, help me to behave in a manner that shows the Father to all I come in contact with. Amen.

August 14

Daily Bible Reading: Romans 13[228]

Verse of the Day: Romans 13:10 – *"Love worketh no ill to his neighbor: love therefore is the fulfilment of the law."*

Continuing in the Description of being a Christian Paul gives us in chapters 12 – 15, we see in this chapter we read that we have two responsibilities. The first is to honor civil law. When we honor the laws of the government, we are honoring God. We show that we understand that all things are under the hand of God, and even the government is under His ultimate control.

Then, beginning in verse 8 of this chapter, we are taught to love others. This is the fulfillment of the law of God. The two great commandments are (according to Jesus) love God and love others.

Today, consider whether others can see Christ in us by how we live as a Christian. How is my scorecard?

Prayer: Jesus, may I portray to the world the life of a Christian by my love for God and for others I come in contact with.

August 15

Daily Bible Reading: Romans 14[229]

Verse of the Day: Romans 14:19 – *"So then let us follow after things which make for peace, and things whereby we may edify one another."*

We are called to edify, or build up, each other. Too often as Christians we fail in this area. Some believe it is their calling to tear down everyone and show them how they are failing God. But, as our verse today in these chapters on being a Christian that Paul writes to the Roman believers shows, we are to build up one another.

So, how do we do this? By seeking to pursue peace. There is enough tribulation and challenges in the world around us. We need to seek out

---

[228] OT Reading – Psalm 99 – 102
[229] OT Reading – Psalm 103 – 104

the things that will develop and produce peace. When we do, we will be building up others, not tearing them down.

Prayer: God of all Peace, make me a minister of peace in this world of tribulation, care, and destruction. Help me to seek out ways to create an atmosphere of growth in peace. Show me how I can bring people to You through the peaceful application of Your love in their lives through mine. Amen.

August 16

Daily Bible Reading: Romans 15:1 – 20[230]

Verse of the Day: Romans 15:13 – *"Now the God of hope fill you with all joy and peace in believing, that ye may abound in hope, in the power of the Holy Spirit."*

The Greek term used for hope in this passage is one that shows a confident expectation or anticipation. In the New Testament the word hope does not carry with it the idea of wishful thinking, as we so often use it today.

Paul in chapters 12 – 15 has been encouraging us to live like believers. We are to display what a Christian looks like. He is speaking in our passage today of glorifying God together. We are to be like-minded with one another (vs. 5) and this will help to display the oneness and glory of God. When we live together as Christians in this life, we give the world a glimpse of what Heaven will be like.

Prayer: Father of Unity, help us today to seek out ways to be like-minded in what we say, do, and plan. If we truly want the world to see we have something different and better, let us live it out before them today. Amen.

August 17

Daily Bible Reading: Romans 15:21 – 33[231]

Verse of the Day: Romans 15:33 – *" Now the God of peace be with you all. Amen."*

Paul is drawing this letter to the Roman believers to a close. He speaks to them about his desire to come and visit with them. He had no idea at this point that his trip would be financed and provided by the Roman government.

---

[230] OT Reading – Psalm 105 – 106
[231] OT Reading – Psalm 107 – 108

Paul has spent a good deal of time and effort writing this special letter. He has shared his heart and his concerns. He starts out by emphasizing that the whole world needs the gospel, possibly because he is writing to people in the city of Rome, the hub of the world at that time. He ends by praying for peace in the lives of those he has been writing to. He has made it evident that peace comes from the grace of God given freely to all who ask. He stresses the need for all to come to salvation. He makes us aware that there is no greater need a person has than their relationship with God.

Prayer: Father, may my heart, mind, and life be in line with You at all times. Amen.

August 18

Daily Bible Reading: Romans 16[232]

Verse of the Day: Romans 16:21 – 23 – *"Timothy my fellow-worker saluteth you; and Lucius and Jason and Sosipater, my kinsmen. I Tertius, who write the epistle, salute you in the Lord. Gaius my host, and of the whole church, saluteth you. Erastus the treasurer of the city saluteth you, and Quartus the brother."*

Paul had gone through a list of 26 people that he mentions by name in the longest list of greetings he has written. About one-third of these are women. Here we find a group of people who are sending their greetings along with Paul to that list.

What is interesting is this shows us that the early church was made up of all levels of society and all nationalities. In this list we see the names of Tertuius and Quartus. These two are apparently slaves. They were given numerical names. Erastus is the treasure of the city. What a range of socio-economical levels of people all working in love and unity together. Do we see this today?

Prayer: Father, may we work in harmony and love with our brothers and sisters in Christ.

August 19

Daily Bible Reading: 1 Corinthians 1[233]

Verse of the Day: 1 Corinthians 1:2 – *"unto the church of God which is at Corinth, even them that are sanctified in Christ Jesus, called to be*

---

[232] OT Reading – Psalm 109 – 111
[233] OT Reading – Psalm 112 – 115

saints, with all that call upon the name of our Lord Jesus Christ in every place, their Lord and ours:"

Corinth. A city whose name became a Greek verb because of their debauchery and vibrant lifestyle. It was fast and vile, yet rich and industrial. Into this wicked and vile city came Paul. I don't believe any ministry has ever faced the challenges to survive as this one did, nor any church experience so much conflict.

In these 16 chapters, Paul emphasizes the need to develop a holy character even in the midst of strife and division. The first six chapters are in response to a report from Chloe, and the remaining chapters deal with specific questions from the Corinthian believers. Even with the very confrontational tone of the letter, Paul ends it with hope.

Prayer: Spirit of the Most Holy God, guide me to glean from this letter the vital truths of how to live a holy life at all times.

August 20

Daily Bible Reading: 1 Corinthians 2[234]

Verse of the Day: 1 Corinthians 2:9 – 10 – *"but as it is written, Things which eye saw not, and ear heard not, And which entered not into the heart of man, Whatsoever things God prepared for them that love him. But unto us God revealed them through the Spirit: for the Spirit searcheth all things, yea, the deep things of God."*

Human knowledge can seem impressive, maybe ever overwhelming at times. But when it comes to knowing about tomorrow, well, at that point it really fails. Our knowledge about tomorrow is guesswork at best.

God has all control over today, and tomorrow. He has hidden what will be tomorrow in His unfathomable plan. He has interwoven it with all the depth and the knowledge that He holds, and we are unable to see it until it unrolls before us. Can we truly trust Him with our future? If we can't trust Him, whom could we trust?

Prayer: Heavenly Father, God of all eternity past and future, help us to trust You to lead and guide us into the plan You have made.

---

[234] OT Reading – Psalm 116 – 118

August 21

Daily Bible Reading: 1 Corinthians 3[235]

Verse of the Day: 1 Corinthians 3:5 – *"What then is Apollos? and what is Paul? Ministers through whom ye believed; and each as the Lord gave to him."*

In true Christian work there is no such thing as "celebrities." We are all equal in the sight of God. We, as human beings, tend to place people up on a pedestal. When they fail in some way (remember that we are all sinners saved by grace), then many become disillusioned and disturbed.

Paul wanted the believers at Corinth to see that all work and workers were equal before God. Some of us have the task of plowing up the soil, others go behind and plant the seed. Some work at watering the seed, and still others are given the privilege to harvest. But it takes all to see it happen.

Prayer: Holy Spirit, You have tasked me with a special assignment in the Kingdom. Don't let me look at others and feel that I am inadequate to do what You have called me to do. I can, through Your power, do what it is that You are calling me to do. Amen.

August 22

Daily Bible Reading: 1 Corinthians 4[236]

Verse of the Day: 1 Corinthians 4:10 – *"We are fools for Christ's sake, but ye are wise in Christ; we are weak, but ye are strong; ye have glory, but we have dishonor."*

Who's fool are you? When I was asked that question the first time, I was insulted. No one likes to be called a fool. Then the person showed me this verse in Paul's letter, and I got his meaning.

Paul was a fool for Christ's sake. He submitted to Christ's strength, glory, and wisdom. We must be careful that we do not seek our own glory, display our own strength, and strive to parade our own wisdom before the world.

If I am to appear foolish to the world around me, I want it to be because I am standing on God's Word. The World doesn't see things as God does, so let me be His fool and not the world.

---

[235] OT Reading – Psalm 119:1 – 48
[236] OT Reading – Psalm 119:49 – 104

Prayer: Jesus, I want to live in your wisdom, strength, and glory. Let the world see You through me. I want to display who You are.

August 23

Daily Bible Reading: 1 Corinthians 5[237]

Verse of the Day: 1 Corinthians 5:12 – " *For what have I to do with judging them that are without? Do not ye judge them that are within?"*

This chapter deals with the Corinthian Church ignoring sin in its ranks. Paul calls them to deal with sin inside the church.

He tells them that not associating with sinners in the world would require "for then must ye needs go out of the world" (verse 10b). He is reminding us that we are sent into the world to challenge them to accept Christ. We are not to imitate or accept for ourselves their sinful lifestyle. We can, as the old saying goes, "Love the sinner and hate the sin."

Too often churches compromise their standards seeking to increase their numbers, however, this goes against the Scriptures. In fact, allowing this mindset can affect the entire church. Paul said, "Know ye not that a little leaven leaveneth the whole lump?" (verse 6b).

Prayer: Jesus, I want to be molded into an image of You. Do not allow the world to take control of my thoughts and lifestyle. Amen.

August 24

Daily Bible Reading: 1 Corinthians 6[238]

Verse of the Day: 1 Corinthians 6:19 – *"Or know ye not that your body is a temple of the Holy Spirit which is in you, which ye have from God? and ye are not your own;"*

The Greek word ναος refers to the building itself. There are other Greek words that refer to the whole complex.

Paul was reminding each of the believers in Corinth that their body was a sanctuary for God. What a privilege it is for us to be the spiritual dwelling place of God. In the Old Testament, the Glory of God filled the Tabernacle (Ex. 40:34) and the Temple (1 Kings 8:10,11).

Today, the Glory of God in the person of the Holy Spirit dwells in each believer. In the New Jerusalem there will not be a need for a

---

[237] OT Reading – Psalm 119:105 – 176
[238] OT Reading – Psalm 120 – 123

physical Temple because God and the Lamb will be the eternal temple (Rev. 21:22).

Prayer: Father, may I be a pure and holy place for Your Spirit to reside in. May I be worthy of the privilege of being the Temple of God today. In Jesus Name I pray, Amen.

August 25

Daily Bible Reading: 1 Corinthians 7:1 – 24[239]

Verse of the Day: 1 Corinthians 7:1a – *"Now concerning the things whereof ye wrote:"*

The first 6 chapters of this letter deal with a report that Paul received from Chloe. At this point, he answers some questions and discusses some areas that the Corinthians had posed to him. From chapter 7 through 14, he deals with a variety of topics. He begins with Marriage Obligation in chapter 7, and ends with a discourse on Spiritual Gifts in chapter 14. In between he will answer their questions on Christian liberties and Proper form of worship.

He has been asked about the area of celibacy and divorce. He speaks of the relationship between a husband and his wife. Our society and churches would do well to listen to the advice given by God through the pen of the Apostle Paul.

Prayer: Heavenly Father, You have designed our lives and know what is the best for each of us. Father, may we put aside our cultural and preconceived views to be open to the words that You have written for us. May we walk in Your way at all times. Amen.

August 26

Daily Bible Reading: 1 Corinthians 7:25 – 40[240]

Verse of the Day: 1 Corinthians 7:33-34 – *"but he that is married is careful for the things of the world, how he may please his wife, and is divided. So also the woman that is unmarried and the virgin is careful for the things of the Lord, that she may be holy both in body and in spirit: but she that is married is careful for the things of the world, how she may please her husband."*

---

[239] OT Reading – Psalm 124 – 127
[240] OT Reading – Psalm 128 – 131

We may be missing the mark when we are quick to tell singles that the ultimate plan of God for them is to get married. We even now have Christian Dating Websites to help this process.

The ultimate plan for a single person is to listen to what He is saying to you. Being single may be the highest spiritual plateau you have ever known in your life. You may be closer to Him being single than you could be as a married person.

Prayer: O Holy One, I pray that I will not interfere with Your plans for the lives I come in contact with. Help me to pray and seek the highest for everyone I see. Amen.

August 27

Daily Bible Reading: 1 Corinthians 8[241]

Verse of the Day: 1 Corinthians 8:9 – *"But take heed lest by any means this liberty of yours become a stumblingblock to the weak."*

Εξουσια. This term in the Greek denotes a right, privilege or authority. In some contexts it means the freedom to exercise one's rights.

Here Paul is using it in the context of eating food dedicated to idols. He has no problem with those who purchased this leftover meat and ate it at home. To Paul, they were not participating in idol worship. They had the freedom to eat this meat with a clean conscience.

However, he does make one exception. If eating this meat would destroy a weaker brother or sister they should abstain. For the weaker believer, Paul says we should not partake in even something that may cause them to stray or fall to the wayside. How many of us want to exercise our rights without consideration of others?

Prayer: Great Spirit of God, guide me to consider others at all times in all ways. Amen.

August 28

Daily Bible Reading: 1 Corinthians 9[242]

Verse of the Day: 1 Corinthians 9:19 – *"For though I was free from all men, I brought myself under bondage to all, that I might gain the more."*

---

[241] OT Reading – Psalm 132 – 135
[242] OT Reading – Psalm 136 – 138

Continuing with his statements to the Corinthian Church that we looked at yesterday, Paul uses himself as an example to show that he followed what he taught.

Paul put his calling to minister to others above his own personal preferences. He was willing to conform to the customs of those he came in contact with (Greek, Jew, etc.) to bring them to Christ. To those under the Law (Jews) he sought to observe the Law. To those outside the Law (Gentiles) Paul did not observe Jewish customs. He went on to clarify this, unless someone misunderstood, in verse 21 he said he obeyed the law through obedience to Christ.

Being free was not a license to sin with others; it was the ability to be with them, yet stay pure in heart.

Prayer: Jesus, may I be available to others, yet remain true to You in all I do and say.

August 29

Daily Bible Reading: 1 Corinthians 10:1 – 13[243]

Verse of the Day: 1 Corinthians 10:10 – *"Neither murmur ye, as some of them murmured, and perished by the destroyer."*

Have you ever stopped to consider how often you may grumble and complain? The word used for murmur means to have a complaining attitude, to speak negatively. Maybe it is because of a boring job. Or maybe you are picking up behind your kids (or husband) for the nth time. Maybe you are complaining about needing to take out the garbage again.

Consider that instead of complaining and griping, do it with a thankful heart. Be thankful that you have a job (many do not), that you have those kids (or husband), and that you are blessed to have enough that you actually have trash to take out.

Prayer: God of all Provision, thank You that I have so many things and people in my life. Thank You that I have the strength to work and to do household chores. I am so grateful for all the many blessings that You have provided in my life. I praise You. Amen.

---

[243] OT Reading – Psalm 139 – 141

August 30

Daily Bible Reading: 1 Corinthians 10:14 – 33[244]

Verse of the Day: 1 Corinthians 10:14 – *"Wherefore, my beloved, flee from idolatry."*

Idolatry. Does that really happen today? Oh yeah, it must be some of those weirdo religions out there. Well, the term used here in the Greek means the worship of false gods, of the formal sacrificial feats held in honor of false gods of avarice, as a worship of Mammon.

What is Mammon? The dictionary defines it as material wealth or possessions especially as having a debasing influence. So, do people tend to honor and worship their wealth today? Do we find people and religious teachings like that today? You bet. So, what do we do when confronted with idolatry? Stand up and rebuke it? Fight it tooth and nail? Debate it?

Well, Paul told the Corinthian believers to run! We need to heed that same advice today. When we are facing the temptation to fall into idolatry, run from it. Don't dabble, don't see how close you can get, don't excuse it and dress it up. RUN!

Prayer: *Father, give me swift feet to run.*

August 31

Daily Bible Reading: 1 Corinthians 11:1 – 15[245]

Verse of the Day: 1 Corinthians 11:1 – *"Be ye imitators of me, even as I also am of Christ."*

Paul makes a bold statement here, imitate me. The Greek word μιμηται means to mimic or to act like. Paul is challenging the Corinthian believers to act like him, to mimic him in what they do.

Would I be so bold to tell others this? How about you? Yet, we inwardly expect others to be like us in church. They need to dress like us, talk like us, act like us, like the same things we do.... Well, you get the picture.

Paul challenged them to mimic him, as he mimicked Christ. What a qualifier. Does everything about me mimic Jesus? Can the world see Jesus in me? Do the things I do look like Jesus? All the time? Do the things I say

---

[244] OT Reading – Psalm 142 – 144
[245] OT Reading – Psalm 145 – 147

mimic Jesus? All the time? We must walk the walk to challenge others to walk like Jesus.

Prayer: Spirit of the Living God, come into my life today and take control. May I be a true reflection of my Savior in all that I think, say, and do. May I walk the walk today. Amen.

SEPTEMBER Working In God's Purpose

September brings us out of the very hot and humid days of summer, and begins to take us into the refreshing days of Autumn.

The students have all gone back to school. The vacations to the beach have come to an end. And, we will continue to see the hand of God working in His Word.

We will be reading letters to three first-century churches. We will finish the first letter to the church at Corinth, and move immediately into Paul's second letter to this church. It is the only church in the New Testament to receive two letters, maybe because of the many problems that they were facing. Following the second letter, we will see God's directions to the churches of Galatia, and finish the month by starting the letter to the church at Ephesus.

We will learn much of how to conduct ourselves in church and how not to in these letters. So, let us settle in for some important lessons.

September 1

Daily Bible Reading: 1 Corinthians 11:16 – 34[246]

Verse of the Day: 1 Corinthians 11:28 – *"But let a man prove himself, and so let him eat of the bread, and drink of the cup."*

Paul is continuing to answer the questions that had been posed to him by the church at Corinth. In this part of chapter 11, he addresses the Lord's Supper. In fact, he starts this section with a condemnation, "But in giving you this charge, I praise you not, that ye come together not for the better but for the worse" (vs. 17).

The place where the Lord's Supper is practiced is not as significant as the condition of the hearts of those taking it. Before any of us takes the cup or bread, we should take the time to ask, "Is there anything between the Lord and me? Is my heart clean?" And if we can't answer wholeheartedly yes, then we must make things right *before* we partake.

Prayer: Holy and Just Father, as I examine my heart, shine your light upon my thoughts, words, and actions. Am I truly clean and pure before You? Have I confessed and accepted Your cleansing and forgiveness today. Amen.

September 2

Daily Bible Reading: 1 Corinthians 12[247]

Verse of the Day: 1 Corinthians 12:1 – *"Now concerning spiritual gifts, brethren, I would not have you ignorant."*

We come to an interesting section of the letter. Paul is discussing the spiritual gifts, their types, and uses. The Greek word used here "των πνευματικων," literally means "the spiritual things."

These graciously given gifts were given by the Lord to various individuals in the church to edify the believers. Every member of the church has been given at least one gift (teaching, prophesying, exercising faith, etc.) to serve in their respective churches.

You might say that God has not given you a gift, but He says in His Word that He has. So, that means that you need to search Him and His Word to discover what the gift is and how to use it in your local body of believers.

---

[246] OT Reading – Psalm 148 – 150
[247] OT Reading – Proverbs 1 – 2

Prayer: Spirit, open my eyes to see what You have gifted me with, and how I am to use that gift where I am. I want to be used by You in the Church that Christ died for. Amen.

September 3

Daily Bible Reading: 1 Corinthians 13[248]

Verse of the Day: 1 Corinthians 13:13 – *"But now abideth faith, hope, love, these three; and the greatest of these is love."*

There have been more songs and poems written about love than any other subject. It has set on fire and broken more hearts than any other passion. Of all these writings, this chapter in Corinthians carries the power of God in its description of what it is.

Paul's description here is short, but very powerful. The word he chose in the Greek shows a love that is based upon the deliberate choice of the one loving and not the worthiness of the one being loved. It is different than the simple human emotion. It is a giving, a selfless, and an expect nothing-in-return kind of love. It is a picture of how we are to love, and a description of how that God loves us.

Prayer: All-loving Father, may the Spirit fill my heart with Your love until it overflows to those around me. May I seek to love as You have loved. May I find the truth of what love is and give it freely to those You place in my way. I thank You for Your unlimited love. Amen.

September 4

Daily Bible Reading: 1 Corinthians 14:1 – 20[249]

Verse of the Day: 1 Corinthians 14:1 – 2 – *"Follow after love; yet desire earnestly spiritual gifts, but rather that ye may prophesy. For he that speaketh in a tongue speaketh not unto men, but unto God; for no man understandeth; but in the spirit he speaketh mysteries."*

One of the problems that the church at Corinth faced was the issue of "speaking in tongues." It had apparently gotten out of context and out of hand. Paul now addresses this issue. The Greek word γλωσση means language, and thus a tongue. On the Day of Pentecost, the believers were given the ability to speak in languages that they did not know to be able to share the message of the gospel with visitors to Jerusalem. It was always a known language in its usage.

---

[248] OT Reading – Proverbs 3 – 4
[249] OT Reading – Proverbs 5 – 6

Paul will emphasize that the gift is used when there are those who can interpret what is said. If it is any value it must be an edifying action for those receiving it.

Prayer: Spirit, I do covet Your gifts, but I seek the most important one, Love. Grant me to use it in abundance daily. Amen.

September 5

Daily Bible Reading: 1 Corinthians 14:21 – 40[250]

Verse of the Day: 1 Corinthians 14:26 – *"What is it then, brethren? When ye come together, each one hath a psalm, hath a teaching, hath a revelation, hath a tongue, hath an interpretation. Let all things be done unto edifying."*

Apparently, things had gotten out of hand at the Church of Corinth. Some believe this may have been a cacophony of sounds and events each time they assembled. It was confusing to many, and cumbersome to truly focus on worship of Jesus.

Paul reminds them that they assemble to worship Jesus and edify each other. Paul will remind them that "God is not *a* God of confusion, but of peace" (vs. 33). Psalm probably refers to their singing; teaching was sharing from the Old Testament or the Apostles lessons. The revelation was probably referring to the message delivered from God.

Prayer: Spirit of the Holy One, guide us as we gather to worship our Lord and Savior Jesus. May we meet in order and focus on Him alone. Give us the hearts to obey and learn of Him.

September 6

Daily Bible Reading: 1 Corinthians 15:1 – 32[251]

Verse of the Day: 1 Corinthians 15:12 – *"Now if Christ is preached that he hath been raised from the dead, how say some among you that there is no resurrection of the dead?"*

The Scriptures often speaks of Christ's resurrection (Greek αναστασις) from the dead. The term literally means a resurrection from out of the dead ones.

This 15th Chapter of the first letter to the Corinthians gives us a great deal of teaching on this vital topic. In verse 4 Paul shows that the Old

---

[250] OT Reading – Proverbs 7 – 8
[251] OT Reading – Proverbs 9 – 10

Testament prophesied this event (Ps. 16:10). He gives judicial proof of the event, Christ being seen of over 500 at one time. Paul teaches that Christ's resurrection is vital to the aspect of our salvation (v. 15:17).

Because Christ has conquered death, we no longer need to fear it (vv. 15:20-26). The last enemy has been conquered. The remainder of the chapter also deals with this important topic.

Prayer: Living Savior, we give praise for what You have accomplished, both on the cross and in Your Resurrection. Amen.

September 7

Daily Bible Reading: 1 Corinthians 15:33 – 58[252]

Verse of the Day: 1 Corinthians 15:55 – 58 – *"O death, where is thy victory? O death, where is thy sting? The sting of death is sin; and the power of sin is the law: but thanks be to God, who giveth us the victory through our Lord Jesus Christ. Wherefore, my beloved brethren, be ye stedfast, unmoveable, always abounding in the work of the Lord, forasmuch as ye know that your labor is not vain in the Lord."*

What a great triumphant set of verses. Death is totally vanquished. The damage that Satan inflicted on Creation in the Garden of Eden has all been reversed for the believer through the death, burial and resurrection of Jesus Christ. When we are changed at Christ's return, we will never face the Spector of death again. We will be in a state of timeless, ageless existence. All will be grand, and we will never again face the trials or horrors of sin.

Prayer: Eternal Son of the Living God, what a grand and glorious future I am beholding in Your Word. I have a future beyond anything I can see or experience here. Hallelujah! Amen.

September 8

Daily Bible Reading: 1 Corinthians 16[253]

Verse of the Day: 1 Corinthians 16:13 – 14 – *"Watch ye, stand fast in the faith, quit you like men, be strong. Let all that ye do be done in love."*

The word "watch" in the New Testament is often used in anticipation of a future event. The admonition to stand fast in the faith was appropriate because the Corinthian church was susceptible to false

---

[252] OT Reading – Proverbs 11 – 12
[253] OT Reading – Proverbs 13 – 14

teaching. Quit you like men spoke to the need of mature bravery in the people. All of this was to be accomplished in love.

The real tests of courage are the inner ones that others cannot see. Remaining faithful when no one is looking. Enduring pain when the room is empty. Standing alone when you are misunderstood. Even when we feel that no one is around or looking, we have a Father in Heaven who sees all that we do. He sees deep inside of us, and even when we fail, He loves us.

Prayer: Heavenly Father, may I be one who You can see a faithfulness, an endurance, a willingness to stand, all made possible by Your love. Count me all in for You.

September 9

Daily Bible Reading: 2 Corinthians 1[254]

Verse of the Day: 2 Corinthians 1:1 – 2 – *"Paul, an apostle of Christ Jesus through the will of God, and Timoth[y] our brother, unto the church of God which is at Corinth, with all the saints that are in the whole of Achaia: Grace to you and peace from God our Father and the Lord Jesus Christ."*

This second letter to the church at Corinth could be considered the letter of a transparent Apostle. This is the most autobiographical letter that we have persevered from the Apostle Paul. Paul's apostleship was under attack, so he writes in a very strong forceful style. Still, as we read his words, we see a man who has a tender heart toward God and a commitment to ministry. He is both steel and velvet in what he writes.

This letter covers crucial concerns for the church, instructions on the offering being collected, and a validation of Paul's ministry.

Prayer: God, there are times that the ones around us may question what You have taught us. If we are truly listening to You, may we be strong and firm in our convictions. Amen.

September 10

Daily Bible Reading: 2 Corinthians 2[255]

Verse of the Day: 2 Corinthians 2:6 – 8 – *"Sufficient to such a one is this punishment which was inflicted by the many; so that contrariwise ye should rather forgive him and comfort him, lest by any means such a one*

---

[254] OT Reading – Proverbs 15 – 16
[255] OT Reading – Proverbs 17 – 18

should be swallowed up with his overmuch sorrow. Wherefore I beseech you to confirm your love toward him."

In the previous letter, Paul had admonished them on dealing with a fellow believer who was living in open sin. The church had taken a very relaxed attitude over it to the point that even unbelievers were talking about it. He pushed them to administer church discipline upon the person responsible.

In this letter, it appears as if the person had repented and sought to be restored to the fellowship of the church. Paul was trying to get them to see that the person no longer needed critics, he needed a place to find healing and refuge.

Prayer: Gracious and Forgiving God, help us to offer forgiveness and healing to those who have repented and come back to You.

September 11

Daily Bible Reading: 2 Corinthians 3[256]

Verse of the Day: 2 Corinthians 3:18 – *"But we all, with unveiled face beholding as in a mirror the glory of the Lord, are transformed into the same image from glory to glory, even as from the Lord the Spirit."*

God is committed to working out His purpose in us. He works in us, developing, rearranging, firming up, and deepening us to look and act like His Son Jesus Christ.

When we received Christ as our Savior, God began the sanctification process in us. In Romans 8:28 – 30, Paul told the Roman believers God's process.

As we see God in His Word, it begins to mirror in us the form and beauty of Jesus. As we go through the gradual process of being changed, molded, transformed, we begin to walk and talk like Jesus. If we aren't getting closer to Him and being like Him, we are the ones who are stopping the process. Let God have full control of your life today.

Prayer: Father, make me like Your Son in all my thoughts, actions, and desires. Amen.

---

[256] OT Reading – Proverbs 19 – 20

September 12

Daily Bible Reading: 2 Corinthians 4[257]

Verse of the Day: 2 Corinthians 4:7 – 10 – *"But we have this treasure in earthen vessels, that the exceeding greatness of the power may be of God, and not from ourselves; we are pressed on every side, yet not straitened; perplexed, yet not unto despair; pursued, yet not forsaken; smitten down, yet not destroyed; always bearing about in the body the dying of Jesus, that the life also of Jesus may be manifested in our body."*

The Greek words οστρακινοις σκευεσιν translated earthen vessels in this passage literally means "clay pots."

In ancient times people would put their valuable items in clay posts and bury them to preserve them. The Dead Sea Scrolls are some of those items stored in clay pots. As these treasures were encased in earthen vessels, so the indwelling Christ lives in our earthen bodies.

Prayer: Spirit of the Living Christ, as You have taken up residence in my physical life today, You have changed my life for now and my soul for eternity. May I be worthy of encasing the Son of God in my life. Amen.

September 13

Daily Bible Reading: 2 Corinthians 5[258]

Verse of the Day: 2 Corinthians 5:21 – *"Him who knew no sin he made to be sin on our behalf; that we might become the righteousness of God in him."*

The work of salvation is complete. There is nothing for me to do except accept that which Christ finished upon the Cross. Think about it as Jesus looking us in the eye saying, "I have paid your debt in full on the Cross. If you come to Me, I will give you perfect righteousness."

The impeccability of Jesus deals with the question: could Jesus have sinned? While it is fundamentally agreed the Bible teaches that Jesus did not sin, there has historically been divided opinion as to whether or not He could have sinned. Because He was sinless, He could exchange our sinfulness for His sinlessness. What a blessing and privilege to be able to stand before God sinless, not by our works, but by Christ's.

---

[257] OT Reading – Proverbs 21 – 22
[258] OT Reading – Proverbs 23 – 24

Prayer: Jesus, thank You for the exchange You were willing to make so that I might become a part of the family of God and be able to stand clean before the Father. Amen.

September 14

Daily Bible Reading: 2 Corinthians 6[259]

Verse of the Day: 2 Corinthians 6:16 – 17 – *"And what agreement hath a temple of God with idols? for we are a temple of the living God; even as God said, I will dwell in them, and walk in them; and I will be their God, and they shall be my people. Wherefore Come ye out from among them, and be ye separate, saith the Lord, And touch no unclean thing; And I will receive you,"*

Some have taken this verse out of context and ascribed to it the need for us to have no dealing with unbelievers. Paul was not encouraging isolation in this passage (consider 1 Cor.9:5-13) but discouraging compromise with the sinful beliefs, values, and practices of the world. He was urging them to maintain integrity in the world just as Christ displayed for us. Christ was involved in the lives of unbelievers without taking on any of their characteristics. That is what we should be doing.

Prayer: Holy Father, guide me in the way to be involved with family and neighbors who need to know Your Son as Savior. Guide me in being with them while maintaining a holy life.

September 15

Daily Bible Reading: 2 Corinthians 7[260]

Verse of the Day: 2 Corinthians 7:5 – 7 – *"For even when we were come into Macedonia our flesh had no relief, but we were afflicted on every side; without were fightings, within were fears. Nevertheless he that comforteth the lowly, even God, comforted us by the coming of Titus; and not by his coming only, but also by the comfort wherewith he was comforted in you, while he told us your longing, your mourning, your zeal for me; so that I rejoiced yet more."*

Paul in this autobiographical book gives us a glimpse of all the suffering and difficulties that he encountered as an apostle of the Lord. Ministry is not always easy or smooth. Often we mistake the idea that if all is going well we are in the will of God, and if there are problems we

---

[259] OT Reading – Proverbs 25 – 27
[260] OT Reading – Proverbs 28 – 29

are outside His will. Paul walked in the will of God and yet met with many struggles.

If you are facing struggles today, make sure that there is nothing that you have done to bring them on. If you are where God wants you, He will see you through.

Prayer: Father, I want to be in Your Will.

September 16

Daily Bible Reading: 2 Corinthians 8[261]

Verse of the Day: 2 Corinthians 8:1 – 2 – *"Moreover, brethren, we make known to you the grace of God which hath been given in the churches of Macedonia; how that in much proof of affliction the abundance of their joy and their deep poverty abounded unto the riches of their liberality."*

The Greek word απλοτητος comes from the root word ἁπλοῦς meaning simple or generous. If the two notions are combined, they present the meaning of glad and generous giving to the mind of the Greek. Paul is the only New Testament writer to use this word. He used it to demonstrate and describe how that certain believers happily gave generous contributions to other believers who were undergoing hardships.

Do we give generously to fellow Christians struggling, or do we tend to think that maybe they are getting what they deserve?

Prayer: Generous and Glorious Spirit, may I be one who will listen to the voice of God, and as He gave generously, give to my fellow believers in their times of need. Amen.

September 17

Daily Bible Reading: 2 Corinthians 9[262]

Verse of the Day: 2 Corinthians 9:7 – *"Let each man do according as he hath purposed in his heart: not grudgingly, or of necessity: for God loveth a cheerful giver."*

Chapters 8 and 9 of this letter deal with giving. Paul doesn't use gimmicks or devices to try to encourage the Church at Corinth in their giving. He gave them the example of the Macedonian believers and called his readers to follow it.

---

[261] OT Reading – Proverbs 30 – 31
[262] OT Reading – Ecclesiastes 1 – 3

I love our verse above. Especially as you look at it in the Greek. The word translated cheerful (ιλαρον) is pronounced the same as our English word hilarious.

When was the last time that you gave so much that you felt hilarious about it? Too often we grumble and complain about giving. God, however, is looking down from Heaven watching for those who find it hilarious to be able to give.

Prayer: Spirit, touch my heart, mind, and life so that I can be one who gives in such abundance that I find it hilarious. Amen.

September 18

Daily Bible Reading: 2 Corinthians 10[263]

Verse of the Day: 2 Corinthians 10:4 – 5 – *"(for the weapons of our warfare are not of the flesh, but mighty before God to the casting down of strongholds); casting down imaginations, and every high thing that is exalted against the knowledge of God, and bringing every thought into captivity to the obedience of Christ;"*

We are in a daily battle. There is a grand war raging, and we are soldiers in it. The problem is that we spend too much time fighting a physical war while the battle is in the realm of the spiritual.

Paul well understood that the real battle was not with those around him, but with the spiritual concepts and teachings. In our passage today he reminds us to get our eyes off the horizontal and place it on the vertical. We need to get away from the human viewpoint and face the eternal issues.

Prayer: Jesus, I spend too much time fighting the physical battles while I need to focus on the spiritual war against the souls of men. Help me focus on what is important.

September 19

Daily Bible Reading: 2 Corinthians 11:1 – 15 [264]

Verse of the Day: 2 Corinthians 11:4 – *"For if he that cometh preacheth another Jesus, whom we did not preach, or if ye receive a different spirit, which ye did not receive, or a different gospel, which ye did not accept, ye do well to bear with him."*

---

[263] OT Reading – Ecclesiastes 4 – 6
[264] OT Reading – Ecclesiastes 7 – 9

Paul was jealous of the Corinthians that they would remain true to what is true. He warns them against believing the wrong truths.

The another Jesus would be one that was a man and not God, or crucified but not risen. The different spirit was one of fear not faith, of bondage not freedom. And the different gospel would be one of law not grace, works not faith.

We can see why Paul was so strong on what he is saying. If anyone believes the wrong Jesus, spirit, or gospel they are lost and separated from God for all eternity. Paul wants his readers and us to look at our beliefs and ourselves closely. Are we in line with the Scriptures, or are we not following the true God?

Prayer: Spirit search my heart for truth.

September 20

Daily Bible Reading: 2 Corinthians 11:16 – 33 [265]

Verse of the Day: 2 Corinthians 11:23 – *"Are they ministers of Christ? (I speak as one beside himself) I more; in labors more abundantly, in prisons more abundantly, in stripes above measure, in deaths oft."*

Paul says that he speaks as one beside himself, in other words, a fool. Paul was hesitant to brag about his spiritual accomplishments because he knew it was only God who made his preaching and service effective. He was the instrument, God was the One who played the melody.

Following this verse through verse 29, Paul recites a long list of physical sufferings, long travels, toils, and weaknesses that he had encountered in the ministry that God granted him. He understood that temporal distresses bring eternal rewards.

Prayer: Father, as I strive to serve, give me the grace and strength to bear up under the various trials and distresses that serving You in this sinful world will come upon me. I know that all that I suffer for You in this world is small compared to the riches of eternity. Amen.

---

[265] OT Reading – Ecclesiastes 10 – 12

September 21

Daily Bible Reading: 2 Corinthians 12[266]

Verse of the Day: 2 Corinthians 12:10 – *"Wherefore I take pleasure in weaknesses, in injuries, in necessities, in persecutions, in distresses, for Christ's sake: for when I am weak, then am I strong."*

Paul says that he takes pleasure in being weak, being injured, in need, persecuted, and in distress. Not exactly what we would expect to hear from someone who has been through all that Paul has been through.

Paul was doing some boasting here, "And he hath said unto me, My grace is sufficient for thee: for *my* power is made perfect in weakness. Most gladly therefore will I rather glory in my weaknesses, that the power of Christ may rest upon me." Paul's weakness made it evident to others that it was not him, but the One who truly deserved the credit. Jesus.

Would I be willing to go through all that Paul went through so that Jesus would be magnified and glorified? Give it some thought today.

Prayer: Jesus, may I be used by You today.

September 22

Daily Bible Reading: 2 Corinthians 13[267]

Verse of the Day: 2 Corinthians 13:14 – *"The grace of the Lord Jesus Christ, and the love of God, and the communion of the Holy Spirit, be with you all."*

This is Paul's benediction or concluding statement to the Corinthian believers. He invokes the blessing of the Triune God. He evokes grace from the Lord Jesus, love from God, and communion (or, fellowship) of the Holy Spirit.

At the end of this letter, Paul identifies the solution to many of their, and our, problems. The Holy Spirit who lived in each of the believers could empower them to live a righteous life. And, in addition, the Holy Spirit could reconcile them to each other. They could love and encourage each other, rather than fighting.

We need God's grace instead of our selfishness, God's love in place of anger, and fellowship instead of conflict.

---

[266] OT Reading – Song of Solomon 1 – 3
[267] OT Reading – Song of Solomon 4 – 5

Prayer: Glorious God, I come to You on bended knee, I fail in being right with others.

September 23

Daily Bible Reading: Galatians 1[268]

Verse of the Day: Galatians 1:6 – 7 – *"I marvel that ye are so quickly removing from him that called you in the grace of Christ unto a different gospel; which is not another gospel: only there are some that trouble you, and would pervert the gospel of Christ."*

Paul was literally shocked at the soon desertion of the Galatian believers from the true gospel message that they had received at his hand. The word translated marvel here is the very first word in the Greek sentence showing the importance of the concept.

They had quickly defected from the gospel of salvation by God's undeserved grace to another message. This second message was not the true message of salvation, and thus they were being led astray in what they believed.

Paul calls those presenting this other message perverters of the truth, and that they did not have a better alternative to offer.

Prayer: Merciful God in Heaven, may I only believe and trust in the true gospel, the truth of Salvation grace through faith. Amen.

September 24

Daily Bible Reading: Galatians 2[269]

Verse of the Day: Galatians 2:19 – 21 – *"For I through the law died unto the law, that I might live unto God. I have been crucified with Christ; and it is no longer I that live, but Christ liveth in me: and that life which I now live in the flesh I live in faith, the faith which is in the Son of God, who loved me, and gave himself up for me. I do not make void the grace of God: for if righteousness is through the law, then Christ died for nought."*

Do you think God ever does anything useless? Would God waste time on anything not necessary? Well, Paul is making the argument here that if I could attain my own righteousness to a level acceptable by God (the Law), then God graciously sending His Son to die was a useless, unnecessary move. In fact, I could call it downright cruel.

---

[268] OT Reading – Song of Solomon 6 – 8
[269] OT Reading – Isaiah 1 – 3

Why sacrifice Your Only Son if there was any other way to accomplish our salvation.

Prayer: Merciful, Gracious Father, I believe that You sent Jesus to die for my sins upon that cruel Cross because I could attain righteousness in no other way. Thank You for Your Love.

September 25

Daily Bible Reading: Galatians 3[270]

Verse of the Day: Galatians 3:24 – 25 – *"So that the law is become our tutor to bring us unto Christ, that we might be justified by faith. But now that faith is come, we are no longer under a tutor."*

The Greek word for tutor used here (παιδαγωγός) carried the meaning of a guardian and guide of boys. Among the Greeks and the Romans the name was applied to trustworthy slaves who were charged with the duty of supervising the life and morals of boys belonging to the better class. The boys were not allowed so much as to step out of the house without them before arriving at the age of manhood. We might call this person a schoolmaster or teacher.

The law acted as an outward check of desires so that our conscience of sin is more acute. Since we can't deal with our own sin, the Law guides us to Christ, our rescuer and Savior.

Prayer: Savior, thank You for the Law that made me see the need I have for You.

September 26

Daily Bible Reading: Galatians 4[271]

Verse of the Day: Galatians 4:4 – 5 – *"but when the fulness of the time came, God sent forth his Son, born of a woman, born under the law, that he might redeem them that were under the law, that we might receive the adoption of sons.*

The "fullness of time" is the perfect time in history, the time that was appointed by God. The perfect time for Jesus to come into time and space and become human and die for us. The perfect time for the Seed of the woman to come (Gen, 3:15).

---

[270] OT Reading – Isaiah 4 – 6
[271] OT Reading – Isaiah 7 – 9

Jesus was born under the law meaning that He was Jewish and subject to the Law. He was identified with mankind, the very ones He came to save. God bought us back from the slave market of sin and then not only bought us but also made us His adopted children. We are no longer slaves to sin, nor children under the tutor of the Law.

Prayer: Great and Glorious Father of Creation, I praise You that You planned from before You created time and space to provide my redemption and adoption. Hallelujah, amen!

September 27

Daily Bible Reading: Galatians 5[272]

Verse of the Day: Galatians 5:16 – *"But I say, Walk by the Spirit, and ye shall not fulfil the lust of the flesh."*

The Spirit versus the flesh. We have all experienced it. We have witnessed the inner battle that we go through. With the flesh in control, we suffer through agitation, irritation, offenses, struggles, and comparisons. When the Spirit is in control, we have true release and relief. We have love that isn't capricious, peace that stays with us, and joy that lasts.

While the Greek word σαρκος usually means the human body, Paul consistently uses it to mean the entire fallen being. Not just the external body but also the mind and soul. The unbeliever can only live in the flesh, but the believer can choose to live in the Spirit or the flesh. Paul continually reminds believers to live in the power of the Spirit and not the flesh.

Prayer: Precious Spirit of God, today I come to You admitting that I often fail and fall into following my flesh. I want to walk in the Spirit. I want to display Your power in my life, in all I think, say, and do. Amen.

September 28

Daily Bible Reading: Galatians 6[273]

Verse of the Day: Galatians 6:10 – *"So then, as we have opportunity, let us work that which is good toward all men, and especially toward them that are of the household of the faith."*

---

[272] OT Reading – Isaiah 10 – 12
[273] OT Reading – Isaiah 13 – 15

As you read this today, consider this: today is unique, it has never happened before and it will never happen again. At midnight tonight it will cease to exist. Quietly, without fanfare, and completely.

However, the hours between when you read this and the end of today are hours filled with opportunities and many possibilities. God wants you to live this day to the fullest. He wants you to have the abundance that He can give as we follow His leading.

We need to seek ways to serve, minister, and love not only our fellow believers today, but also the unbelievers God places in our path. Plan to let God surprise you with these opportunities today.

Prayer: Father, overwhelm me with the ways that I can serve my fellow human beings with Your Love and care. Amen.

September 29

Daily Bible Reading: Ephesians 1[274]

Verse of the Day: Ephesians 1:9 – *"making known unto us the mystery of his will, according to his good pleasure which he purposed in him"*

The mystery of His will. The word translated "mystery" in the NT it denotes, not the mysterious (as with the English word), but that which, being outside the range of unassisted natural apprehension, can be made known only by Divine revelation, and is made known in a manner and at a time appointed by God, and to those only who are illumined by His Spirit. In the ordinary sense, a "mystery" implies knowledge withheld; its Scriptural significance is truth revealed.

The Will of God had been hidden or obscure, but through Jesus Christ it has been manifested for all to see. In the preceding verses (7 and 8) Paul spells out what that Will is.

Prayer: Jesus, great Revealer of God and His Will, may I spend time with You today gaining insight and wisdom in Your will and purpose in my life. I seek to fulfill what You have purposed for me in this world. Amen.

---

[274] OT Reading – Isaiah 16 – 18

September 30

Daily Bible Reading: Ephesians 2[275]

Verse of the Day: Ephesians 2:10 – *"For we are his workmanship, created in Christ Jesus for good works, which God afore prepared that we should walk in them."*

Ποίημα. The Greek word used here for "workmanship" is used only two times in the New Testament, both times by Paul. The word literally means that which has been made or a work. It is the word from which we get our English word "poem". It indicates a masterpiece. In days past, a young person would be apprenticed to a Master craftsman. When they had finished their education under them they had to produce a piece of work that displayed their knowledge and skill (think Doctrinal Thesis). This was their "masterpiece."

Here Paul tells us that we are God's masterpiece. We are His crowning work through Jesus Christ.

Prayer: Heavenly Father, may I display to the world around me a pleasing picture of Your masterful work done in me through Your grace and finished work of Your Son Jesus. I praise You for what You have finished in me. Amen.

---

[275] OT Reading – Isaiah 19 – 21

OCTOBER Autumn Assurance of God's Presence

October brings up images of colorful leaves, pumpkins, and so many memories of the season before Winter. We celebrate Columbus Day in October. We hold Fall Festivals and other celebrations in this season of harvest.

The harvest. That time of year when the hard work of preparing the soil, planting, weeding, watering, and constant vigilance over the fields yield the crops that we so seek.

As I stop to think about the harvest, I realize that God has been faithful in my (your) life and all that He has invested in us can now be reaped.

We can move into the cooler evenings, the beautiful colors, and the fullness of the harvest with the reminder that God is ever-present in our lives.

October 1

Daily Bible Reading: Ephesians 3[276]

Verse of the Day: Ephesians 3:20 – 21 – *"Now unto him that is able to do exceeding abundantly above all that we ask or think, according to the power that worketh in us, unto him be the glory in the church and in Christ Jesus unto all generations for ever and ever. Amen."*

I get chills every time I read these verses. Wow. This is a doxology or praise that Paul writes. Spend a little time camping out on what this says.

In the Greek we find the words literally state that He can do beyond measure, exceedingly beyond measure, over and above, more than is necessary, superadded. It is the Greek way of giving the highest superlative. That is not only dealing with what we ask, but what we might even think. Neither God's love nor His power is limited by the human imagination.

Prayer: Superlative God, may I see your great Love and Power at work in my life today. May others see You through my imitating Jesus in all I say and do. I praise You today!

October 2

Daily Bible Reading: Ephesians 4[277]

Verse of the Day: Ephesians 4:26 – *"Be ye angry, and sin not: let not the sun go down upon your wrath:"*

Paul uses Psalm 4:4 to illustrate that all anger is not sinful. However, we must be careful that anger does not fester or continue too long. We might respond in a controlled anger to injustice and sin being careful not to be consumed with this anger. We need to seek out the opportunities to display Christ's love to everyone.

Any anger that moves out of the realm of control, or that plans to hurt another person is sinful. Anger that leads to thoughts of revenge is sinful. As Christians, we are never to seek to extract justice or revenge. This is God's realm. When we seek to do this we are putting ourselves in God's place. God will not honor any feelings or plans like these.

Prayer: Gracious Father, I am so thankful that You do not treat me as I often treat others. Help me to remember how You forgive and behave

---

[276] OT Reading – Isaiah 22 – 23
[277] OT Reading – Isaiah 24 – 26

toward me in my actions and words to others. Forgive me as I have sinned so often.

October 3

Daily Bible Reading: Ephesians 5[278]

Verse of the Day: Ephesians 5:15 – 16 – *"Look therefore carefully how ye walk, not as unwise, but as wise; redeeming the time, because the days are evil."*

Are you too busy? Are you caught in the busyness trap? Not necessarily doing bad things, just too many things. I have to be careful in my life not to allow too many things to come between the Lord and me.

Being too busy is not a positive mark. It is not a friend but an enemy to what is best. Even when we are busy doing good things, it can be an evil, selfish, demanding force that demands our time, thoughts, and other things that we have no business surrendering up. God warns us in this passage that there is a wise and unwise use of our time.

Ever feel that you need more time? Maybe what you really need is to learn to use your time more wisely. Make that your goal today and every day that follows.

Prayer: Creator of Time, teach me to use my days wisely for You and Your goal for me.

October 4

Daily Bible Reading: Ephesians 6[279]

Verse of the Day: Ephesians 6:18 – *"with all prayer and supplication praying at all seasons in the Spirit, and watching thereunto in all perseverance and supplication for all the saints,"*

The battle rages around us. We are caught up in it. What battle? The spiritual battle between God and Satan. We know who wins, but that doesn't mean that we aren't faced with some major battles.

Paul in Ephesians 6 speaks of the Christian Armor that we are to put on. We must be equipped and aware daily of the fight for our faith. Notice in our verse today that Paul encourages us to pray. Pray in all seasons (all the time) while watching (being aware) continuously.

---

[278] OT Reading – Isaiah 27 – 28
[279] OT Reading – Isaiah 29 – 30

One of my mentors of the past always taught that nothing of eternal significance ever happened outside of prayer. The quest may be, "How much time do I devote to prayer each day?"

Prayer: Lord of Hosts, open my eyes to the importance of prayer in my life. Amen.

October 5

Daily Bible Reading: Philippians 1[280]

Verse of the Day: Philippians 1:25 – 26 – "*And having this confidence, I know that I shall abide, yea, and abide with you all, for your progress and joy in the faith; that your glorying may abound in Christ Jesus in me through my presence with you again.*"

We come to one of my favorite letters in the New Testament, Philippians. This is a short letter (four chapters and only 104 verses), yet it resounds over and over with encouragement and challenges to be joyful in all circumstances.

As you read this short letter from Paul, we quickly learn that he is not sitting in a glamorous resort dining on prime steak. Paul is in a Roman prison. This is one of the four "Prison Epistles" that Paul penned.

This is a vivid reminder to us that our joy is not in our circumstances or experiences, but in whom we know ... Jesus Christ.

Prayer: Jesus, Joy of our Salvation, as I muse over the words of Paul these next few days, may I find the courage to be joyful no matter what I am going through. Amen.

October 6

Daily Bible Reading: Philippians 2[281]

Verse of the Day: Philippians 2:3 – 4 – "*doing nothing through faction or through vainglory, but in lowliness of mind each counting other better than himself; not looking each of you to his own things, but each of you also to the things of others.*"

Have you ever noticed how that people who affect us the most are those who pay least attention to themselves. They constantly notice the needs of others and seek to reach out and help. They carry an honest concern for us.

---

[280] OT Reading – Isaiah 31 – 33
[281] OT Reading – Isaiah 34 – 36

These are the people who we rarely hear them say "I'" "me", "my", or "mine". They generally speak about "we", "you", etc. We often come across those who are selfish, and draw close to those who are unselfish.

So, do we find people drawing close to us? Is it because we are unselfish, or self-centered? Ponder it today, and seek God for the right way to be with people.

Prayer: Jesus, I know that You gave all for me, now may I give for others. True joy comes from being unselfish and concerned for others.

October 7

Daily Bible Reading: Philippians 3[282]

Verse of the Day: Philippians 3:13 – 14 – *"Brethren, I count not myself yet to have laid hold: but one thing I do, forgetting the things which are behind, and stretching forward to the things which are before, I press on toward the goal unto the prize of the high calling of God in Christ Jesus."*

Some days we may feel up, and then other days not so much. Sometimes this comes from our memory. We are all guilty for sin that we have committed. Paul could not undo all the things he had done, but he had learned on a daily (he uses the present tense form of the word in the Greek) basis to forget those things that have been forgiven by the shed blood of Jesus Christ.

We need to move on. We need to strive to do what God is calling us to do. We are to seek Him, to serve Him, and to savor the joy that comes from our close personal relationship with Him.

Prayer: Father, I rest in Your Grace and Mercy today. May I draw close and bask in Your Joy. I thank You for this, Amen.

October 8

Daily Bible Reading: Philippians 4[283]

Verse of the Day: Philippians 4:8 – *"Finally, brethren, whatsoever things are true, whatsoever things are honorable, whatsoever things are just, whatsoever things are pure, whatsoever things are lovely, whatsoever things are of good report; if there be any virtue, and if there be any praise, think on these things."*

---

[282] OT Reading – Isaiah 37 – 38
[283] OT Reading – Isaiah 39 – 40

The Greek word αρετη translated virtue in this verse was used generously in Greek writings, but is actually rarely used in the New Testament. It appears only 5 times. It means (moral) goodness or excellence. Peter used it in 1 Peter 2:9 and is translated praises.

It generally is used of a person of excellence that is a quality only available from God. Only receiving the divine power to live and be morally excellent upon this earth. (2 Peter 1:3).

Prayer: Father, I long to be a person who can be labeled as a person of virtue. I seek this quality in my life. I know from Your Word that this is only available from You. As one of your children, I pray and seek to be a person of virtue, of moral excellence in this world that I live in. Cleanse me, fill me, use me. Amen.

October 9

Daily Bible Reading: Colossians 1[284]

Verse of the Day: Colossians 1:28 – 29 – *"whom we proclaim, admonishing every man and teaching every man in all wisdom, that we may present every man perfect in Christ; whereunto I labor also, striving according to his working, which worketh in me mightily."*

C.I. Scofield has been quoted as saying, "Pure Christianity lives between two dangers ever present: the danger it will evaporate into a philosophy … and the danger that it will freeze into a form."

We are going to spend a few short days in this letter to the church at Colossae that Paul penned. It will help us to maneuver between these ever-present dangers. It can be our map and compass. This book seeks to focus our attention on Jesus as Lord of All and that He is adequate for all of life and its circumstances.

Prayer: Father as I read Your written Word, help me to continually see the Living Word … Jesus, Your precious Son. Help me to steer clear of the rocks of philosophical Christianity and the rapids of Christianity as a form without the Savior and Creator. Amen.

---

[284] OT Reading – Isaiah 41 – 42

October 10

Daily Bible Reading: Colossians 2[285]

Verse of the Day: Colossians 2:9 – 10 – *"for in him dwelleth all the fulness of the Godhead bodily, and in him ye are made full, who is the head of all principality and power:"*

Here we see Paul speaking about the doctrine we call the Incarnation of Christ. This is the understanding that God entered time and space in bodily form. Jesus stepped out of heaven and into His Creation. Paul is refuting a Gnostic concept of the first century that God could not be physical, and if He was physical He couldn't be God.

Because of Jesus, we have everything we need when we have accepted Him into our lives. We are made complete when Jesus comes in as our Savior and Lord. Many of Paul's day thought that you needed special secret knowledge to be made complete. Paul stresses that when we receive Christ we become complete in all ways.

Prayer: Heavenly Father, thank You that Jesus came in the flesh to provide the fulfillment that I need in all areas of my life. I am so thankful that I have the fullness of Him.

October 11

Daily Bible Reading: Colossians 3[286]

Verse of the Day: Colossians 3:15 – *"And let the peace of Christ rule in your hearts, to the which also ye were called in one body; and be ye thankful."*

The Greek word ειρηνη has a variety of meanings: tranquility, unity, harmony, and corresponds to the Hebrew word שָׁלוֹם (shalom) that holds a primary meaning of wholeness. In the New Testament, it generally is used to denote a harmonious relationship between people.

The Greek word for rule used here, βραβευετω means to act as an umpire or to be an arbitrator. So, the unifying, harmonious, wholeness of God work in our lives as an umpire when the concepts of anger, envy, and other such passions arise.

Prayer: Father, I seek You to so live in my life that every time passions that are not in line with the reconciliation that You have produced in my life through Christ may be controlled. Look into my heart and any such

---

[285] OT Reading – Isaiah 43 – 44
[286] OT Reading – Isaiah 45 – 47

passions that I am harboring today remove and cleanse my thoughts and intents. Amen.

October 12

Daily Bible Reading: Colossians 4[287]

Verse of the Day: Colossians 4:2 – 6 – *"Continue stedfastly in prayer, watching therein with thanksgiving; withal praying for us also, that God may open unto us a door for the word, to speak the mystery of Christ, for which I am also in bonds; that I may make it manifest, as I ought to speak. Walk in wisdom toward them that are without, redeeming the time. Let your speech be always with grace, seasoned with salt, that ye may know how ye ought to answer each one."*

Seize the day! Make the most of every opportunity! Be ready at all times! Be watchful! Be full of thanksgiving! Walk in wisdom!

As we spend time today moving about in our sphere of influence in the world (no matter how great or small it may be), God calls us to not let another day go by without taking action in the area that God has prompted you to do.

Prayer: Spirit of the Holy One, as I live my life today, may I make the most of every opportunity You place before me. May I have eyes wide-open looking for where You want me to work for You. Surprise me. Amen.

October 13

Daily Bible Reading: 1 Thessalonians 1[288]

Verse of the Day: 1 Thessalonians 1:2 – 3 – *"We give thanks to God always for you all, making mention of you in our prayers; remembering without ceasing your work of faith and labor of love and patience of hope in our Lord Jesus Christ, before our God and Father;"*

John Maxwell often talks about leadership being influence. The degree to which we influence others, we lead them.

Paul told the Thessalonian Church that he often gave thanks in prayer for them. Why? Because as he says here of their faith, love and hope. Later in verses 6 – 7 Paul states they became the model church for others to follow.

---

[287] OT Reading – Isaiah 48 – 49
[288] OT Reading – Isaiah 50 – 52

If we realize how important our modeling Christ in this world really is, we probably would change a lot of things we do. If so, then understand that we are the visual image of Christ that so many may see. Live like it.

Prayer: Jesus, I want to model You to others. I must spend time in Your presence daily. I must read the Bible and pray each day. Amen.

October 14

Daily Bible Reading: 1 Thessalonians 2[289]

Verse of the Day: 1 Thessalonians 2:12 – *"to the end that ye should walk worthily of God, who calleth you into his own kingdom and glory."*

There is always room for improvement in this life. That is true in our Christian walk. Too often we can find ourselves (at least subconsciously) assuming that we have arrived.

We need to heed Paul's admonitions that we continue to grow in areas of love for each other. We need to be aware of our short-comings in our lives, our need to seek after a desire that our hearts be blameless in holiness.

And this walk is not only in our outward appearances before men, but in our very heart observed only by God. Until we stand in His Presence one day, we will never "have arrived." So, constantly watch our walk, and tame our talk. Let Him take charge today.

Prayer: Righteous Father, I want to walk in a worthy manner before You. You have called me, saved me, and equipped me to walk the walk and talk the talk. I am Yours forever.

October 15

Daily Bible Reading: 1 Thessalonians 3[290]

Verse of the Day: 1 Thessalonians 3:11 – 13 – *"Now may our God and Father himself, and our Lord Jesus, direct our way unto you: and the Lord make you to increase and abound in love one toward another, and toward all men, even as we also do toward you; to the end he may establish your hearts unblamable in holiness before our God and Father, at the coming of our Lord Jesus with all his saints."*

---

[289] OT Reading – Isaiah 53 – 55
[290] OT Reading – Isaiah 56 – 58

Paul here talks about the coming (Greek παρουσια) of Jesus Christ. The word used means presence, the coming, arrival, advent, and thus carries the meaning in the New Testament of the future visible return from heaven of Jesus, to raise the dead, hold the last judgment, and set up formally and gloriously the kingdom of God. The question today is simply this, Are you ready for His return?

Prayer: Lord Jesus, I know Your word tells of Your Second Coming. May I be ever ready for that event. Each day brings us one day closer to that great climatic revealing of You. I long to see You face-to-face. I long for Your Presence in all of it's fullness. Come, Lord Jesus!

October 16

Daily Bible Reading: 1 Thessalonians 4[291]

Verse of the Day: 1 Thessalonians 4:13 – *"But we would not have you ignorant, brethren, concerning them that fall asleep; that ye sorrow not, even as the rest, who have no hope."*

Death brings sorrow. I am a Chaplain with Hospice and a Disaster Relief team. Often in these encounters with people who have friends and loved ones who have died there are tears. Tears are a normal part of the grieving process. God designed it that way.

God never tells us not to grieve or not to cry. But, He does tell us that we do not have to grieve like those in the world who do not have any hope. As believers, we have a hope and an answer to our grief. We know Who holds what is beyond the grave. And in the midst of our tears and grief, knowing the One waiting will help to bring comfort in these times.

Prayer: God of all comfort, we come to You with our tears and grief. We come to You with empty hearts and hands, You take us in Your loving arms and hold us with Your comforting hands of grace and mercy. Amen.

October 17

Daily Bible Reading: 1 Thessalonians 5[292]

Verse of the Day: 1 Thessalonians 5:16 – 18 – *"Rejoice always; pray without ceasing; in everything give thanks: for this is the will of God in Christ Jesus to you-ward."*

Do you ever say, "I wish I knew what God's Will is for me?"

[291] OT Reading – Isaiah 59 – 61
[292] OT Reading – Isaiah 62 – 64

Different from other "gods" who appear to be arbitrary, mysterious, and changeable in what they want, Yahweh is consistent and very open. When we study God's Word, we come to find His will portrayed to us in many places. Here is one place where the writer tells us this is God's Will for us, every one of us.

We are to rejoice, pray, and give thanks. When we apply this to our situations, we can be assured that we are in the very center of His Will, no matter what the circumstances. Consider Job in the Old Testament, he lived this in his life. Do we? If not, that may be why we struggle finding His Will.

Prayer: Precious Holy Spirit, bring constantly to my mind the reminder to rejoice, pray and give thanks each moment of the day.

October 18

Daily Bible Reading: 2 Thessalonians 1[293]

Verse of the Day: 2 Thessalonians 1:4 – *"so that we ourselves glory in you in the churches of God for your patience and faith in all your persecutions and in the afflictions which ye endure;"*

The word translated here as patience from the Greek (υπομονης) can also be translated as perseverance. It carries the connotation of a patient, steadfast waiting for, a patient enduring, a sustaining, and in the New Testament it is the characteristic of a man who is not swerved from his deliberate purpose and his loyalty to faith and piety by even the greatest trials and sufferings.

God is calling us to not lose heart because of the events of today. Some days will be tough, don't quit. Stand firm. Be strong and seek to see it through. Ask God today to put His protective shield around you, steadying you in all that you face.

Prayer: Father, I seek to be a steady influence in the place where You have put me. I can only do this by holding to Your Hand, seeking to persevere no matter what comes up.

---

[293] OT Reading – Isaiah 65 – 66

October 19

Daily Bible Reading: 2 Thessalonians 2[294]

Verse of the Day: 2 Thessalonians 2:8 – *"And then shall be revealed the lawless one, whom the Lord Jesus shall slay with the breath of his mouth, and bring to nought by the manifestation of his coming;"*

The Greek word ανομος literally means "without law." Thus, the word is depicting the man of rebellion who will be in contrast to Jesus Christ.

Jesus Christ displays righteousness, is the One who personifies true righteousness, the "lawless one" will be the exact opposite. He will personify rebellion against God and all that He is. He will rebel against God's righteous law.

Many see this as the one John calls the "Antichrist" (1 John 4:2,3) and the "beast" (Revelation 13:1). He will come in open defiance of the Supreme Sovereign of the Universe, thus displaying and being the fulfillment of evil and opponent of Jesus Christ and His Kingdom.

Prayer: Sovereign God, let me see through the teachings and leadings of the "lawless one."

October 20

Daily Bible Reading: 2 Thessalonians 3[295]

Verse of the Day: 2 Thessalonians 3:1 – *"Finally, brethren, pray for us, that the word of the Lord may run and be glorified, even as also it is with you;"*

Paul prayed often and fervently for many he had the privilege of working with. His letters are full of the reminders to the recipients that he was praying and remembering them before God.

Also, he frequently asked for them to remember him in prayer. And, when he does, the request is for the ability to continue to spread the Gospel and build the Kingdom of Christ.

Do you pray often for those you minister with and to? Do you spend time thanking God for them? And, in turn, do you request them to pray for you as you seek to build the Kingdom of God in your sphere of influence?

---

[294] OT Reading – Jeremiah 1 – 2
[295] OT Reading – Jeremiah 3 – 4

Prayer: Heavenly Father, I pause today and offer prayers of thanksgiving for _____. May You empower them to build Your Kingdom right where they are today. Amen.

October 21

Daily Bible Reading: 1 Timothy 1[296]

Verse of the Day: 1 Timothy 1:1 – 2 – *"Paul, an apostle of Christ Jesus according to the commandment of God our Saviour, and Christ Jesus our hope; unto Timothy, my true child in faith: Grace, mercy, peace, from God the Father and Christ Jesus our Lord."*

This is the first of three letters that we commonly call the "Pastoral Letters" of Paul. This one, 2 Timothy, and Titus are written to give instructions on being a shepherd of God's flock. Timothy was an understudy, a student of the Apostle Paul, and Paul left him at Ephesus to lead the fledgling church in that city.

Paul's letter can be divided into three sections; chapter 1 is personal in encouragement and advice, chapters 2 and 3 speak to the ministry, and the remaining chapters speaks to the one who ministers.

Prayer: Father, as we read this letter over the next few days, let us pray that God will help us to see truths that will encourage us and help us to encourage those who we know minister for Jesus Christ. Amen.

October 22

Daily Bible Reading: 1 Timothy 2[297]

Verse of the Day: 1 Timothy 2:1 – 4 – *"I exhort therefore, first of all, that supplications, prayers, intercessions, thanksgivings, be made for all men; for kings and all that are in high place; that we may lead a tranquil and quiet life in all godliness and gravity. This is good and acceptable in the sight of God our Saviour; who would have all men to be saved, and come to the knowledge of the truth."*

Paul is now beginning to elaborate on what will build up the church. He says that supplications (personal needs), prayers, intercessions (praying for the needs of others), and thanksgivings (an attitude of gratitude and praise for what God has done) should be a part of the ministry of the church.

---

[296] OT Reading – Jeremiah 5 – 6
[297] OT Reading – Jeremiah 7 – 8

He says that these expressions of prayer must be made for all men (the term used here means male and female alike). Of all ranks in life. Why? Because it is God's Will for everyone to come to Him.

Prayer: Today I will spend time with You, Father, in prayer for everyone You bring to my mind. I praise You for this special time. Amen.

October 23

Daily Bible Reading: 1 Timothy 3[298]

Verse of the Day: 1 Timothy 3:1 – *"Faithful is the saying, If a man seeketh the office of a bishop, he desireth a good work."*

The Greek word used here for bishop is επισκοπης and means one who oversees. In the New Testament, this term is sometimes translated as Elders.

Elders were responsible for the internal affairs of the New Testament Church. It appears from the context in other places (Acts 14; 20; Titus 1) that there was a plurality of men in positions of responsibility in any given congregational unit.

After the New Testament times, it became the custom in the church to select one of these Elders and name him the bishop, like our present day role of the Pastor.

Paul says it is a worthy position and goes on to describe the qualifications and in his letters, the responsibilities of these men.

Prayer: Father, today may I spend time in prayer for my Pastor and leaders in my local church assembly. I hold them up to You.

October 24

Daily Bible Reading: 1 Timothy 4[299]

Verse of the Day: 1 Timothy 4:13 – *"Till I come, give heed to reading, to exhortation, to teaching."*

Paul here is encouraging Timothy in his role in the church at Ephesus. Paul has encouraged him to not let his youth deter him from fulfilling the call that God has placed upon his life.

Paul challenges him to hold fast to the things that are needed. Don't neglect the [public] reading of the Scripture, this would be followed with

---

[298] OT Reading – Jeremiah 9 – 10
[299] OT Reading – Jeremiah 11 – 13

exhortation (the encouragement to obey what was read), and also the formal teaching and instruction in the Word of God.

Paul urges Timothy throughout this letter (and in connection, all ministers of God's Word, ordained or not) to be diligent in doing what God has called us to do.

Prayer: Holy Spirit, I come to You today asking for You to work in my life and heart so that I may go out and share Your Word with those in my sphere of influence in this world. May I encourage others with Your Word today.

October 25

Daily Bible Reading: 1 Timothy 5[300]

Verse of the Day: 1 Timothy 5:17 – *"Let the elders that rule well be counted worthy of double honor, especially those who labor in the word and in teaching."*

The primary function of the elders was to rule well. The word we have translated as honor (τιμης) carries a double meaning - the honor which one has by reason of rank and state of office which he holds, and also in writings outside of the New Testament the idea of financial remuneration. So, Paul's statement of "double honor" can carry both of the connotations at the same time – respect for a job well done, and adequate pay for the work they do.

Do we pay this type of "honor" to our Pastors today? Do we respect them for the work they do (preaching and teaching), and do we pay them adequately for this work? Muse over this in your sphere of life today.

Prayer: Spirit of God, keep us in line with what You desire for our Pastors and their families. May we honor them doubly today. We lift them up in prayer and praise to You.

October 26

Daily Bible Reading: 1 Timothy 6[301]

Verse of the Day: 1 Timothy 6:20 – *"O Timothy, guard that which is committed unto thee, turning away from the profane babblings and oppositions of the knowledge which is falsely so called;"*

---

[300] OT Reading – Jeremiah 14 – 16
[301] OT Reading – Jeremiah 17 – 19

The Greek word παραθηκην translated committed in this verse is used only here and in 2 Timothy 1:12, 14. It is the word used for a deposit, a trust or thing consigned to one's faithful keeping. What Paul was calling upon Timothy to guard was the truths that Paul entrusted to him in this letter. He was to guard against the false knowledge (Gnosticism) that had infiltrated the Ephesian Church. This system of teaching taught that a person received salvation only when they had "knowledge" of deep spiritual mysteries. Paul tells Timothy plainly and directly to stay away from this teaching.

The gospel is plain, "Believe on the Lord Jesus, and thou shalt be saved." (Acts 16:31)

Prayer: Spirit, keep me focused on the truth, all the truth, and only the truth of the gospel message. Christ and Him alone.

October 27

Daily Bible Reading: 2 Timothy 1[302]

Verse of the Day: 2 Timothy 1:7 – *"For God gave us not a spirit of fearfulness; but of power and love and discipline."*

σωφρονισμου. A Greek word that means an admonishing or calling to soundness of mind, to moderation and self-control. Some translations use the words "sound mind" in this place. The Holy Spirit of God gives to believers spiritual gifts and then empowers us to use them. God's Spirit does not give us a spirit of cowardice, but one that empowers us for the scope of ministry.

It is by God's Spirit that we have the strength or ability (power) to do the work of the ministry. It is by this same Spirit that we have the agape love that flows from God to do His work. And, because of this, He gives us the self-discipline necessary to minister in His name.

Today, prayerfully seek God to fill you with His Love, His Grace, His Mercy, His Power, His abilities to serve as He calls you.

Prayer: Holy Father, fill me, equip me, use me in Your service today. Guide me and direct me to walk and work in Your desired plan.

---

[302] OT Reading – Jeremiah 20 – 22

October 28

Daily Bible Reading: 2 Timothy 2[303]

Verse of the Day: 2 Timothy 2:15 – *"Give diligence to present thyself approved unto God, a workman that needeth not to be ashamed, handling aright the word of truth."*

It seems that our world today, in general, lacks biblical truth. It is not due to a lack of Bibles. What is lacking is people who carefully handle the Word of Truth.

We need more students of the Scriptures. We need people who study them to be sound in theology and interpretation of the Scriptures. And, this only comes from spending time in devoted study, not just a casual reading of the Bible. If we are careful in our approach to the Word, study it under the inspiration of the Holy Spirit, and live what we learn, we will be able to teach without fear or shame.

Prayer: Most Holy God, Father of Creation, Giver of Eternal Life, may I take the time today to spend it with You and Your precious Word. I seek You to speak into my life the life-giving words of Your Holy Scriptures. Teach me Your Truth, Your Promises, Your Plan, and Your Direction for my life as I speak for You.

October 29

Daily Bible Reading: 2 Timothy 3[304]

Verse of the Day: 2 Timothy 3:16 – *"Every scripture inspired of God is also profitable for teaching, for reproof, for correction, for instruction which is in righteousness:"*

Paul uses a Greek term translated "inspired of God" in this place which is made up of two words – one translates as God and the other translates as breathed. This term θεοπνευστος is difficult to understand in our terms, it carries two concepts.

The first concept is that they are breathed out by God. This shows the divine origin of the words. The second is that God inspired (or inbreathed) the words. This gives us the picture that God is present in His Word. The Bible is not a simple library of books, it is a supernatural collection of truth from He who is Truth for all mankind. It will make us complete (verse 17) if we will just let it.

---

[303] OT Reading – Jeremiah 23 – 24
[304] OT Reading – Jeremiah 25 – 26

Prayer: Precious Living Word of God, Jesus, through Your Spirit speak life into my soul that I may be able to spread the truth of life to others that I come in contact with. Empower me with Your Spirit and Word to minister for You today.

October 30

Daily Bible Reading: 2 Timothy 4[305]

Verse of the Day: 2 Timothy 4:2 – *"preach the word; be urgent in season, out of season; reprove, rebuke, exhort, with all longsuffering and teaching."*

Preach. Ah, that means a preacher, right? It is an admonition only to those who stand in the pulpit, doesn't it?

Not fully. Paul is challenging his young student Timothy to be bold and ready to share at any moment. But the word translated preach in this passage can mean to publish or proclaim openly. It is not held only to those who we call Pastors. It is for all of us. We need to be ready at any moment to share the good news with anyone we come in contact with.

We need to be ready to take a stand, to be alert, to be prepared with the message of hope and salvation that the world needs. God can, and will, use us to be His mouth to those He places around us. Today, be ready, and watch what He will do.

Prayer: Father, I am standing ready and willing before You, use me as You see fit today.

October 31

Daily Bible Reading: Titus 1[306]

Verse of the Day: Titus 1:4 – *"to Titus, my true child after a common faith: Grace and peace from God the Father and Christ Jesus our Saviour."*

This short letter is to Titus, a Greek who was converted under the ministry of Paul. He was an associate and helped on some of Paul's missionary tours. Paul may have established a church on the island of Crete following his first imprisonment. He left Titus there to minister to the church (1:5) and set things in order. This is a short letter (only 46 verses) that contains a variety of theological topics.

---

[305] OT Reading – Jeremiah 27 – 28
[306] OT Reading – Jeremiah 29 – 30

Look for three important lessons in this letter as you read it. First, deeds will either deny or defend our teaching. Second, grace elevates godliness, not cheapens it. And finally, God's kindness should change the way that we act. See if you recognize them in the three chapters of this letter.

Prayer: Spirit of the Holy One, open my eyes that I may see the multitude of lessons You provide for me in Your Word. Give me understanding as I read and apply it.

NOVEMBER Thanks Giving and Thanks Living

November. The time of year, where we focus on being thankful for what God has done in, to, with, and for us.

This month, find ways to thank God for all He has provided – and for what He has held back from us.

We will continue in the Letter to Titus and go through the short letter to Philemon, a beautiful picture of forgiveness. We will then see the "betters" that the writer of Hebrews bring before us. We travel with James and see how we can be assured of our salvation. Peter teaches on trials and tribulations in his two letters.

So, in the midst of these vital letters, let us focus upon thanking God for the plethora of blessings, the multitude of grace, the wonder of His great care for us. And, in return thank Him for all of this.

November 1

Daily Bible Reading: Titus 2[307]

Verse of the Day: Titus 2:11 – 14 – *"For the grace of God hath appeared, bringing salvation to all men, instructing us, to the intent that, denying ungodliness and worldly lusts, we should live soberly and righteously and godly in this present world; looking for the blessed hope and appearing of the glory of the great God and our Saviour Jesus Christ; who gave himself for us, that he might redeem us from all iniquity, and purify unto himself a people for his own possession, zealous of good works."*

Zealous of good works. Our human nature is actually the opposite of this. We swear, scream, get angry, pout, fight, argue, become irritated with minor things.

We need to learn to pause and be still and quiet before the Lord. Learn from Him. Consciously turn it all over to Him. Let Him be in control. It might surprise you how different it appears when it is in His hands.

Prayer: Gracious and Loving Savior, today I seek to turn my nature over to You to control and direct. I am letting You take the wheel and steer me through this day. Praise You!

November 2

Daily Bible Reading: Titus 3[308]

Verse of the Day: Titus 3:5 – 7 – *"not by works done in righteousness, which we did ourselves, but according to his mercy he saved us, through the washing of regeneration and renewing of the Holy Spirit, which he poured out upon us richly, through Jesus Christ our Saviour; that, being justified by his grace, we might be made heirs according to the hope of eternal life."*

Consider this, can we lose the free gift of salvation? No way! If we had to work for it, then we could lose it. In fact, if we worked for it then it is not a gift, we had earned it.

We miss the mark when we turn the free gift of God's grace into a wage that we have earned. (By the way missing the mark is what the Greek word that we translate to mean sin). If we could work, how much

---

[307] OT Reading – Jeremiah 31 – 32
[308] OT Reading – Jeremiah 33 – 35

do we have to do? And then, how little do we need to do to lose it? Enjoy, it is a gift that we can't lose.

Prayer: Jesus, thank You for the gift of salvation, the precious grace given by faith to those of us who chose to believe. I am thankful that it doesn't rest upon me or my acts.

November 3

Daily Bible Reading: Philemon[309]

Verse of the Day: Philemon 10 – 11 – *"I beseech thee for my child, whom I have begotten in my bonds, Onesimus, who once was unprofitable to thee, but now is profitable to thee and to me:"*

This very short, personal letter from Paul to Philemon is a plea for a Christian love on behalf of Philemon in relation to the cultural institution of his day, slavery. It is a letter that displays true concepts of forgiveness. Philemon had every right according to the culture of his day to put Onesimus to death for running away.

It speaks to us today personally. Consider that every one of us were once fugitives from God. Our guilt was great and the penalty would be severe. Grace opened up the door of appeal to us. Jesus is our mediator (like Paul) before the Father. He paid our debt (as Paul offers for Onesimus) to provide the forgiveness needed. Have you received Jesus' provision?

Prayer: Jesus, I thank You for providing the payment for my debt. I am grateful for Your provision that I can be restored to the Father in full, adopted into His family forever. Amen.

November 4

Daily Bible Reading: Hebrews 1[310]

Verse of the Day: Hebrews 1:1 – 3 – *"God, having of old time spoken unto the fathers in the prophets by divers portions and in divers manners, hath at the end of these days spoken unto us in his Son, whom he appointed heir of all things, through whom also he made the worlds;"*

As we study the letter to the Hebrews, we find that the writer is calling us to see the superiority. The writer wants us to see that Jesus is superior to the prophets, angels, Joshua, the Sabbath, and Priests. He will

---

[309] OT Reading – Jeremiah 36 – 37
[310] OT Reading – Jeremiah 38 – 39

encourage us that Jesus is better than any earthly priesthood, animal sacrifices, and the Old Testament Mosaic system of the priesthood.

This letter is written to encourage us to cling to Jesus and not slip away from the truth. We must persevere even in the face of hardships. So, as we study this letter, let us learn to have Faith to believe in Jesus, Hope to endure the trials of life, and Love to encourage others in these truths,

Prayer: Father, may I see Jesus as Superior to all other things in Your Creation. Amen.

November 5

Daily Bible Reading: Hebrews 2[311]

Verse of the Day: Hebrews 2:9 – *"But we behold him who hath been made a little lower than the angels, even Jesus, because of the suffering of death crowned with glory and honor, that by the grace of God he should taste of death for every man."*

We say that we glory in the cross; however, it is not the literal cross that we bow to. We bow humbly to the One who hung upon that cross. It is not the cross, it is what the cross represents that we reverence. It is our Substitute, the One who took our place that we look to. He paid the price for our sins. He suffered, bled, and died to provide the full payment for our sin-debt before the Father. He was willing to go into the depth of agony and suffering for me (and you) so that we can be reconciled with the Heavenly Father.

Prayer: Jesus, I pause today to ponder the great superior Love that You had for all mankind that You would freely give Your Life, Your Blood, Your Righteousness for us. As I now think upon my sinful condition before You, I accept Your grace in faith for my salvation.

November 6

Daily Bible Reading: Hebrews 3[312]

Verse of the Day: Hebrews 3:13 – *"but exhort one another day by day, so long as it is called To-day; lest any one of you be hardened by the deceitfulness of sin:"*

The Greek word παρακαλειτε is translated here as "exhort" also carries the connotation of comfort, appeal, to implore, or to plead. The writer of this letter uses the imperative form of the word and expresses a

---

[311] OT Reading – Jeremiah 40 – 42
[312] OT Reading – Jeremiah 43 – 45

command to the hearer to perform a certain action by the order and authority of the one commanding.

He is stressing that unbelief leads to a loss of all the superior benefits of our relationship with Christ. He warns that this unbelief comes because of the delusion that sin will create in the believer. The word translated "harden" here means to become obstinate or stubborn. We can develop a stubborn refusal to obey the Word of God.

Prayer: May my heart, mind, and soul continually be soft, may I continually seek to obey Your Word. Remove from my life any sin that will create this hardened heart in me. Father, I want to be Yours forever and ever.

November 7

Daily Bible Reading: Hebrews 4[313]

Verse of the Day: Hebrews 4:12 – *"For the word of God is living, and active, and sharper than any two-edged sword, and piercing even to the dividing of soul and spirit, of both joints and marrow, and quick to discern the thoughts and intents of the heart."*

Look at the descriptors applied to the Bible. Ponder slowly each one. Alive. Active. Sharp. Piercing. This book that you hold in your hand is unlike any other book ever written. It is the only book that every time you begin to read it, the Author will speak directly into your life.

It still touches lives and changes hearts. Sometimes it feels as if the Heavenly Surgeon is painfully and deeply cutting away the dead flesh that holds us back. He probes our thoughts, intents, and beliefs as we read His words to us.

Prayer: Heavenly Father, I submit to Your sharp, probing look into my life and heart. Discover and remove all that stands between me and my being fully used by You. I want the cancerous growth of sin fully eradicated from my being. I am willing to accept the pain for the freedom to be healthy in You alone.

November 8

Daily Bible Reading: Hebrews 5[314]

Verse of the Day: Hebrews 5:8 – *"though he was a Son, yet learned obedience by the things which he suffered;"*

---

[313] OT Reading – Jeremiah 46 – 48
[314] OT Reading – Jeremiah 49 – 50

The wisest of God's saints on this Earth are those who have been educated in the School of Suffering. They have learned through the endurance of pain the deep lessons that God has prescribed in their course of study.

Jesus was familiar with suffering (Isaiah 53:3). And many of His followers have been through this set of lessons. He experienced everything that a person goes through here on Earth. He understands how hard it is for a person to completely obey God, He knows about the attractions of temptations. Yet, through all that He encountered He persisted in leading an obedient life, and led a sinless life. He did all this to be the perfect sacrifice to die in my place, to take my sin, to exchange my sinfulness for His sinlessness.

Prayer: Father, I am thankful that Christ was able to do what I couldn't. I am grateful that He suffered, and that He successfully stayed the course for my salvation. Amen.

November 9

Daily Bible Reading: Hebrews 6[315]

Verse of the Day: Hebrews 6:4 – 6 – *"For as touching those who were once enlightened and tasted of the heavenly gift, and were made partakers of the Holy Spirit, and tasted the good word of God, and the powers of the age to come, and then fell away, it is impossible to renew them again unto repentance; seeing they crucify to themselves the Son of God afresh, and put him to an open shame."*

Some use this passage to refute the concept of eternal security. They teach you can lose your salvation and gain it back again. However, if you read the passage closely you see that it says if one could lose their salvation, it would be impossible for them to gain salvation again.

We can be encouraged that the truth is, our salvation is not our doing, and Jesus did everything necessary for our salvation. And, because of this, we can count on Him to hold and maintain our position in Him. He holds me, not me holding Him. And He won't let go.

Prayer: Jesus hold me tight, I am trusting totally in You for my Eternal future. Thank You for doing what I couldn't and can't do. Amen.

---

[315] OT Reading – Jeremiah 51 – 52

November 10

Daily Bible Reading: Hebrews 7[316]

Verse of the Day: Hebrews 7:25 – *"Wherefore also he is able to save to the uttermost them that draw near unto God through him, seeing he ever liveth to make intercession for them."*

The word translated "uttermost" is from the Greek word παντελες which can be translated "completely." It is speaking of a complete or whole salvation.

This verse is in the present tense and means that Jesus Christ is presently interceding before the Father for any and all who will come to Him. Our justification is a once-for-all event, yet on a daily (hourly) basis, Jesus is involved in the continuing process of our sanctification.

We come to the Cross once, but we come to the Savior constantly for continuous cleansing and forgiveness.

Prayer: Jesus, I thank You for Your continuous standing by the Father interceding for me. I am a sinner saved by Grace, but I constantly need your prayers for my continued relationship with the Heavenly Father. Amen.

November 11

Daily Bible Reading: Hebrews 8[317]

Verse of the Day: Hebrews 8:11 – *"And they shall not teach every man his fellow-citizen, And every man his brother, saying, Know the Lord: For all shall know me, From the least to the greatest of them."*

This is part of a passage from Jeremiah 31 that the writer of Hebrews is quoting. In this, we find the word "know" used twice. In the Greek, two different words are used. The first "know" is the Greek word γνωθι. This means to know personally, it is an on-going knowledge which carries the concept of a personal relationship.

The second "know" is the Greek word ειδησουσιν. This one comes from a root word meaning "to see", and means to perceive, experience, or to know absolutely. It suggests a complete knowledge of someone, while the first word carries the idea of a growing knowledge.

---

[316] OT Reading – Lamentations 1 – 2
[317] OT Reading – Lamentations 3 – 5

Prayer: Father, I thank You that I can have a complete knowledge of You based upon this growing knowledge of You in our relationship. I long to know You more and more each day.

November 12

Daily Bible Reading: Hebrews 9[318]

Verse of the Day: Hebrews 9:27 – 28 – *"And inasmuch as it is appointed unto men once to die, and after this cometh judgment; so Christ also, having been once offered to bear the sins of many, shall appear a second time, apart from sin, to them that wait for him, unto salvation."*

Unlike the repeated sacrifices of the old Levitical system, as men die once, Jesus died once. Unlike men, Jesus did not face the judgment – He was sinless.

As a man, I am aware that there will come a day of my death (if Christ doesn't come first), and it is a sobering thought of needing to stand before a Holy God and be judged because of my sinful nature. But, Praise the Lord, I do not have to fear this because Jesus was offered on my behalf. His sinlessness has been transferred to take away my sinfulness. I am redeemed, restored, and remade in His image.

Prayer: Jesus, as I ponder on Your Great Sacrifice, I become more and more in awe of what You did for me. May I never lose sight of the greatness of Your Sacrifice on my behalf.

November 13

Daily Bible Reading: Hebrews 10:1 – 23[319]

Verse of the Day: Hebrews 10:14 – *"For by one offering he hath perfected for ever them that are sanctified."*

In verse 10 of this passage, we read "By which will we have been sanctified through the offering of the body of Jesus Christ once for all." The sanctification spoken of in this verse is a positional one – referring to our justification or the fact we have been declared righteous. In our passage above, the sanctification is referring to the gradual process whereby believers are made more and more perfect.

We are once declared righteous when we accept Jesus Christ as our Lord and Savior. However, we are involved in a daily process of being sanctified by Jesus so that we will one day become perfect, just as He is.

---

[318] OT Reading – Ezekiel 1 – 3
[319] OT Reading – Ezekiel 4 – 6

This final fulfillment will not happen while in these mortal bodies but will be completed when we die and receive our glorified bodies.

Prayer: Father. I thank You that You took me just as I was – "warts and all." I also thank You that You love me too much to leave me like that. Change me as You wish – I'm all Yours.

November 14

Daily Bible Reading: Hebrews 10:24 –39[320]

Verse of the Day: Hebrews 10:24 – 25 – *"and let us consider one another to provoke unto love and good works; not forsaking our own assembling together, as the custom of some is, but exhorting one another; and so much the more, as ye see the day drawing nigh."*

Interesting concept in this verse. Notice the word "provoke." παροξυσμον is the Greek word used here. Some translate it as to stimulate, encourage, etc. It is the same word that we get our English word paroxysm from. That word means any sudden, violent outburst; a fit of violent action or emotion. The Greek carries the idea of an irritation.

The writer of this passage was trying to show us how important it is for us to help one another – even if we are irritating or highly emotional. Our time together shaping and developing each other is of prime importance. So, even if we create an irritation in our encouragement – do it.

Prayer: Father, help us to see how important our relationship to You and each other is. Amen.

November 15

Daily Bible Reading: Hebrews 11:1 –19[321]

Verse of the Day: Hebrews 11:16 – *"But now they desire a better country, that is, a heavenly: wherefore God is not ashamed of them, to be called their God; for he hath prepared for them a city."*

As I was reading our passage for today, I came across an interesting statement. That is the last part of our reading today – *"wherefore God is not ashamed of them, to be called their God."*

---

[320] OT Reading – Ezekiel 7 – 9
[321] OT Reading – Ezekiel 10 – 12

In this chapter of those who are in the Hall of the Faithful, because of their strong faith and belief in their God, God was proud of them. He was proud to be called their God.

I got to thinking, is God proud of me? Is He not ashamed to be called my God? Have I been faithful? Have I been obedient? Have I maintained my part of the relationship? Do I sometimes seem ashamed to admit God is my God?

Prayer: God, it is my desire to please You. I know I must have faith to please You – increase my faith. Draw me close to You. Amen.

November 16

Daily Bible Reading: Hebrews 11:20 –40[322]

Verse of the Day: Hebrews 11:36 – 38 – *"and others had trial of mockings and scourgings, yea, moreover of bonds and imprisonment: they were stoned, they were sawn asunder, they were tempted, they were slain with the sword: they went about in sheepskins, in goatskins; being destitute, afflicted, ill-treated (of whom the world was not worthy), wandering in deserts and mountains and caves, and the holes of the earth."*

In the first half of this chapter God lists those whose stories encourage and excite us. They were blessed physically as well as spiritually. In our passage today we see a shift in what those who had faith received. In this life, not always will we be rewarded, however, as this chapter ends it says – *"And these all, having had witness borne to them through their faith, received not the promise, God having provided some better thing concerning us, that apart from us they should not be made perfect."*

Prayer: Father, may I be strong to receive Your reward, perfection in a much better world.

November 17

Daily Bible Reading: Hebrews 12[323]

Verse of the Day: Hebrews 12:24 – *"and to Jesus the mediator of a new covenant, and to the blood of sprinkling that speaketh better than that of Abel."*

The Greek word used here for mediator is μεσιτη and means one who intervenes between two, either in order to make or restore peace and friendship, or form a compact, or for ratifying a covenant. The writer

---

[322] OT Reading – Ezekiel 13 – 15
[323] OT Reading – Ezekiel 16

of this letter describes Moses as the mediator of the first (or Old) Covenant. He acted as a liaison between God and the Israelites.

In similar fashion, the writer pictures Jesus as our mediator, or liaison between God and man. He established this by His death. He then sent out the Disciples to spread the good news. Now we find that He is sitting at the right hand of God interceding for us daily (Heb. 7:25). What a better, more apt mediator we have in Jesus.

Prayer: Jesus, I thank You that today You stand at the right hand of the Father interceding on my behalf. You purchased this right through Your death and resurrection. I am Yours. Amen.

November 18

Daily Bible Reading: Hebrews 13[324]

Verse of the Day: Hebrews 13:15 – *"Through him then let us offer up a sacrifice of praise to God continually, that is, the fruit of lips which make confession to his name."*

The Old Testament animal sacrifices have been done away with by the once-for-all sacrifice of our Savior, Jesus Christ. Yet, as New Testament believers we are still challenged to bring sacrifices to God. This time the sacrifices are praise and our lives (Romans 12:1,2). God wants living sacrifices that proclaim praise and worship.

The word sacrifice carries with it the meaning of giving up something highly valued for the sake of something else considered to have a greater value or claim. So, our sacrifice is giving up ourselves (which we highly value) to proclaim praise and worship of Jesus. Today, see how often you can give Him praise in your circumstances and activities.

Prayer: Jesus, I give all praise to You today. I seek to see You in all events in my life today. You are worthy of all my honor and admiration. Thank You for all You have done.

November 19

Daily Bible Reading: James 1[325]

Verse of the Day: James 1:13 – 15 – *"Let no man say when he is tempted, I am tempted of God; for God cannot be tempted with evil, and he himself tempteth no man: but each man is tempted, when he is drawn*

---

[324] OT Reading – Ezekiel 17 – 19
[325] OT Reading – Ezekiel 20 – 21

away by his own lust, and enticed. Then the lust, when it hath conceived, beareth sin: and the sin, when it is fullgrown, bringeth forth death."

Notice four downward "D's" in this passage. This is the path that leads us to a dangerous development. First is Desire. This is found in the phrase "his own lust." The temptations come into our lives because of our sinful nature. Following this understanding, the next step down is Deception. We are shown this in the word "enticed." This word pictures being caught by a baited trap. What is the bait? Our lust. Lust is a strong desire for what is forbidden. The third D is Disobedience (conceived sin). Our desires lead us to deception and this bring us to disobey God, and it ends in death, or horrible consequences.

Prayer: Spirit, keep me aware and wary of my desires. Let me only desire what God wants.

November 20

Daily Bible Reading: James 2[326]

Verse of the Day: James 2:10 – *"For whosoever shall keep the whole law, and yet stumble in one point, he is become guilty of all."*

The Pharisees of Jesus day were guilty of selective obedience. They would pick and choose which parts of the law they would obey. They were strict on keeping the Sabbath or tithing, yet ignore or excuse away other parts. Unfortunately today, we are often guilty of this same thing. We condemn sin in others and excuse away sin in our lives.

God does not allow for "selective obedience." Sin is sin is sin. The whole law has to be accepted, and any violation of any part of it means we have broken it. The Law is not a list of individual items it is a complete whole. This is why we cannot work our way, or earn our way into heaven. Having this bent to sin, I am guilty of breaking the Law of God. That is why we need the sacrifice of Jesus to make us right with God.

Prayer: Jesus, thank You for dying for me. Thank You for providing the way for me to be reconnected with the Father. Thank You!

---

[326] OT Reading – Ezekiel 22 – 23

November 21

Daily Bible Reading: James 3[327]

Verse of the Day: James 3:17 – *"But the wisdom that is from above is first pure, then peaceable, gentle, easy to be entreated, full of mercy and good fruits, without variance, without hypocrisy."*

In this chapter, James presents some warnings about how we misuse our tongues. He challenges us to consider how that we praise God one moment and then curse or call down doom on those around us. We speak good of God, and speak badly of our fellow men.

He calls us to consider that nature does not display this type of behavior. What is good is good, and what is bad is bad. There is no room for a mixture. In our verse today, James convicts us that true wisdom has these eight values in it. If, and this is a strong line of understanding, the wisdom you are living by does not line with these eight attributes, then it is not from God. Perhaps we need to pause and consider what we are looking at to guide our lives.

Prayer: Open my eyes that I might see the truth around me, O Spirit of Truth. Amen.

November 22

Daily Bible Reading: James 4[328]

Verse of the Day: James 4:10 – *"Humble yourselves in the sight of the Lord, and he shall exalt you."*

The Greek word translated as humble in this verse means to make oneself low before others. The voice of this word is that one is doing this to themselves. God, through James, is telling us that we need to make the decision and act on it to hold our view of ourselves as being subservient to those around us.

When we do this, God will exalt us. The word in the Greek means to raise to the very summit of opulence and prosperity, to raise to dignity, honor, and happiness. I don't know about you, but I would love to have this done to me.

What we can learn from this is that if we try to make ourselves appear important, it won't last. But, if we abase ourselves, God will honor us, and that will last for eternity.

---

[327] OT Reading – Ezekiel 24 – 26
[328] OT Reading – Ezekiel 27 – 28

Prayer. Spirit of the Father, come into my life, I give You full control over my body, soul, and spirit. I seek to humble myself in Your sight.

November 23

Daily Bible Reading: James 5[329]

Verse of the Day: James 5:16 – 18 – "*Confess therefore your sins one to another, and pray one for another, that ye may be healed. The supplication of a righteous man availeth much in its working. Elijah was a man of like passions with us, and he prayed fervently that it might not rain; and it rained not on the earth for three years and six months. And he prayed again; and the heaven gave rain, and the earth brought forth her fruit.*

How often do we put the heroes of the faith upon pedestals and feel that they are closer to God because they are so much more righteous than we are. Moses, David, Elijah, Paul, they were all remarkable men, however, they were exactly that – men. This verse reminds us of the power of the prayers of Elijah, but it first establishes that he was just like we are.

So, what made the difference? His earnest (fervent) approach to prayer. Do we earnestly bring our petitions to God?

Prayer: Father, today I bring to You my earnest prayer for-_____. Amen.

November 24

Daily Bible Reading: 1 Peter 1[330]

Verse of the Day: 1 Peter 1:16 – "*because it is written, Ye shall be holy; for I am holy.*"

The Greek word for holy, αγιοι, means a most holy thing, a saint. It appears well over 220 times in the New Testament. Paul frequently calls believers saints. Peter starts his letter off with this admonition.

When we see this word "because" we need to look back to see what it connects to. In this case, it is verses 13 – 15. Peter under the Spirit's influence is challenging us to be obedient and live as God would have us live. And he tells us it is because God has told us to do this (Lev. 11:44f; 19:2; 20:7.) Since God is working to conform us into the likeness of His

---

[329] OT Reading – Ezekiel 29 – 31
[330] OT Reading – Ezekiel 32 – 33

Son (Romans 8:29), He expects us to be obedient and to be what He is changing us into.

Prayer: Father, You are Holy. You are working on me and changing me. It is Your desire that I become like the image of Your Son. I will give myself over to You. I will submit to Your shaping and redefining me. I will give You full reign over my being. Make me like Jesus. Make me worthy of the title Saint. Amen.

November 25

Daily Bible Reading: 1 Peter 2[331]

Verse of the Day: 1 Peter 2:9 – 10 – *"But ye are an elect race, a royal priesthood, a holy nation, a people for God's own possession, that ye may show forth the excellencies of him who called you out of darkness into his marvellous light: who in time past were no people, but now are the people of God: who had not obtained mercy, but now have obtained mercy."*

Peter here lists six descriptions of believers in Jesus Christ. (1) He calls us an elect race, the Greek word means chosen. We have been chosen by God. (2) We are described as a kingly priesthood. A priest was one who represented God to man. (3) We are a saintly multitude (a holy nation). (4) Preserved by God (literal of the Greek "for God's own possession). (5) The great population that are for God (the people of God). And, (6) those who have experienced mercy.

If that doesn't brighten your day, I'm not sure what will.

Prayer: Father, thank You for what we are and have in You through Your Son Jesus. We have such a blessing and destiny because of Him.

November 26

Daily Bible Reading: 1 Peter 3[332]

Verse of the Day: 1 Peter 3:12 – *"For the eyes of the Lord are upon the righteous, And his ears unto their supplication: But the face of the Lord is upon them that do evil."*

Interesting thoughts expressed in today's verse. Eyes, ears, and mouth are attributed to God as He observes the world around us – and us.

This says the "eyes" of God are upon the righteous. The term used here can be a metaphor for the eyes of the mind, the faculty of knowing

---

[331] OT Reading – Ezekiel 34 – 35
[332] OT Reading – Ezekiel 36 – 37

someone. He knows who are righteous. His "ears" is a term that can denote the faculty of perceiving with the mind, the faculty of understanding and knowing. God knows our deepest thoughts and desires in our prayers. Finally, the "face" of the Lord is a term that is used in expressions which denote to regard the person in one's judgment and treatment of men. He stands in judgment of those who are evil.

Prayer: Father, I seek your eyes, ears, and not Your face upon me today and forever.

November 27

Daily Bible Reading: 1 Peter 4[333]

Verse of the Day: 1 Peter 4:17 – 18 – "*For the time is come for judgment to begin at the house of God: and if it begin first at us, what shall be the end of them that obey not the gospel of God? And if the righteous is scarcely saved, where shall the ungodly and sinner appear?*"

Too often we lay the blame for the way that things are happening in our country to those who are pagans. We seek God's judgment upon those who don't want anything to do with God.

The problem is, the problems in our land are not necessarily because of the pagans, after all, pagans can only do what pagans do. The problem lies at the door of the church. We as believers are not doing what the gospel deems we should be doing. And, if this is so, the above verse should cause us to repent and return to the way of the Cross.

Prayer: Most Gracious God, we admit our sin. We come before You in humble contrition and seek Your mercy and grace. Forgive us, restore us, raise up Your Standard in our land.

November 28

Daily Bible Reading: 1 Peter 5[334]

Verse of the Day: 1 Peter 5:1 – 4 – "*The elders therefore among you I exhort, who am a fellow-elder, and a witness of the sufferings of Christ, who am also a partaker of the glory that shall be revealed: Tend the flock of God which is among you, exercising the oversight, not of constraint, but willingly, according to the will of God; nor yet for filthy lucre, but of a ready mind; neither as lording it over the charge allotted to you, but making yourselves ensamples to the flock. And when the chief Shepherd*

---

[333] OT Reading – Ezekiel 38 – 39
[334] OT Reading – Ezekiel 40

shall be manifested, ye shall receive the crown of glory that fadeth not away."

Today, the verses speak to Pastors and Spiritual Leaders. We need to heed God's challenge and warning. Also, we can be blessed in a great way.

If you are not a Pastor or Spiritual Leader, your task is to pray for your leaders. They hold a great responsibility before God, and to those are given much, much is required.

Prayer: Jesus, we pause today to pray for Your leaders in the church. Put a hedge of protection around them, and bless them today.

November 29

Daily Bible Reading: 2 Peter 1[335]

Verse of the Day: 2 Peter 1:5 – 11 – *"Yea, and for this very cause adding on your part all diligence, in your faith supply virtue; and in your virtue knowledge; and in your knowledge self-control; and in your self-control patience; and in your patience godliness; and in your godliness brotherly kindness; and in your brotherly kindness love. For if these things are yours and abound, they make you to be not idle nor unfruitful unto the knowledge of our Lord Jesus Christ. For he that lacketh these things is blind, seeing only what is near, having forgotten the cleansing from his old sins. Wherefore, brethren, give the more diligence to make your calling and election sure: for if ye do these things, ye shall never stumble: for thus shall be richly supplied unto you the entrance into the eternal kingdom of our Lord and Saviour Jesus Christ."*

Prayer: Today as I read only Your Word, Father, may it challenge me to apply the truth in this passage in my life today. May I accept this as a goal in my life. I want to be more like Christ in my daily walk and in my inner being.

November 30

Daily Bible Reading: 2 Peter 2[336]

Verse of the Day: 2 Peter 2:15 – *"forsaking the right way, they went astray, having followed the way of Balaam the son of Beor, who loved the hire of wrong-doing;"*

---

[335] OT Reading – Ezekiel 41 – 42
[336] OT Reading – Ezekiel 43 – 44

Balaam. An interesting prophet in the Old Testament. After being told over and over again that he would not be allowed to curse the people of Israel, Balaam seemed dead-set on disobeying God.

Peter warned against "the way of Balaam," Jude against "the error of Balaam" and John against "the doctrine of Balaam" (II Peter 2:15; Jude 11; Revelation 2:14). God evidently considers these warnings necessary and appropriate for Christians even today. The way of Balaam" was a readiness to prostitute his high spiritual gifts and privileges for "The wages of unrighteousness" (II Peter 2:14), being willing to preach something contrary to God's Word for personal gain.

Prayer: Father, may I by the power of Your Spirit never sell myself and the gift You have given me for the wages of man. May I be true to Your Word no matter the consequences.

DECEMBER His Birth Our Promises

December, the month that we celebrate the birth of Jesus, the month of festivities, fun, food, family, and so much more. As we approach this special season, let us not lay aside our time spent in the precious word of God. The world and the events of this season can so easily steal our time of fellowship with the Father in His Word.

Jesus entered time and space to become the "Living Word" that we read about in His "Written Word." The little baby in the manger did not come to stay that way. He came to live, die, and rise again to provide our means of restoration with the Father.

Celebrate? Definitely. But, do not forget to remember the real reason for the season and connect through His Word.

December 1

Daily Bible Reading: 2 Peter 3[337]

Verse of the Day: 2 Peter 3:8 – 9 – *"But forget not this one thing, beloved, that one day is with the Lord as a thousand years, and a thousand years as one day. The Lord is not slack concerning his promise, as some count slackness; but is longsuffering to you-ward, not wishing that any should perish, but that all should come to repentance."*

Jesus is coming again. He promised it, thereby it is sure. But, too many may argue that it has been over 2,000 years and He has not come back. Maybe He isn't coming back. After all, what is He waiting for? The world is in a mess. Things keep getting worse. Where is He?

This verse reminds us that God's not willing that any should go to Hell; He is patient trying to woo each one back to Him. He is patient, however, that will come to an end and Jesus will come back. And, those who reject Him will be left to their choice of an eternity separated from the Father.

Prayer: Father, give me the words to turn many back to You. May I be Your voice, that shows Your Patience and Love. Amen.

December 2

Daily Bible Reading: 1 John 1[338]

Verse of the Day: 1 John 1:1 – *"That which was from the beginning, that which we have heard, that which we have seen with our eyes, that which we beheld, and our hands handled, concerning the Word of life."*

John writes this letter to expose the false teachers and to give believers an assurance of salvation. He starts the letter with a verse that has four great verbs to stimulate our thoughts and understanding.

The words: heard (which means to attend to, consider what is or has been said), seen (to see, i.e. become acquainted with by experience, to experience), beheld (to behold, look upon, view attentively, contemplate often used of public shows), and handled (to handle, touch and feel) all emphasize to us that John personally knew and had closely investigated the One he is about to write about.

---

[337] OT Reading – Ezekiel 45 – 46
[338] OT Reading – Ezekiel 47 – 48

Do you personally know the Savior?

Prayer: Jesus I want to know You in a personal and up-close way. I want You to be so real in my life that I could never ever deny You.

December 3

Daily Bible Reading: 1 John 2[339]

Verse of the Day: 1 John 2:1 – *"My little children, these things write I unto you that ye may not sin. And if any man sin, we have an Advocate with the Father, Jesus Christ the righteous:"*

The Greek word translated as Advocate in this passage is παρακλητον. The word means one who pleads another's cause with one, an intercessor. It is also used in the Scriptures describing the Holy Spirit.

In this passage, it is used to describe the intercessory work of the Son of God. When we sin (and we will), Jesus represents us before the Father in Heaven's Court. Satan is the accuser of the brethren (Rev.12:10) and comes before God pointing out our every flaw and sin. Jesus comes next to us and pleads our defense based upon our position received by accepting Him. His shed blood removes the stain of sin and presents us blameless before God the Father.

Prayer: Thank You, Blessed Jesus, my Savior and Advocate. I could not stand before a Holy God except by Your intervention. May I continually praise Your Name.

December 4

Daily Bible Reading: 1 John 3[340]

Verse of the Day: 1 John 3:1 – *"Behold what manner of love the Father hath bestowed upon us, that we should be called children of God; and such we are. For this cause the world knoweth us not, because it knew him not."*

The Apostle John stands in grand amazement at the love of God. The Apostle often referred to himself as the disciple whom Jesus loved (John 13:23) had a close relationship with the Savior. He was called a Son of Boanerges (Son of Thunder) by Jesus early on, and later was known as the Disciple of Love. He has become an example of the change that happens when a person allows Jesus into their life. We get a glimpse of

---

[339] OT Reading – Daniel 1 – 2
[340] OT Reading – Daniel 3 – 4

the power of the love of God in John, and he can only stand in awe and amazement.

Are you a child of God? If you are, the very wonder of His love should overwhelm you. We are privileged to be called His children and receive His love.

Prayer: I stand in awe of Your great and marvelous love. It is overwhelming to be Your chosen child. Father, thank You.

December 5

Daily Bible Reading: 1 John 4[341]

Verse of the Day: 1 John 4:18 – 19 – *"There is no fear in love: but perfect love casteth out fear, because fear hath punishment; and he that feareth is not made perfect in love. We love, because he first loved us."*

A person once said that the opposite of fear is not courage; it is love. He was basing his comment upon this passage. John informs us that when we are totally in the perfect love of God we have nothing to fear.

Jesus told us not to fear those who could kill our bodies, but to fear the One who could destroy our bodies and souls in Hell. And, when we come into a perfect knowledge of the great wonderful love of the Father, we no longer need to fear. When we belong to Him, His perfect love for us will make sure that all things work for our good. He will eventually make all things right. We need only trust Him.

Prayer: Glorious, Good, and Holy Father, the One Who is Love, the One Who gives Love, The One Who pervades our whole being with Your Love, overwhelm me in Your precious and perfect Love today. Let it flow through me!

December 6

Daily Bible Reading: 1 John 5[342]

Verse of the Day: 1 John 5:13 – *"These things have I written unto you, that ye may know that ye have eternal life, even unto you that believe on the name of the Son of God."*

The phrase used here "These things" refer us back to verses 11 and 12. John wrote, "And the witness is this, that God gave unto us eternal life,

---

[341] OT Reading – Daniel 5 – 6
[342] OT Reading – Daniel 7 – 8

and this life is in his Son. He that hath the Son hath the life; he that hath not the Son of God hath not the life."

We can have assurance of our salvation by trusting in the Word of God that our salvation comes by God's Son, Jesus the Christ. Those who have put their trust in Jesus can rest assured that they have salvation because God says that we have it.

Where is your faith? In yourself? In words, deeds, or actions? In your church, your baptism, your dogma? Only faith in Jesus as Savior can provide salvation. Jesus plus anything else does not equal salvation.

Prayer: Jesus I trust in You and You alone. You are where I place my faith and trust. Amen.

December 7

Daily Bible Reading: 2 John[343]

Verse of the Day: 2 John 1:1 – 3 – *"The elder unto the elect lady and her children, whom I love in truth; and not I only, but also all they that know the truth; for the truth's sake which abideth in us, and it shall be with us for ever: Grace, mercy, peace shall be with us, from God the Father, and from Jesus Christ, the Son of the Father, in truth and love."*

John continues to encourage us to love in this short letter. He speaks about the fact that the mark of Christianity is our continuing to show love one to another. Let it flow. Give it away. Show it in every circumstance.

He also stresses in this letter that we are to take an uncompromising stand against error. But, you think, how can I act loving and stand in opposition to wrong thinking and acts? We must live in the balance of truth and grace. We are to walk in truth and extend grace to those around us, all the while maintaining our integrity and stand for what is true.

Prayer: Father, it is a balancing act of being gracious and loving, yet firm in my stand against evil and error. Balance me in Your hand.

---

[343] OT Reading – Daniel 9 – 10

December 8

Daily Bible Reading: 3 John[344]

Verse of the Day: 3 John 1:11 – "*Beloved, imitate not that which is evil, but that which is good. He that doeth good is of God: he that doeth evil hath not seen God.*"

The proof of our commitment to God is that we live a life modeled after the good and we reject evil. It is so easy today to fall into the trap of modeling our lives after the world, and not after God. The lifestyle that we live reflects the extent of our focus upon God. Whatever we focus on will be what we behave like.

Watch little children to see this truth. They seek to act and do the things that those around them do. For good or bad, they imitate those they are watching. We do the same. Our eyes on the world, and we act like the world. Our eyes on God, and we act like Him.

Prayer, Gracious and Marvelous God, help me to keep my mind and eyes upon You. You are the Truth, and I want to live a life of truth. You are Holy, and I want to live a life that is separated unto You. You are Love, and I want to display Your love to a lost and dying world around me. May I focus on You at all times.

December 9

Daily Bible Reading: Jude[345]

Verse of the Day: Jude 1:17 – 19 – "*But ye, beloved, remember ye the words which have been spoken before by the apostles of our Lord Jesus Christ; that they said to you, In the last time there shall be mockers, walking after their own ungodly lusts. These are they who make separations, sensual, having not the Spirit.*"

Deterioration is not sudden. It happens slowly over time. My garden does not become overgrown with weeds overnight (although sometimes it seems that way). No church suddenly leaves the faith. No person suddenly walks away from God. It is a slow, gradual process of accepting things that once were rejected. They may appear to be harmless or non-essential. Yet, they become a wedge that slowly produces a gap that widens and widens, until there is a total break. The slow moral erosion produces a total spiritual decay.

---

[344] OT Reading – Daniel 11 – 12
[345] OT Reading – Hosea 1 – 4

Prayer: Spirit, watch over me, and keep me in the right path at all times. Strengthen my hearing to hear Your small, still voice directing me. May I set my life upon the tracks of Your guidance.

December 10

Daily Bible Reading: Revelation 1[346]

Verse of the Day: Revelation 1:19 – *"Write therefore the things which thou sawest, and the things which are, and the things which shall come to pass hereafter;"*

The Book of Revelation. Notoriously considered the most difficult book in the Scriptures. While the book certainly provides a declaration of God's plan for the future, it was not designed to be used as a calendar for predicting what is happening and will happen next.

This is the Apocalypse (the revealing), so named because it is the revealing of Jesus Christ (vs.1) to show us what will take place. The outline of the Book is in the verse we read today and consists of (1) what John was seeing, (2) what are in existence now, and (3) what will come to pass in the future.

Read and be blessed (vs. 3), but remember to read from this Book, not into it. Don't try to make it fit your personal preferences.

Prayer: Spirit, open my eyes that I might see and glean what is in this precious book .

December 11

Daily Bible Reading: Revelation 2[347]

Verse of the Day: Revelation 2:1 – *"To the angel of the church in Ephesus write: These things saith he that holdeth the seven stars in his right hand, he that walketh in the midst of the seven golden candlesticks:"*

We begin a series of seven letters addressed to seven existing churches in John's day. Each church receives a message just for them, yet, this being a circular letter would be read by all of them. Thus, the warning and commendations are a challenge to each church, just as it is to us today.

---

[346] OT Reading – Hosea 5 – 8
[347] OT Reading – Hosea 9 – 11

In this chapter, the letters are sent to: (1) Ephesus, the preoccupied church, (2) Smyrna, the persecuted church, (3) Pergamum, the compromising church, and (4) Thyatira, the socially accepted church.

In the next chapter, we will read about the remaining three churches.

Prayer: Spirit, give me insight and understanding of how these four churches speak to me today. May I take the warnings and challenges that are presented here.

December 12

Daily Bible Reading: Revelation 3[348]

Verse of the Day: Revelation 3:13 – *"He that hath an ear, let him hear what the Spirit saith to the churches."*

Continuing with what we were looking at yesterday, consider the final three churches.

We begin with (5) Sardis, the powerless church, (6) Philadelphia, the persevering church, and (7) Laodicea, the lukewarm or nauseating church.

To make sure that we understand that we all are to take heed from the messages sent to these churches, Jesus said five times the statement given in our reading today. Having an open spirit to listen to the Word of God helps the believer to understand the destiny that God has for them.

Prayer: Spirit of Understanding, I pray that You will open my heart, mind, and whole being to study and understand the truths that You have presented in this precious Word of God. It is my desire to delve into the depths of wisdom and life lessons that You have placed before me in this marvelous Book. Amen.

December 13

Daily Bible Reading: Revelation 4[349]

Verse of the Day: Revelation 4:7 – *"And the first creature was like a lion, and the second creature like a calf, and the third creature had a face as of a man, and the fourth creature was like a flying eagle."*

In today's reading, we come upon four living creatures who are around the throne of God. These creatures show us a continuity within the Scriptures. We first find these descriptions in Ezekiel 1: 4 – 10. They are introduced as Cherubim or angels.

---

[348] OT Reading – Hosea 12 – 14
[349] OT Reading – Joel 1 – 3

We can also see in this description that the four living creatures carry a connection to the four Gospel accounts. Matthew portrays Jesus as a king, or we could see a lion. In Mark, Jesus is portrayed as a servant. In Luke, Jesus is portrayed as the perfect man, and finally, in John, Jesus is shown as Deity. Deity is often represented as a mighty Eagle.

Only under the unifying hand of God could writers so far separated maintain a beautiful imagery.

Prayer: Spirit, may I see Jesus in all the Bible.

December 14

Daily Bible Reading: Revelation 5[350]

Verse of the Day: Revelation 5:12 – *"saying with a great voice, Worthy is the Lamb that hath been slain to receive the power, and riches, and wisdom, and might, and honor, and glory, and blessing."*

The Lamb that was slain. One of the many names and titles ascribed to Jesus throughout the Scriptures. In this passage today, the title is attached to the idea that as the Lamb that was slain, Jesus is shown to have great worth. And this worth ascribed to Him is explained by seven descriptive words. In the Bible the number seven is considered to portray completeness or wholeness. In this verse, the worth of the Lamb is complete.

Worthy to receive our complete accolades, He receives power, riches, wisdom, might, honor, glory, and blessing.

Prayer: Heavenly Father, we pause today to look at our Lamb that was slain. The One who was the complete and perfect sacrifice for our sins. We cannot say enough to deliver worship and praise to Your Son. He is worthy of all our praise and worship. Amen.

December 15

Daily Bible Reading: Revelation 6[351]

Verse of the Day: Revelation 6:8 – *"And I saw, and behold, a pale horse: and he that sat upon him, his name was Death; and Hades followed with him. And there was given unto them authority over the fourth part of the earth, to kill with sword, and with famine, and with death, and by the wild beasts of the earth."*

---

[350] OT Reading – Amos 1 – 3
[351] OT Reading – Amos 4 – 6

Hades. In the Greek, it means the place of the unseen. Literally, it means "not seen." It is used to designate the invisible world of the dead. The Hebrew equivalent in the Old Testament is Sheol. It is natural that it is connected here with death. All people who die go into Hades, or the invisible place of the dead. Unfortunately, it has been associated with the word hell, or place of eternal torment. The Greek word for that is gehenna (Mark 9:43 – 45). We all go into Hades, but we can avoid hell by believing in Jesus.

Prayer: Father, unless Jesus comes back first, I will go through the act of dying. I will go into the invisible world of the dead, but knowing Jesus means I will go into Paradise and not Hell. I thank You for Your great provision for me.

December 16

Daily Bible Reading: Revelation 7[352]

Verse of the Day: Revelation 7:9 – 10 – *"After these things I saw, and behold, a great multitude, which no man could number, out of every nation and of all tribes and peoples and tongues, standing before the throne and before the Lamb, arrayed in white robes, and palms in their hands; and they cry with a great voice, saying, Salvation unto our God who sitteth on the throne, and unto the Lamb."*

Throughout the chapter we read today, there is a marked amount of worship. In these verses, we see the multitude of believers proclaiming praise to Jesus. We see that heaven will be made up of all nations, people groups, languages gathered in one place. There will not be separations of people.

I believe that it will be a majestic swelling chorus of voices in many dialects and languages all proclaiming the same thing, that our presence there is because of the Salvation provided by Jesus Christ, our Lord.

Prayer: Jesus, may I praise you now for what You did. I want to practice my praises today in preparation for that day. Amen.

December 17

Daily Bible Reading: Revelation 8[353]

Verse of the Day: Revelation 8:1 – 2 – *"And when he opened the seventh seal, there followed a silence in heaven about the space of half an*

---

[352] OT Reading – Amos 7 – 9
[353] OT Reading – Obadiah

hour. And I saw the seven angels that stand before God; and there were given unto them seven trumpets."

In our chapter today we move from the Seven Seal judgments into the Seven Trumpet judgments. The opening of the first six seals brought great devastation upon the Earth and mankind. When the seventh seal was opened, there was an eerie silence that enveloped all creation. Like the quiet before the storm, the silence was overwhelming in light of what had already taken place. And now, after about a half of an hour of total silence in creation, the first four trumpet judgments are unleashed in rapid succession. Then, as if they weren't distressing enough, an angel flew announcing that the final three were even greater woes.

Prayer: I thank You that You hold me in Your Hand. I find that You will protect me from the horrific judgments brought upon this world and Your Creation. I am Yours.

December 18

Daily Bible Reading: Revelation 9[354]

Verse of the Day: Revelation 9:11 – *"They have over them as king the angel of the abyss: his name in Hebrew is Abaddon, and in the Greek tongue he hath the name Apollyon."*

The "locusts" released upon the Earth are from the αβυσσου, a Greek word that basically means bottomless. This was considered to be a very deep gulf or chasm in the lowest parts of the earth used as the common receptacle of the dead and especially as the abode of demons.

These demonic creatures were under the leadership of one that John made sure was identified in both the Hebrew and the Greek languages. The reference to the Hebrew concept of Abaddon means destruction, and is understood as being the name of the angel-prince of the infernal regions, the minister of death and the author of havoc on the earth. Apollyon is the angel of the bottomless pit, the Destroyer. We consider this to be Satan, the great deceiver and opponent of the righteous.

Prayer: Father, I am totally Yours. Do not allow the Deceiver to come and kill and destroy my life with You.

---

[354] OT Reading – Jonah

December 19

Daily Bible Reading: Revelation 10[355]

Verse of the Day: Revelation 10:5 – 6 – *"And the angel that I saw standing upon the sea and upon the earth lifted up his right hand to heaven, and sware by him that liveth for ever and ever, who created the heaven and the things that are therein, and the earth and the things that are therein, and the sea and the things that are therein, that there shall be delay no longer:"*

This angel was about to make a great proclamation based upon the authority of the One who holds all Authority. The Creator of all that is was about to finish the great mystery. The seventh trumpet would be sounding without delay, and the events that would culminate the return of Christ were to take place.

Prayer: Father, as I have been reading this book, I so thank You that You will not allow Your children to face this massive punishment. It is a frightening reminder that so many of those going through this still shake their fist at You, curse You, and totally reject who You are. This shows me the full depravity of sinfulness.

December 20

Daily Bible Reading: Revelation 11[356]

Verse of the Day: Revelation 11:10 – *"And they that dwell on the earth rejoice over them, and make merry; and they shall send gifts one to another; because these two prophets tormented them that dwell on the earth."*

In our reading today we come across two men who are only identified as the Two Witnesses. We know very little for certain about them, and much speculation has arisen over their identification. Moses, Elijah, Enoch, or John the Baptist are various ideas presented. God has chosen not to disclose their identity, so we waste a lot of time trying to discern them.

In our verse today, we see the depravity of people on earth at this time. They have heard the prophetic warnings issuing from these two, and they seek to destroy the messengers. When they succeed, they do not allow a proper burial, but instead they have a time of celebration, almost

---

[355] OT Reading – Micah 1 – 3
[356] OT Reading – Micah 4 – 5

like our Christmas parties. Revelers are astonished 3 days later when they are resurrected and raptured.

Prayer: Holy Spirit, I pray for those who refuse to listen and believe God's message.

December 21

Daily Bible Reading: Revelation 12[357]

Verse of the Day: Revelation 12:11 – "*And they overcame him because of the blood of the Lamb, and because of the word of their testimony; and they loved not their life even unto death.*"

We are reminded in this passage that believers are victorious in Jesus Christ. We do not need to have any fear. We are shown that we have "overcoming" power. Not in ourselves, but through the One who died that we could live.

The victory comes from the death of Christ upon the Cross, and is proclaimed by our verbal testimony in any and all circumstances. We will have the victory through the believers that remained strong even to giving up their own lives. Often we are not sure if we could be a martyr, but we should be constantly looking to see if we are willing to give up our choices for the ones that God wants. Are we willing to center our all on the desires and directions of our Savior?

Prayer: Jesus, I fail often in making my way more important than Your way. I surrender all.

December 22

Daily Bible Reading: Revelation 13[358]

Verse of the Day: Revelation 13:18 – "*Here is wisdom. He that hath understanding, let him count the number of the beast; for it is the number of a man: and his number is Six hundred and sixty and six.*"

666. A number that has caused many to speculate upon who this man of sin is. Many different people have been ascribed as being this personification of the Antichrist. And, time has proven each one incorrect. We must be careful in trying to make people fit. When the final beast is here, it will be highly obvious.

---

[357] OT Reading – Micah 6 – 7
[358] OT Reading – Nahum

Six as a numerological point is one short of seven. Seven is the number of completion and perfection. This man (the beast is a man) is identified in intensity, 666, meaning he is a very powerful man. His power is beyond any that has been. This will be a key to identifying this man of sin.

Prayer: Father, may I not speculate on that which You have not disclosed. May I seek to only speak and teach that which You have given. Give me wisdom to interpret and teach only what is true from Your Word.

December 23

Daily Bible Reading: Revelation 14[359]

Verse of the Day: Revelation 14:12 – *"Here is the patience of the saints, they that keep the commandments of God, and the faith of Jesus."*

The Christian life is often compared to a marathon that we must run. I like to think of it as an obstacle course. There are many demanding twists, turns, and trials that we must confront and live through.

The Bible makes it clear that we are in a battle. We are the soldiers in the trenches. Most of our battles do not come with fanfare and applause. We fight the good fight (1 Timothy 6:12) on an ongoing basis. Our walk with Christ is one that requires endurance.

We need to be determined as we face each day. God is our helper, He gives us strength, He provides our way of escape (1 Cor. 10:13). Yet, we must make the decision to follow and obey. As we go through this life, we must intensify our determination to walk in the steps of Jesus.

Prayer: Father, strengthen me. I have good goals to walk as Jesus walked, yet I too often walk the way of the world. Amen.

December 24

Daily Bible Reading: Revelation 15[360]

Verse of the Day: Revelation 15:3 – *"And they sing the song of Moses the servant of God, and the song of the Lamb, saying, Great and marvellous are thy works, O Lord God, the Almighty; righteous and true are thy ways, thou King of the ages."*

---

[359] OT Reading – Habakkuk
[360] OT Reading – Zephaniah

The Almighty (Greek παντοκρατωρ), means he who holds sway over all things, the ruler of all, one who has power over everything. We would say that He has total control.

Our God is the One who commands all the hosts, the powers in Heaven and Earth. Because of this, He is able to overcome all His foes. Eight times this word appears in the Book of Revelation. It shows the unveiling of God's awe-inspiring control over the entire universe and throughout all of history.

Prayer: Almighty Father, Almighty Son, Almighty Spirit, what an awesome and majestic view is painted for us in Your Word. You disclose a small glimpse of Your might, Your power, Your presence, Your knowledge, and we then say we totally know You. Continue to open our eyes, hearts and minds to see You.

December 25

Daily Bible Reading: Revelation 16[361]

Verse of the Day: Revelation 16:15 – *"(Behold, I come as a thief. Blessed is he that watcheth, and keepeth his garments, lest he walk naked, and they see his shame.)*

Christmas Day. The day we celebrate the entrance of Jesus into time and space. He came from His throne on Heaven, robed Himself in human flesh, and began the one-way trek to the Cross of Calvary.

As I pondered upon this verse in our reading today, I know the setting is the preparation for the Battle of Armageddon, but I couldn't help but think that this statement of Jesus could have been made that night in Bethlehem. The Creator of the Universe slipped into time and space hardly noticed but by a few shepherds. Today, in the midst of the celebration, don't let Jesus be ignored, not noticed like a thief. Make Him the center of the Day and Celebrations. Focus on Him. Pause and worship the One who makes all things possible.

Prayer: Jesus, I make You the center of my thoughts, thanks, and total celebration today. You are the Reason for the Season, and my life.

---

[361] OT Reading – Haggai

December 26

Daily Bible Reading: Revelation 17[362]

Verse of the Day: Revelation 17:5 – "*and upon her forehead a name written, Mystery, Babylon the Great, the Mother of the Harlots and of the Abominations of the Earth.*"

Babylon. The word means confusion. It is first found in the account of the Tower of Babel, It then became a very large and famous city, the residence of the Babylonian kings, situated on both banks of the Euphrates. Cyrus had formerly captured it, but Darius Hystaspis threw down its gates and walls, and Xerxes destroyed the temple of Belis. At length the city was reduced to almost solitude, the population having been drawn off by the neighboring Seleucia, built on the Tigris by Seleucus Nicanor. Allegorically, it speaks of Rome, the most corrupt seat of idolatry and the enemy of Christianity in John's day. This introduction of the city in today's reading sets the stage for the destruction we will see tomorrow.

Prayer: The world constantly seeks to go away from You, Gracious Father. It seeks to do all that its ruler, Satan, will present to seek to defeat You and Your plan. We know they can't.

December 27

Daily Bible Reading: Revelation 18[363]

Verse of the Day: Revelation 18:10 – "*standing afar off for the fear of her torment, saying, Woe, woe, the great city, Babylon, the strong city! for in one hour is thy judgment come.*"

In today's reading, we find the pronouncement of the fall and total destruction of the city Babylon. In this verse, we find the statement "woe, woe...." The Greek word used here, ουαι, is a primary exclamation of grief, which in this instance is repeated to double the emphasis of the exclamation. It could be translated as alas, or how dreadful. It marks the impact that this city's destruction would have.

Considered a strong city, the world will marvel that in such a short time the city would be destroyed. The power of God in His judgment is demonstrated in this event. We know that God is a God of Love, but we forget that He is also a God of Judgment.

---

[362] OT Reading – Zechariah 1 – 3
[363] OT Reading – Zechariah 4 – 6

Prayer: Father, I want to be on Your side of Love in all of my life. I do not want to face Your Judgment. I have accepted the provision You have made through Jesus , Your Son.

December 28

Daily Bible Reading: Revelation 19[364]

Verse of the Day: Revelation 19:16 – *"And he hath on his garment and on his thigh a name written, King of Kings, and Lord of Lords."*

In the Greek language, they do not have superlatives for words. To create the ultimate superlative, the speaker or writer would repeat the word. We would say, good, better, best, they would say good good.

In today's reading, we see Jesus coming back on a White Horse with a sharp sword (this is in contrast to the first White Horse and rider in Revelation 6:2). Jesus' garment had His name or title written on it, He is the superlative King (King King) and the superlative Lord (Lord Lord).

The Battle is the Lord's, He defeats the Beast and all of his armies by the sword that comes out of His mouth. The Word of God is powerful (Heb. 4:12).

Prayer: Amazing and Powerful Savior, I bow in humble submission to You and Your Will for me today. I seek to walk only in Your Way. Guide me, direct me, lead me in all things.

December 29

Daily Bible Reading: Revelation 20[365]

Verse of the Day: Revelation 20:2 – *"And he laid hold on the dragon, the old serpent, which is the Devil and Satan, and bound him for a thousand years,"*

This chapter we are reading today describes the Millennial Reign of Jesus Christ on the Earth. It begins with the binding of Satan. He is called the Devil (Greek διαβολος) or the deceiver, and Satan (Greek σατανας) the accuser. Throughout the Scriptures we have seen that these names describe him so well. From Genesis chapter 3 where he lied to Eve and Adam, in Job as he stood and made accusations against Job, up to today, he has consistently sought to thwart God's glorious plan for man. Satan tried to stop Christ's coming, His Death, and even His church's task of sharing the Good News.

---

[364] OT Reading – Zechariah 7 – 9
[365] OT Reading – Zechariah 10 – 12

Prayer: Almighty God, as I ponder today the depth that Satan has gone to cause Your plan to be subverted, I am in awe of Your constant and direct provision and protection of Your people. I thank You that You overshadow me, You protect me from the Evil One, and meet my every need to accomplish Your work.

December 30

Daily Bible Reading: Revelation 21[366]

Verse of the Day: Revelation 21:6 – "*And he said unto me, They are come to pass. I am the Alpha and the Omega, the beginning and the end. I will give unto him that is athirst of the fountain of the water of life freely.*"

Alpha and Omega are the first and last letters of the Greek alphabet. It is an idiom that encompasses the whole. It is like our saying from A to Z, or from the start to the finish, or the whole 9 yards, or the whole enchilada, or... well, I am sure you get the picture.

It stresses God's fullness, completeness, comprehensiveness, and his all-inclusiveness. He has always existed and will always exist. He is Omnipotent, Omniscient, and Omnipresent. He is the source of all things and will see all things to their completion. God was in the beginning of our year, and is in the end of our year.

Prayer: Almighty Alpha and Omega, I can rest in assurance of all of Your promises. Your promises are backed by all of You. You never change. You have been and will be. I can hold on to every word that this Bible speaks, You say what You mean and mean what You say.

December 31

Daily Bible Reading: Revelation 22[367]

Verse of the Day: Revelation 22:18 – 19 – "*I testify unto every man that heareth the words of the prophecy of this book, If any man shall add unto them, God shall add unto him the plagues which are written in this book: and if any man shall take away from the words of the book of this prophecy, God shall take away his part from the tree of life, and out of the holy city, which are written in this book.*"

We end our ponderings on the New Testament realizing that if Jesus were to make Himself visible and speak audibly; His message would be in total accord with the Bible.

---

[366] OT Reading – Zechariah 13 – 14
[367] OT Reading – Malachi

His counsel, His commands, His opinions, His warnings, His desires, His promises, all would be in complete alignment with what we are privileged to have. The Bible is God's true, perfect message to you and to me. Continue to read, heed, and believe what God says to us.

Prayer: As I see this year come to a close Gracious Father, may I be called into a continual reading, studying, and learning from You in this Blessed Holy Writ. I thank You for Your provision for me in this Sacred Scriptures.

DAILY DEVOTIONAL Daily Musings From the Old Testament

THOMAS MARSHALL

DAILY MUSINGS FROM THE OLD TESTAMENT

DAILY DEVOTIONAL

About the Author

Dr. Thomas Marshall was saved in April of 1962 on a Sunday morning in Silver Spring, MD. He has been in church since he was three years old. Tom is married to a wonderful lady, Linda, and has three grown daughters and the four greatest grandchildren in the world. Family is at the center of his heart and in his ministry.

In 2014, he celebrated over 34 years in the ministry. He is a licensed and Ordained Baptist minister since 1980. His vision is to see more Kingdom Builders added each year. We have a world that needs to hear and receive the message of the Gospel of Jesus Christ. Our purpose is to fulfill the mission that Jesus Christ gave the Church in Matthew 28. We need to develop the Acts 1:8 mentality and move forward.

Dr. Marshall has degrees and diplomas from Andersonville Baptist Seminary, Liberty Theological Seminary, Liberty University, Johns Hopkins University, Texas Baptist Institute and Seminary, Mid-Atlantic Baptist Institute, and Light University. He currently holds earned doctorates in Theology (D.Min; ThD.) and Biblical Counseling (DBC). He has Masters degrees in Church Ministry, Educational Administration and Supervision, and Pastoral Ministry.

He has a heart and passion for education. Since 1995 he has been involved in Christian Education – from University Professor to Middle School teacher. He has been an administrator at two different Christian Schools, instrumental in starting one of them. He was a presenter at the ACSI Conferences in Washington, D.C. for a number of years. His work as an on-line instructor with Liberty University teaching *Educational Philosophy for Teachers*, helps future teachers discover a proper Christian educational worldview to take into the classroom.

His interests are in the areas of reading, studying, spending time with family, and exercising. He has worked as an editor for LUPress and is the author of *A Student's New Testament Survey* (second-place winner of the 2014 Christian Writers Award in Theology) published by Tate Publishing Co. He is the author of *BOOK OF PHILIPPIANS: CPH New Testament Commentary* published by Christian Publishing House. He has written articles for *Christian Education Bulletin* of the American Baptist Association, the *Laurinburg Exchange* newspaper, and the NC Baptist state paper – the *Biblical Recorder*. He is a Chaplain Volunteer for the NC Baptist Men's

Disaster Relief Team and the New Hope Baptist Church Baptist Builders Team. He volunteers as a Chaplain for the local area hospitals and Scotland County Hospice. He is currently an on-line Adjunct Professor for Liberty University, and Chief Editor (Academics) for Christian Publishing House.

You can follow him at his on-line blog – *Doc's Musings* located on the web at http://tfmarshall.blogspot.com

Bibliography

Akin, Daniel L. *The New American Commentary: 1, 2, 3 John.* Nashville, TN: Broadman & Holman , 2001.

Anders, Max. *Holman New Testament Commentary: vol. 8, Galatians, Ephesians, Philippians, Colossians.* Nashville, TN: Broadman & Holman Publishers, 1999.

—. *Holman Old Testament Commentary - Proverbs .* Nashville: B&H Publishing, 2005.

Anders, Max, and Steven Lawson. *Holman Old Testament Commentary - Psalms: 11.* Grand Rapids: B&H Publishing, 2004.

Anders, Max, and Trent Butler. *Holman Old Testament Commentary: Isaiah.* Nashiville, TN: B&H Publishing, 2002.

Andrews, Stephen J, and Robert D Bergen. *Holman Old Testament Commentary: 1-2 Samuel.* Nashville: Broadman & Holman, 2009.

Barker, Kenneth L., and Waylon Bailey. *The New American Commentary: vol. 20, Micah, Nahum, Habakkuk, Zephaniah.* Nashville, TN: Broadman & Holman Publishers, 2001.

Bergen, Robert D. *The New American Commentary: 1-2 Samuel.* Nashville: Broadman & Holman, 1996.

Blomberg, Craig. *The New American Commentary: Matthew.* Nashville, TN: Broadman & Holman Publishers, 1992.

Boa, Kenneth, and William Kruidenier. *Holman New Testament Commentary: Romans.* Nashville: Broadman & Holman, 2000.

Borchert, Gerald L. *The New American Commentary: John 1-11 .* Nashville, TN: Broadman & Holman Publishers, 2001.

Borchert, Gerald L. *The New American Commentary vol. 25B, John 12–21.* Nashville: Broadman & Holman Publishers, 2002.

Brand, Chad, Charles Draper, and England Archie. *Holman Illustrated Bible Dictionary: Revised, Updated and Expanded.* Nashville, TN: Holman, 2003.

Breneman, Mervin. *The New American Commentary, vol. 10, Ezra, Nehemiah, Esther.* Nashville: Broadman & Holman Publishers, 1993.

Brooks, James A. *The New American Commentary: Mark (Volume 23).* Nashville: Broadman & Holman Publishers, 1992.

Butler, Trent C. *Holman New Testament Commentary: Luke.* Nashville, TN: Broadman & Holman Publishers, 2000.

Butler, Trent C. *Holman Old Testament Commentary - Hosea, Joel, Amos, Obadiah, Jonah, Micah* . Nashville: Broadman & Holman Publishers, 2005.

Cole, R. Dennis. *THE NEW AMERICAN COMMENTARY: Volume 3b Numbers.* Nashville: Broadman & Holman Publishers, 2000.

Cooper, Lamar Eugene. *The New American Commentary, Ezekiel, vol. 17.* Nashville, TN: Broadman & Holman Publishers, 1994.

Cooper, Rodney. *Holman New Testament Commentary: Mark.* Nashville: Broadman & Holman Publishers, 2000.

Dockery, David S. *HOLMAN CONCISE BIBLE COMMENTARY Simple, straightforward commentary on every book of the Bible.* Nashville: Broadman & Holman, 1998.

Dockery, David S., and Trent C. Church, Christopher L. Butler. *Holman Bible Handbook* . Nashville, TN: Holman Bible Publishers, 1992.

Easley, Kendell H. *Holman New Testament Commentary, vol. 12, Revelation.* (Nashville, TN: Broadman & Holman Publishers, 1998.

Elwell, Walter A. *Baker Encyclopedia of the Bible.* Grand Rapids: Baker Book House, 1988.

Elwell, Walter A, and Philip Wesley Comfort. *Tyndale Bible Dictionary.* Wheaton, Ill: Tyndale House Publishers, 2001.

Gangel, Kenneth O. *Holman New Testament Commentary: Acts.* Nashville, TN: Broadman & Holman Publishers, 1998.

Gangel, Kenneth O. *Holman New Testament Commentary, vol. 4, John* . Nashville, TN: Broadman & Holman Publishers, 2000.

Garrett, Duane A. *The New American Commentary: Vol. 14 (Proverbs, Ecclesiastes, Song of Songs).* Nashville: Broadman & Holman Publishers, 1993.

George, Timothy. *The New American Commentary: Galatians* . Nashville, TN: Broadman & Holman Publishers, 2001.

Knight, George W. *The Layman's Bible Handbook.* Uhrichsville: Barbour Publishing, 2003.

Larson, Knute. *Holman New Testament Commentary, vol. 9, I & II Thessalonians, I & II Timothy, Titus, Philemon.* Nashville, TN: Broadman & Holman Publishers, 2000.

Lea, Thomas D. *Holman New Testament Commentary: Vol. 10, Hebrews, James.* Nashville, TN: Broadman & Holman Publishers, 1999.

Lea, Thomas D., and Hayne P. Griffin. *The New American Commentary, vol. 34, 1, 2 Timothy, Titus.* Nashville: Broadman & Holman Publishers, 1992.

Martin, D Michael. *The New American Commentary 33 1, 2 Thessalonians* . Nashville, TN: Broadman & Holman, 2001, c1995 .

Mathews, K. A. *The New American Commentary vol. 1A, Genesis 1-11:26* . Nashville: Broadman & Holman Publishers, 2001.

Matthews, K. A. *The New American Commentary Vol. 1B, Genesis 11:27-50:26.* Nashville: Broadman and Holman Publishers, 2001.

Melick, Richard R. *The New American Commentary: vol. 32, Philippians, Colissians, Philemon.* Nashville, TN : Broadman & Holman Publishers, 2001.

Miller, Stephen R. *The New American Commentary: Volume 18 Daniel.* Nashville: Broadman & Holman Publishers, 1994.

Mounce, Robert H. *Romans: The New American Commentary 27.* Nashville: Broadman & Holman, 2001, c1995.

Mounce, Robert H. *The New American Commentary: Vol. 27 Romans.* Nashville, TN: Broadman & Holman Publishers, 2001.

Mounce, William D. *Mounce's Complete Expository Dictionary of Old & New Testament Words.* Grand Rapids, MI: Zondervan, 2006.

Myers, Allen C. *The Eerdmans Bible Dictionary* . Grand Rapids, Mich: Eerdmans, 1987.

Polhill, John B. *The New American Commentary 26: Acts.* Nashville: Broadman & Holman Publishers, 2001.

Pratt Jr, Richard L. *Holman New Testament Commentary: I & II Corinthians, vol. 7.* Nashville: Broadman & Holman Publishers, 2000.

Richardson, Kurt. *The New American Commentary Vol. 36 James.* Nashville: Broadman & Holman Publishers, 1997.

Rooker, Mark F. *The New American Commentary, vol. 3A, Leviticus.* Nashville: Broadman & Holman Publishers, 2000.

—. *Holman Old Testament Commentary: Ezekiel.* Nashville: Broadman & Holman Publishers, 2005.

Schreiner, Thomas R. *The New American Commentary: 1, 2 Peter, Jude.* Nashville: Broadman & Holman, 2003.

Stuart, Douglas K. *The New American Commentary: An Exegetical Theological Exposition of Holy Scripture EXODUS.* Nashville: Broadman & Holman, 2006.

Taylor, Richard A, and Ray E Clendenen. *The New American Commentary: Haggai, Malachi, , vol. 21A .* Nashville, TN: Broadman & Holman Publishers, 2007.

Vine, W E. *Vine's Expository Dictionary of Old and New Testament Words.* Nashville: Thomas Nelson, 1996.

Walls, David, and Max Anders. *Holman New Testament Commentary: I & II Peter, I, II & III John, Jude.* Nashville: Broadman & Holman Publishers, 1996.

Weber, Stuart K. *Holman New Testament Commentary, vol. 1, Matthew.* Nashville, TN: Broadman & Holman Publishers, 2000.

Wood, D R W. *New Bible Dictionary (Third Edition).* Downers Grove: InterVarsity Press, 1996.

Zodhiates, Spiros. *The Complete Word Study Dictionary: New Testament.* Chattanooga: AMG Publishers, 2000, c1992, c1993.

www.ingramcontent.com/pod-product-compliance
Lightning Source LLC
Chambersburg PA
CBHW022004090426
42741CB00007B/888